THE
VEST
POCKET
INVESTOR

EVERYTHING YOU NEED
TO KNOW TO INVEST
SUCCESSFULLY

THE
VEST
POCKET
INVESTOR

EVERYTHING YOU NEED
TO KNOW TO INVEST
SUCCESSFULLY

Jae K. Shim & Joel G. Siegel

IRWIN
Professional Publishing®
Chicago, London, Singapore

IRWIN Concerned about Our Environment

In recognition of the fact that our company is a large end-user of fragile yet replenishable resources, we at IRWIN can assure you that every effort is made to meet or exceed Environmental Protection Agency (EPA) recommendations and requirements for a "greener" workplace.

To preserve these natural assets, a number of environmental policies, both companywide and department-specific, have been implemented. From the use of 50% recycled paper in our textbooks to the printing of promotional materials with recycled stock and soy inks to our office paper recycling program, we are committed to reducing waste and replacing environmentally unsafe products with safer alternatives.

Irwin Professional Book Team

Executive editor:	Kevin Commins
Marketing manager:	Marissa Ramos
Manager, direct marketing:	Rebecca S. Gordon
Production supervisor:	Laurie Kersch
Assistant manager, desktop services:	Jon Christopher
Project editor:	Christina Thornton-Villagomez
Designer:	Matthew Baldwin/Laura Hunter
Compositor/ interior design:	Lisa King
Typeface:	10/12 Palatino
Printer:	Buxton Skinner Printing Company

Times Mirror
Higher Education Group

Library of Congress Cataloging-in-Publication Data

Shim, Jae K.
  The vest pocket investor : everything you need to know to invest successfully / Jae K. Shim, Joel G. Siegel.
    p.   cm.
  Includes index.
  ISBN 1-55738-813-X
  1. Investments--Handbooks, manuals, etc. I. Siegel, Joel G. II. Title.
HG4527.S45   1996
332.6--dc20   95–23361

Contents

PREFACE

In investing money, the amount of interest you want should depend on whether you want to eat well or sleep well.

J. Kenfield Morley. Some Things I Believe

Before you can manage money to maximize your wealth you must learn the basics of investing. What is the difference between mutual funds? What is the difference between stocks or fixed income securities? How does appreciation in value differ from current fixed income? As a layperson, should you pick your own investments or should you let professional managers in mutual funds do it? Probably, as a beginning investor you should invest in mutual funds before investing directly in stocks or bonds. What investment style and comfort level is appropriate for you? What is a diversified investment portfolio and how can your assets be allocated?

Our level of discussion will be elementary because this is a basic reference for the beginning investor. *The Vest Pocket Investor* tells you what vehicles are available to invest in, the features of each type of investment, the advantages and disadvantages of each investment category, and when a particular investment type might be suitable for you. This primer covers investor objectives, security markets, security transactions, sources of investment information, appraisal of risk and return, financial analysis, tax-deferred savings plans, investment strategies, including active and passive (e.g., indexing), and retirement accounts. There is a thorough explanation of the investment selection process, basic investment terms, indicators, and statistics. Illustrations are rendered in a user-friendly manner.

You may refer to this book when you need a basic definition or explanation of an investment topic, or when your broker calls and suggests a new investment opportunity.

Successful investing is facilitated by obtaining the right information at the right time. The investor should know where to obtain relevant information on specific investments and how to read and interpret the various sources of data. Specific sources of investment information (publications, media outlets, etc.) are provided, and you are guided on how to use these sources in making informed investment decisions.

This book can be used by the inexperienced investor to make everyday investment decisions. It contains easy-to-follow examples from daily life which show you step-by-step what has to be done to realistically achieve your objectives. This book is designed in a question-and-answer format in order to address the issues that come up when investing. The questions are typical of those asked by lay investors such as yourself. The answers are clear, concise, and to the point. In short, this is a workable, easy reference of guidelines, illustrations, checklists, worksheets, charts, graphs, practical applications, recommendations, and how-to's for you, the novice investor. Throughout, you'll find this book practical, quick, useful, and reader-friendly. Another important feature of the guide has to do with how to use a computer for investing. Computerized investing, which is a vital aspect of investing in this day and age, is stressed throughout the book.

We cover every topic a basic investor might run up against. However, advanced topics probably not appropriate for the layperson are limited to a very brief discussion or a definition in the glossary.

The index makes it easy to find what you are looking for and to cross reference. A glossary defining important investment terms is also provided.

This book will help you understand investments. Keep it handy for easy reference when you want to make money!

Jae K. Shim
Joel G. Siegel

ACKNOWLEDGMENTS

We express our sincere thanks to Dr. Yojin Jung of International Investment Advisors, Los Angeles, California, for his coauthoring Chapter 9. We also thank Steve Gramme, a graduate assistant at California State University, Long Beach, for his excellent computer skills and editorial assistance on this book.

CHAPTER 1

INTRODUCTION

Before you invest any funds, you should evaluate your present financial condition. Consider your income, expenses, taxes, future prospects for higher earnings, and all other details that affect your monetary situation. Decide how much you want to invest. Then very carefully formulate your investment aims. Will you invest in order to earn a profit? As a hedge against economic fluctuations? To build up a retirement income? To prepare for your children's college fund?

Your next step should be to examine the investment choices presented in this book and then decide which kinds of investments are best for you.

Set up your long-term goals first, thinking in terms of the middle and distant future. Then establish short-term financial objectives that are consistent with the longer-term aims. After six months or a year, if you haven't been able to meet your short-term goals, you may have to reevaluate the long-term objectives. If, however, you have done much better than you expected to do, you may want to formulate more ambitious goals.

WHAT ARE THE SOURCES OF MONEY FOR INVESTING?

If possible, try to invest 15 percent of after-tax income. Also, before starting to invest in securities such as stock, your total assets should be two times your liabilities.

What are the possible sources of money available for investing?

- *Discretionary income.* After-tax income left after spending to meet living expenses.

- *Life insurance.* Amount of cash value to be borrowed against policy.

- *Gift* from your parents or other source.

- *Profit sharing and pension.* Amount of pension which may be borrowed against at a low interest.

- Other people's money (OPM).

- *Home equity loan or equity line.*

WHAT ARE THE TYPES OF INVESTMENTS?

Investments can be classified into two forms: *fixed-income* and *variable-income.* Simply stated, fixed-income investments promise you a stated amount of income periodically. These include corporate bonds and preferred stocks, U.S. government securities (Treasury bills), municipal bonds, and other savings instruments (savings account, certificate of deposit). On the other hand, variable-dollar investments are those where neither the principal nor the income is contractually set in advance in terms of dollars. That is, both the value and income of variable-income investments can change in dollar amount, either up or down, with changing internal or external economic conditions. These include common stocks, mutual funds, real estate, and variable annuities.

Investments can be viewed as *financial* or *real assets.* Financial assets refer to intangible investments—things you cannot touch or wear or walk on. They are your equity interest in a company, or evidence of money owed to you, or a right to buy or sell an ownership interest. Real assets have tangible, physical substance. Table 1 lists the various forms of financial and real assets.

Table 1—

Overview of Investment Vehicles

(1) Financial assets:
   1. Equity claims—direct
      — Common stock
      — Options, rights, and warrants
   2. Equity claims - indirect
      — Mutual funds
   3. Creditor claims
      — Savings accounts and certificates of deposit (CDs)
      — Treasury bills
      — Money market funds
      — Commercial paper
      — Corporate and government bonds
   4. Preferred stock
   5. Commodities and financial futures
   6. Annuities—variable and fixed

(2) Real assets:
   1. Real estate
   2. Precious metals and gems
   3. Collectibles

Direct and Indirect Investments

When you make a *direct* investment, you acquire a claim on a particular investment vehicle. When you choose an *indirect* investment, you have a portfolio of stocks, bonds, or properties. A popular indirect investment is shares of a mutual fund, which holds a portfolio of securities issued by mutual fund investment companies, or shares of *Real Estate Investment Trusts (REITs)*. You can have a portfolio of securities representing diversified investment types. This variety of investments minimizes risk while bringing in a satisfactory return.

Long-Term and Short-Term Investments

An investment may be *short-term* or *long-term*. Short-term investments last for one year or less. Long-term investments last more than one year. A short-term investment might be a three-month Treasury bill. A long-term investment might be a five-year Treasury note. Some long-term investments do not mature, such as equity securities. However, you can buy a long-term investment and treat it as a short-term one by disposing of it within one year. How many of your investments are short-term? How many are long-term? Is that the combination you consider best for you?

Short-term securities involve little risk and offer liquidity. They include the liquid investments listed earlier in this chapter: Savings accounts, certificates of deposit, money market certificates, mutual funds, U.S. Treasury bills, and commercial paper.

Long-term securities are debt or equity instruments with a maturity of more than one year. A debt instrument is a certificate or security showing that you loaned funds to a company or to a government in return for future interest and repayment of principal. Equity securities are those in which you have ownership interests.

WHAT ARE THE FEATURES OF BONDS?

Bonds are one type of debt instrument—a certificate of corporate or government obligation to you in return for your loan (investment). Bonds are usually sold in $1,000 denominations. You can purchase or sell a bond before maturity at a price other than face value. The bond indenture specifies the terms of the borrowing arrangement. Many bonds are callable at the command of the issuing company. This means that the issuing firm can buy back the debt prior to maturity.

The interest you receive on a bond equals the nominal interest rate times the face value. Suppose, for example, that you buy a 10-year $40,000 bond at 8 percent interest. You pay 94 percent of face value. Interest is payable semiannually, which is typical. The purchase price is $37,600 (94% x $40,000). You receive a semiannual interest payment of $1,600 (4% x $40,000). At maturity, you will receive the full maturity value of $40,000.

Corporate bonds are riskier than government bonds because companies can fail. Most individuals in high tax brackets do not find corporate bonds attractive because interest received is fully taxable.

U.S. government obligations include Treasury notes and Treasury bonds. Treasury notes are U.S. obligations having a maturity from 2 to 10 years. The yield is slightly higher than on Treasury bills. Treasury bonds are long-term obligations for over 10 years. They usually pay a higher interest rate than do Treasury notes. The risk default is nonexistent.

The interest on local (state and city) bonds, as discussed earlier, is exempt from federal and local

taxes. However, to be free from state tax you must
buy bonds issued by your home state. For example,
interest on California state bonds is exempt from
California state tax, but interest on New York bonds
is not exempt from California state tax. Municipal
bonds appeal to high-tax-bracket investors because
the interest received is tax free. If you are in a high
tax bracket, you should consider buying municipal
bonds.

Zero-coupon bonds pay no interest and are issued at a discount and redeemed at face value at
maturity. They can be risky, but of some interest to
longer-term investors.

WHAT ARE THE FEATURES OF STOCK?

An equity investment is ownership in a business
(evidenced by a security) or property (evidenced
by title). You obtain an equity interest by buying
stock. Equity securities have no maturity date. You
purchase them in order to receive income (dividends) and capital gain. The types of stock are common and preferred.

Common stock is an equity investment reflecting ownership in a company. If you hold 1,000
shares of common stock in a firm that has 100,000
shares outstanding, you own a 1 percent ownership
interest in that company. Thus, you can control the
company. In many instances, an investor can gain
control by owning a considerably smaller percentage than this.

Here are some of the advantages of owning
common stock:

- Inflation hedge.

- You can vote.

- If the company does well, your stock price will
  appreciate and your dividends will increase.

Owning common stock also carries disadvantages, however, including the following:

- When the firm isn't thriving, your earnings will drop and price stability will suffer—meaning that the stocks' resale value will decrease.
- You may not receive sizable dividends.
- Common stock is riskier than debt securities and preferred stock, since you will be the last to receive money if the company fails. (Debt holders come before equity holders in liquidation, and in this instance you are an equity holder.)

Common stock owners have the preemptive right, which allows them to maintain their proportionate share in the company. Thus, they can buy new shares issued before they go on sale to the general public. This way they can maintain their percentage of ownership.

Preferred stockholders have no voting rights buy they do receive a fixed dividend rate. They also take precedence over common stockholders in the receipt of dividends and in the event of liquidation. Preferred stock may be callable at the company's option, and it generally provides only dividend income, with no capital gain potential. See Table 2 for a comparison of debt instruments, preferred stock, and common stock.

Table 2—

Comparison of Securities

	Debt	Preferred Stock	Common Stock
Voting rights	No	No	Yes
Risk	Low	Medium	High

(continued)

Table 2—*continued*

	Debt	Preferred Stock	Common Stock
Appreciation in value of company	No	Yes	Yes
Fixed annual return	Yes	Yes	No
Partial tax exclusion for interest or dividends	No	Yes	Yes

WHAT ARE THE TYPES OF DIVIDENDS?

There are three types of dividends: Cash, stock, and property dividends. Cash dividends are taxable. They are usually paid quarterly. If a stock dividend differs from the security receiving the dividend (in other words, if you own common stock but get a preferred stock dividend), you must pay taxes on the dividends you receive. If they are the same (in other words, if you own common stock and get common stock dividends), you do not pay taxes on those dividends. You can look up the dividend records and ratings of companies in *Standard and Poor's Stock Guide*.

WHAT ARE CONVERTIBLE SECURITIES?

Convertible securities can be converted into common stock at a later date. Two examples of these securities are convertible bonds and convertible preferred stock. These securities give you fixed income in the form of interest (convertible bonds) or dividends (convertible preferred stocks). They also let you benefit from the appreciation value of the common stock.

WHAT ARE DERIVATIVE PRODUCTS?

Derivatives are instruments whose value depends on the value of the underlying securities, foreign currencies, commodities, or market indexes. Options and futures are derivative instruments. Their value is derived from the underlying security. Options and futures are also *leverage*-inherent investments that can be used to increase potential return or to reduce risk. An option is the right to buy or sell a security or property at a given price during a specified time period. An option is neither a debt nor equity; it is an opportunity to acquire securities. You might buy options in order to take advantage of an anticipated change in the price of common stocks. You should know, however, that you, as an option holder, have no guaranteed return; the option may not be attractive to exercise, because the market price of the underlying common stock has not increased, for example, or the option time period may elapse. If this happens, you will lose your entire investment. Hence, options involve considerable risk.

Commodity (e.g., cocoa) and financial (e.g., Treasury bills, foreign currency) futures are seller commitments to deliver a specific commodity or financial instrument at a set price by a given date. The contract specifies the amount, valuation method, quality, standardized unit, and means of delivery. The profitability of these investments depends on many uncontrollable factors linked to the world economy. Therefore, futures are high-risk investments.

WHAT IS THE DIFFERENCE BETWEEN COMMON STOCKS AND MUTUAL FUNDS?

A mutual fund is a diversified group of stocks, bonds, or other assets contributed by investors and managed by professional money managers. The primary appeal of mutual funds is that they are professionally managed and provide diversification.

Table 3 summarizes the differences between stocks and mutual funds.

Table 3—

Differences Between Stocks and Mutual Funds

	Stocks	*Mutual funds*
Ownership	Shares of a single company	Shares in the fund; fractional ownership of a group of assets
Voting rights	Yes	No
Value	Per share price	Net asset value (NAV)
Professional management	No	Yes
Diversification	No	Yes
Liquidity	3 business days	Almost immediate
Dividends and capital gain	Direct	Can be reinvested
Investment decision by	Yourself	Fund manager
Choice of investment goals	No	Yes
Accessibility	Via broker	Yes; via a toll-free phone

	Stocks	*Mutual funds*
Flexibility	No	Yes, exchange privileges; check-writing services
Commission	Full or discount	Load or no-load

WHAT OTHER TYPES OF INVESTMENTS EXIST?

There are many other forms of investments. Some are real assets, such as real estate, precious metals and gems, and collectibles. Some are tax-advantaged investments whose income grows tax-deferred. They include Individual Retirement Accounts (IRAs), Keoghs, and annuities. Limited partnerships provide tax shelters with passive participation and limited liabilities.

WHAT ARE THE FACTORS TO BE CONSIDERED IN INVESTMENT DECISIONS?

Your financial situation and future expectations are essential in formulating an investment strategy. Consideration should be given to safety, return and risk, stability of income, and marketability and liquidity.

Risk and security of principal. You will want to know the degree of risk involved in a particular investment, as you will not want to lose part or all of your initial investment. The primary purpose of investing is to earn a return on your money in the form of interest, dividends, rental income, and capital appreciation. However, increasing total returns would entail greater investment risks. Thus, yield and degree of risk are directly related. Greater risk also means sacrificing security of principal. You have to choose the priority that fits your financial circumstances and objectives.

Return needs. When steady income is a most important consideration, you may opt for high-yielding stocks. If you are searching for capital appreciation, you may look toward smaller, emerging growth stocks.

Marketability and liquidity. This is the ability to find a ready market to dispose of the investment at the right price.

Tax Factors. Investors in high tax brackets will have different investment objectives than those in lower brackets. If you are in a high tax bracket, you may prefer municipal bonds (interest is not taxable), or investments that provide tax credits or tax shelters, such as those in oil and gas.

In addition, there are many other factors to be considered as they relate to a specific situation, including:

- Current and future income needs—funds for college education or retirement
- Level of risk tolerance—conservative, neutral, or speculative
- Capacity for risk—ability to withstand financial losses
- Amount of investment (for example, some REITs require a $5,000 minimum investment)
- Hedging against inflation (for example, fixed-income securities are generally bad against inflation)

- Ease of management (for example, mutual funds save management and bookkeeping troubles)
- Diversification (for example, you can enjoy owning many investment vehicles through a mutual fund)

In the beginning, look for liquid investments that provide a good return (high interest or dividends) and are at the same time immediately salable. That's what liquid means—that you can sell the investment quickly in case you need the money for another, more important purpose. Here are some popular liquid investments:

- Certificates of deposit
- U.S. Treasury bills (T-bills)
- Money market certificates
- Mutual funds
- Savings accounts
- Commercial paper

Liquidity is not your only consideration. You must also take into account the return you will receive on an investment—especially in relation to its risk. The higher the risk, the higher the return should be; this is an unfailing rule of the investor.

Income on investments comes in one of three forms:

- Ordinary income: Interest or dividends
- Short-term capital gain: The profit you earn when you sell an investment you've held for one year or less
- Long-term capital gain: The profit you earn when you sell an investment you've held for longer than one year.

WHAT TAX ASPECTS SHOULD YOU CONSIDER WHEN INVESTING?

Your tax situation will affect your investment choices. Many people in the lower income-tax brackets choose to invest for the purpose of increasing ordinary income, which is fully taxable. Those in higher-tax brackets, however, often choose long-term investments because they carry certain tax advantages.

Here is a look at the way some securities are taxed:

- Ordinary income (interest and dividends) is fully taxable.
- Short-term capital gain is fully taxable.
- Long-term capital gain gives you a tax advantage in that only 28 percent of this gain is taxable.
- Income on U.S. government securities is subject to federal income tax but exempt from state and city taxes.
- Income from municipal securities (issued by your state or city) is exempt from both federal and local taxes.
- Individual Retirement Accounts (IRAs) and Keogh plans provide taxable income when payments are received after retirement. Prior to retirement, interest income earned on the accounts is accumulated in the fund and is nontaxable.

WHAT ARE THE DRAWBACKS AND BENEFITS OF BUYING MUNICIPAL BONDS?

Now we will look more closely at some of these investments. Municipal securities, for example, look good in the list above because of the tax benefit. There is a slight catch, however. These investments usually have a long maturity period; in other words, you have to tie up your money for several years before you receive your profit. They are neverthe-less attractive to some investors, depending on their tax bracket. An investor in the combined federal and state 40 percent bracket, for example, may hold municipal securities that provide a 10 percent return; this person will receive a before-tax return of 16.7 percent calculated as follows:

$$\frac{10\%}{1 - \text{tax rate}} = \frac{10\%}{1 - .4} = \frac{10\%}{.6} = 16.7\%$$

Tax-exempt municipal bonds, tax-deferred investments, and tax shelters such as limited partnerships are attractive to high-tax-bracket investors.

WHAT ABOUT RETIREMENT?

Retired people generally favor safe investments that provide fixed yearly returns. Appreciation in the price of a security is not as important to them as a stable, guaranteed income. For example, a long-term government bond will satisfy most retirees' needs. Risky investments are not desirable because of the uncertainty.

You have to plan for sufficient income during your retirement. In addition to Social Security and your job's pension plan, you can invest in annuities and self-sponsored retirement plans like IRAs and Keoghs. You can deposit as much as $2,000 a year in an individual retirement account (IRA), the income from which is nontaxable. If you are self-employed, or if you earn significant income from self-employment in addition to your salaried job, you can deposit up to 25 percent of that part of your income in a Keogh Plan, also nontaxable. However, payments you receive from the fund after retirement are taxable.

HOW ARE CAPITAL LOSSES TREATED FOR TAX PURPOSES?

Earlier we discussed capital gain and the conditions under which it is taxable. How about capital loss? This loss is the negative difference between the price you pay for an investment and the price you receive for it when you sell it. In other words, if you buy ten shares of a certain stock for a total of $500 and later sell those shares for $350, you take a capital loss of $150. You can deduct capital losses in full up to $3,000. If your losses exceed $3,000, you can carry the excess forward to the succeeding years.

HOW DO RISK AND RETURN RELATE?

How much financial risk should you be willing to take on an investment? Risk is the chance you take of losing money on an investment; it is the uncertainty regarding the investment's final payoff. The more an investment can vary in value during the maturity period, the greater the risk you take when you buy and hold onto it.

All investments involve some degree of risk. In general, you will have to find a balance between risk and return; the higher the risk, the greater must be the return. Figure 1 illustrates a risk-return tradeoff.

Figure 1—

Risk Chart

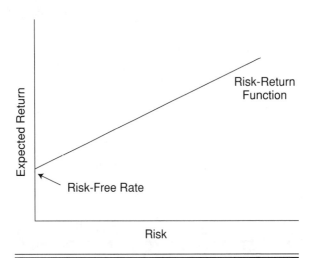

WHAT IS THE DIFFERENCE BETWEEN MARKETABILITY AND LIQUIDITY?

Marketability is different from liquidity. Marketability means there is an available market to sell the investment. Liquidity means marketability exists and market price is stable.

Liquidity is important when you need money immediately, such as for an emergency. However, liquid investments usually provide a lower return than illiquid ones. Liquid investments include savings accounts and money market funds.

Table 4 shows marketability and liquidity for various investments.

Table 4—

Investment Marketability and Liquidity

	Marketability	Liquidity
Savings accounts	Not applicable	High
Corporate bonds	High	Medium
Short-term U.S. government securities	High	High
Long-term U.S. government securities	High	Medium
Common stock	High	Low
Real estate	Medium	Low

HOW DO INTEREST RATES AFFECT THE MARKET VALUE OF YOUR INVESTMENT?

Bonds are responsive to changes in interest rates. When interest rates increase, bond prices decrease. If you paid $1,000 (par) for a bond that paid 7 percent, or $70 interest per annum, and then interest rates increased so that newly issued bonds were paying 9 percent, or $90 interest, no one would desire to purchase your bond for $1,000. Why would anyone take 7 percent if that person could get 9 percent? The price of your bond would have to drop so someone might buy it at a discount (less than $1,000), so he could make a profit on the lower price paid and receive $1,000 at maturity.

Stocks are sensitive to interest rate changes. For example, as interest rates increase, stock prices also tend to decrease because:

- Dividends are less attractive, prompting stock sales.

- It is more expensive to purchase stock on margin (credit), depressing investment in stocks.
- It results in higher cost of a company to borrow, cutting profits.

WHAT ARE THE EXPENSES ASSOCIATED WITH YOUR INVESTMENTS?

You might want to take into account investment expenses associated with various investment instruments, because they do vary widely. Table 5 summarizes these.

Table 5—

High- and Low-Expense Investments

High-expense investments:

- Over-the-counter (OTC) and inactive stocks
- Load mutual funds
- Unit investment trusts (UITs)
- Zero coupon bonds
- Limited partnerships
- Collectibles
- CDs, if withdrawn before maturity

Low-expense investments:

- No load mutual funds
- Actively traded stocks and bonds.

Note: You should consider using discount brokers unless you need investment advice. There are substantial savings in commission. Also, buy in volume to obtain discounts. For example, as you increase the number of shares bought, the brokerage commission per share drops. The greater the dollar purchase of a Treasury bill, the less the commission. If you buy a Treasury bill of $50,000 or more, there is a minimal commission. The smaller the purchase, the greater the per share commission rate.

HOW AGGRESSIVE—OR CONSERVATIVE—SHOULD YOU BE?

Aggressive investing seeks to obtain the highest return at above-normal risk. Defensive investing seeks to minimize risk, but generates less return. An aggressive strategy involves more trading. A defensive strategy holds for the long term.

Aggressive investments include buying securities on margin (credit) to use leverage to maximize return. Defensive investments do not normally use credit (or leverage).

Aggressive investing may involve a few securities at one time seeking high return, but this is risky. Sometimes the more you invest in one item, such as a jumbo certificate of deposit, the higher the return. Diversification—spreading your funds among various securities—is a defensive policy.

How aggressive or conservative you should be depends on a number of factors, including your risk profile and investment goals. For example, retirees want safety and constant annual returns. Appreciation is not as essential as stable, guaranteed income. Risky investments involve uncertainty.

STEPS IN INVESTMENT PLANNING

In a broad sense, investment planning involves constructing and monitoring an investment portfolio. This requires a systematic approach that follows a series of steps, as indicated in Figure 2.

First, you, as an investor, must determine the risk level you are willing to accept. It depends to a great extent on your stage in the lifecycle. For example, the younger you are, the more risk you can afford to assume.

The next step is to determine your investment objectives, such as liquidity, current income versus capital growth, tax exposure, college funding, and retirement planning. These variables dictate your choice of investment vehicles. The need for adequate diversification must be considered when types of investments are selected. You should determine asset allocation proportions and overall risk.

Next, the resulting portfolio is periodically evaluated and monitored to determine if it is achieving your investment objectives in accordance with the changing market and economic environment. If it is not, a portfolio revision is in order. The revision may be based on changes in your investment status, such as tax brackets, and might include selling some assets and purchasing others. Investment planning should be an ongoing process within a well conceived risk-return framework.

Figure 2—

Steps in Investment Planning

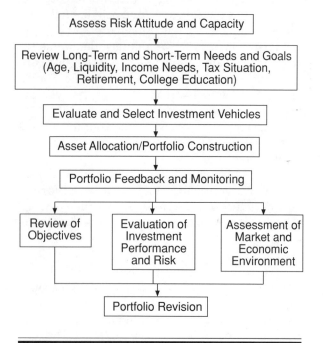

CHAPTER 2

FINANCIAL MARKETS AND INVESTMENT PROCESS

Suppliers and buyers of funds make their investment transactions in financial markets. Financial markets consist of the money market and the capital market. In the money market, short-term debt securities with a life of one year or less are bought and sold. Transactions in long-term securities like stocks and bonds are made in the capital market, which is composed of several security exchanges.

WHAT ARE THE CAPITAL MARKETS?

Capital markets are either primary or secondary. In the primary market, new shares are issued to the public. A new security issuance usually involves an investment banking firm that specializes in selling new security issuances for compensation. In large issues, the investment bankers act as stockbrokers that sell a percentage of the issue. The lead investment banker is the originating house, and all other investment bankers are the syndicate.

The secondary market is where securities are traded after original issuance, when the original holders sell their shares to other buyers. The secondary markets include the organized security exchanges—New York, American, and regional—and the over-the-counter market. These organized exchanges serve as clearinghouses for those who supply securities and those who demand them. The listing requirements for companies on the New York Stock Exchange are more restrictive than those for the other exchanges.

"Listed" securities are traded on the organized exchanges. Trading is done on the floor of the exchange by members who are for the most part brokerage firms. Brokers bring together the buyer and seller of a stock. The New York Stock Exchange accounts for about 80 percent of the total volume of shares traded on organized exchanges. Regional exchanges include the Pacific Stock Exchange, which is an auction market, and the Philadelphia Stock Exchange.

What Is the Over-the-Counter Market?

The *over-the-counter (OTC)* market is the market characterized by trading through a broker-dealer without using the facilities of an exchange. Although it is not an auction market, it does provide a forum where new unlisted issues are sold. Traders (dealers) use a telecommunications network called the *National Association of Security Dealers Automated Quotation System (NASDAQ)* for transactions in these securities. The over-the-counter market trades a higher dollar volume of securities than do the national and regional exchanges.

Each over-the-counter trader makes a market in certain securities by offering to buy or sell them at specified prices. Dealers are the second party to a transaction. The bid price is the maximum price the dealer offers for a security. The ask price is the lowest price for which the dealer will sell the security. The dealer's profit is the spread—the difference between the bid price and the ask price.

What are the advantages of purchasing stocks in the over-the-counter market?

- Some securities are traded only in this market.

- Some securities have significant potential for return, but with high risk.

- Over-the-counter dealers have the excellent communications network known as NASDAQ, which results in a high degree of marketability for their stocks and a better reflection of true price.

The disadvantage of buying on the over-the-counter market is that the companies whose stocks are sold there are generally lower-quality firms than those listed on the New York Stock Exchange and the American Stock Exchange.

Some New York Stock Exchange listed securities are traded on the over-the-counter market. These transactions constitute the third market. The fourth market comprises the trading of securities between institutions without the use of middlemen. Especially large issues are traded on this fourth market.

What About the Futures Market?

Future contracts for future delivery of a commodity or financial instrument at a given price for a specified time period are traded on several exchanges, principally the *Chicago Board of Trade*. This exchange has the most comprehensive listing of commodities and financial future contracts. Other futures exchanges exist, some of which specialize in particular commodities. Futures in foreign currency are primarily traded on the *International Monetary Market*, which is part of the *Chicago Mercantile Exchange*.

WHAT DO SECURITY TRANSACTIONS INVOLVE?

Before you invest, you should learn the procedures for acquiring an investment, the associated costs, the characteristics of your chosen investment, and the advantages and disadvantages of alternative investment opportunities.

Stockbrokers can buy and sell securities for you. They also provide price quotations and other investment information, and they will give you stock and bond guides that explain and summarize the activity of securities.

Stockbrokers work for the brokerage houses that own seats on the organized exchanges. Members of the exchange execute orders placed by their brokers. Orders for over-the-counter securities are carried out by dealers who specialize in certain securities. Regardless of which market your security is being sold in, you have to place your order with a broker. He or she will send you a monthly statement listing the stocks you've bought and sold, the commission fees you've paid your broker, the interest charges, your dividend and interest income, and your final balance.

You have the option to hold stock or bond certificates in your own name, or allow a brokerage firm to hold them in the firm's "street name." If the firm holds on to certificates, the broker can sell them without having to get your signature. If you hold certificates in your own name, you can participate directly in a company's dividend reinvestment program without paying brokerage commissions.

Some of the major brokerage firms are Merrill Lynch, Paine Webber, Salomon Brothers, and Prudential-Bache.

Here are the different types of brokerage accounts from which you can choose:

1. *Single or joint.* Are you single or married?

2. *Cash.* You must make full payment for securities purchased within three business days. When you sell your securities, the brokerage house has three days to give you your money.

3. *Margin.* You make partial payment for securities purchased, with the remainder on credit. The broker retains the securities as collateral.

4. *Discretionary.* You give your broker permission to buy and sell securities at his or her discretion.

WHAT ARE THE TYPES OF SECURITIES TRANSACTIONS?

Types of securities transactions include:

1. *Long purchase.* You buy a security expecting it to increase in value (buy low and sell high). Your return will come in the form of dividend and interest income over the maturity period plus capital gain at the time of sale minus brokerage fees.

2. *Short selling.* Here you sell high and buy low. In a short sale, you'll earn a profit if the market price of the security declines. To make a short sale, the broker borrows the security from someone else and then sells it for you to another. Later on, you buy the shares back. If you buy the shares back at a lower price than the broker sold them for, you will make a profit. You "sell short against the box" when you sell short shares you actually own (not borrowed shares). You lose money when the repurchase price is higher than the original selling price.

Example 1—

Suppose that you sell short 50 shares of stock having a market price of $25 per share: The broker borrows the shares from you and sells them to someone else for $1,250. The brokerage house holds onto the proceeds of the short sale. Later on, you buy the stock back at $20 a share, earning a per-share profit of $5, or a total of $250.

3. *Buying on margin.* A margin purchase is made partly on credit. Margin requirements are generally about 50 percent cash and 50 percent credit. Typically, you have to pay more cash for stock than for bonds because of the increased risk. You must pay interest to the brokerage house on the money you owe them. When you buy on margin, you can make a high return— or incur a significant loss, so be careful.

Example 2—

You purchase 100 shares of Texas Instrument stock at $50 per share, ($5,000). The margin requirement is 70 percent, so you pay $3,500. The $1,500 balance represents a loan from the brokerage house. If the interest rate is 10 percent, you'll pay an annual interest charge of $150 (10% x $1,500). The brokerage fee is $60. A margin purchase magnifies return, because only a part payment is made for security. If the stock goes to $55 next year, you will receive from sale $5,500 ($55 x 100 shares). Your net return before interest and commission is

$2,000 ($5,500 - $3,500). After interest and commission you earn $1,790 ($2,000 - $210). Your net rate of return is 51.1 percent ($1,790/$3,500).

---

4. *Odd lots and round lots.* An odd-lot transaction is one having fewer than 100 shares of a security. A round-lot transaction is in multiples of 100. If you purchase 50 shares of Company XYZ, for example, you make an odd-lot purchase. If you buy 235 shares of Company DEF, you make a combination round-lot and odd-lot transaction.

5. *Block trade.* A block trade is an order for a minimum of 10,000 shares.

WHAT KINDS OF ORDERS ARE FILLED BY BROKERS?

Brokerage commissions are tied to the number of shares ordered and the total market value of the shares bought and sold. The types of orders you may place for stock transactions are as follows:

1. *Market order.* You transact a market order when you purchase or sell stock at the existing market price.

2. *Limit order.* This means purchasing at no more than a specified price or selling at no less than a specified price. The order remains open for a stated time period or until withdrawn. A higher commission is usually charged for this privilege.

Example 3—

You give a limit order to purchase at $10 or less a security now selling at $11. If the stock goes up to $20, your broker will not buy it; if it falls to $10 or less the broker buys. *Note:* Such an order may be suitable when market prices vary or uncertainty exists.

3. *Day order.* Your order is good only for the present day.
4. *Good till canceled (GTC).* An order open until consummated or withdrawn.
5. *Stop-loss order.* This is an order to purchase or sell a security when it rises to or drops below a specified price.

Example 4—

Suppose that you own 1,000 shares of Avis, having a market price of $50 per share. You give your broker a stop-loss order to sell this if it decreases to $46. Because you originally bought it at $26 a share, your stop-loss order locks in a gain of $20 ($46 - $26).

By selling the shares at a present price, you are insulated from later stock price declines. This order cannot be used for over-the-counter securities. *Note:* It is advisable to set the order at about 18 percent below your initial cost or the highest price over the last 52 weeks.

6. *Time order.* This order tells your broker to sell at a specified price during a prescribed time or until withdrawn.

Example 5—

You want to sell 50 shares of ABC at $30 per share, and you expect the price of the stock to increase to $30 in one month. You execute a time order with your broker to sell your shares at $30 within a month period.

---

7. *Scale order.* You execute an order to buy or sell a security in given amounts at various prices.

WHEN IS THE SETTLEMENT DATE?

A settlement for a stock transaction occurs on the third full business day subsequent to the trade. It is known as "T plus three" for "trade plus three days." For example, if you purchase shares you must pay for them by the third business day (settlement date) subsequent to the date of purchase (trade date).

Example 6—

If you buy stock on March 7 (Monday), then the settlement date is March 10 (Thursday).

The same rule applies to bonds, municipal securities, mutual funds (closed-end), and limited

partnerships that trade on an exchange. Options and
government securities such as Treasury bills must
be settled within *one* business day after the trade.

HOW DO YOU PICK A STOCK BROKER?

Brokerage fees are incurred when you purchase or
sell a security. The brokerage fee is typically from 2
to 5 percent of the amount of the transaction. On
sale of a security you pay nominal federal fees.

You can save a lot of money through a discount
broker if you make your own stock choices or you
do not require brokerage reports and services. You
can also negotiate commissions with your broker.
Some discount brokers will do research for clients
for a fee. *Note:* In the past, brokerage recommendations have not been better than random investing.
Furthermore, there is much "sales talk." Before picking a full service or discount broker, do some home-
work, including the following:

1. Look at several brokerages and their fees. Com-
    pare rates and the range of services offered.
    Many brokerages—discount as well as full ser-
    vice—charge a minimum commission rates,
    which means you will pay at least that amount
    for any trade. *Note:* Check out the competition.
    You can get the information about rates from
    Mercer Inc., 80 Fifth Avenue, New York, NY
    10011.

2. Determine how your brokerage house sets its
    rates. Some use the dollar amount of the trans-
    action, some base it on the number of shares.
    The rate also can depend on the type of secu-
    rity traded. For example, it will cost more to
    execute an option trade. Some offer rebates or
    discounts based on the volume of trades.

3. How often and what types of information do you get? Some only mail the statement quarterly, others do it monthly. Some include balances, stock positions, dividends, and interest earned.

ARE YOU BETTER OFF WITH STOCK SPLITS AND STOCK DIVIDENDS?

A company may issue more shares by a stock split and/or stock dividend. A stock split reduces the cost per share proportionately. For example, a two-for-one split means that for each share you had before, you now have two; however, the cost per share is halved so the total cost is identical. A stock split takes place when a business feels its stock price is excessive and wishes to reduce the per share cost to stimulate buying by smaller investors.

A stock dividend is a pro rata distribution of more shares of a firm's stock to investors. For example, a 20 percent stock dividend means that for each 1 share owned you receive .20 share. If you owned 500 shares, you would have 600 shares after the stock dividend.

WHAT MUST YOU KNOW ABOUT CASH DIVIDENDS?

Most companies declare more than half of their net income in dividends. Review a company's dividend trend over the years to anticipate what future dividends might be. Is the firm's dividend policy in conformity with your wants? Refer to Standard and Poor's *Stock Guide* for dividend records and ratings by company.

You pay tax on cash dividends. Such dividends are usually issued quarterly. Important dates for dividends are:

1. *Declaration date.* When the board of directors declare a dividend. At such time, the company obligates itself.
2. *Date of record.* The date you must own the stock to receive the dividend. If you sell your stock before the record date, you forfeit the dividend.
3. *Payment date.* The date the dividend will be mailed to you—typically several weeks subsequent to the date of record.

Example 7—

A company declares a dividend on March 10 (date of declaration) payable April 25 (date of payment) to all shareholders of record April 1 (date of record).

---

4. *Ex-dividend date.* This is three business days before the record date. It determines who is eligible to receive the declared dividend. The ex-dividend date is the one on and after which the privilege to receive the current dividend is not automatically transferred from the seller to the buyer. The stock starts to be traded ex-dividend. The dividend is payable to the shareholder of record prior to the ex-dividend date.

ARE DIVIDEND REINVESTMENT AND CASH OPTION PLANS FOR YOU?

A benefit of a dividend reinvestment plan is that the firm reinvests your dividends to purchase additional shares with little or no brokerage fee. You get more shares at a discount (e.g., 10 percent) off market price. Identify companies having a dividend reinvestment plan by examining Moody's *Annual Dividend Record.*

A disadvantage to dividend reinvestment is the delay in selling reinvested shares, because the company usually retains the reinvested shares. Additionally, the company prohibits you from selling some of the reinvested shares. If you sell, you may be required to sell your entire holdings to terminate the dividend reinvestment account. A delay may exist in purchasing stock via the purchase plan. Additionally, reinvested dividends are treated as ordinary income when paid for tax purposes, regardless of whether the distributions are not received or not in cash. Some plans permit investing more cash (than the dividend payment).

A cash option plan also allows the investment of more money without charges being assessed.

An automatic reinvestment plan is like *dollar-cost averaging*: It gives you the opportunity to buy shares in good and bad markets, thus "averaging out" your cost per share.

IS BUYING STOCK ON MARGIN (CREDIT) A GOOD IDEA?

If you buy shares on margin (credit), interest is assessed on the unpaid balance in your brokerage account. The interest usually is 3 percent above the prevailing interest rates at banks. You can borrow up to 50 percent of the total value of stocks, up to 70 percent for corporate bonds, and up to 90 percent for U.S. Government securities. More must be deposited for stock than for bonds because there is more risk. If your portfolio's value declines significantly, you will get a *margin call* to send in more cash or securities, or sell some stock. There must be at least $2,000 in cash (or equity in securities) on deposit to open a margin account.

Using margin (credit) provides the chance to increase return through leverage. You make a part payment for a security that increases in market price. But your loss may deepen if the market price of the stock portfolio drops.

═══════════════════════════════════════

Example 8—

You purchase 100 shares of TGY Company at $50 per share, ($5,000). You pay 70 percent down ($3,500) with $1,500 on credit. The interest rate is 10 percent. The per annum interest charge is $150 ($1,500 x .10). Assuming per-share price appreciates to $60 and brokerage charges are $100, your return rate equals:

Net return = $1,000 - $150 - $100 = $750

Rate of return = $750/$3,500 = 21.4%

Example 9—

You purchased 200 shares of Ace Company at $30 per share on margin last year. The brokerage commission was $100. You paid 70 percent down with the balance on credit subject to 10 percent in interest charge. You now sell the security for $40 per share minus a brokerage commission of $150. The gain or loss and the return without and with margin appears below:

	Without Margin	With Margin
Cash paid	$6,100	$4,270 (a)
On credit	0	1,830 (b)

	Without Margin	*With Margin*
Initial Cost	$6,100	$6,100
Interest	0	183 (c)
Total cost	$6,100	$6,283
Net sales proceeds	$7,850 (d)	$7,850
Gain or loss	$1,750	$1,567
Return on initial cash investment	28.7% (e)	36.7% (f)

(a) $6,100 x 70% = $4,270

(b) $6,100 x 30% = $1,830

(c) $1,830 x 10% = $183

(d) $8,000 - $150 = $7,850

(e) Gain/Initial cash investment = $1,750/$6,100 = 28.7%

(f) Gain/Initial cash investment = $1,567/$4,270 = 36.7%

IS SELLING SHORT A STOCK ADVISABLE?

In short selling, you gain if stock price declines. To engage in a short sale, your broker borrows stock from someone and then sells it on your behalf to someone else. When market price per share drops, you purchase shares to replace those borrowed. If you buy the shares back at a lower price than the broker sold them for, you make a profit. "Selling short against the box" is when you sell short shares you own rather than borrow. You can only make a short sale on an "up-tick," when the stock's price is increasing. The reason for the up-tick requirement is to prevent further selling that would exacerbate the effect of sharply declining stock prices.

You need a margin account with cash or securities valued at least 50 percent of the market value of the securities you wish to sell short. You must keep the proceeds from the short sale in your brokerage account. Brokerage commissions are incurred on both the sale and repurchase.

Some reasons for short selling include:

1. You expect a declining stock price.
2. You want to delay a gain to postpone taxes on it from one year to another.

You may want to issue a limit order instead of a market order when selling short. A problem in shorting a stock "at the market" is the up-tick rule (i.e., when the current price exceeds the prior one). However, you can always sell short over-the-counter stocks. If market price declines drastically, it may take a while for there to be an up tick.

Example 10—

If GEF Company was initially at $50 per share when you put your order in, and sharply declined when you sold short, the price might fall to, say, $42. You could have insulated yourself from this by placing a limit order to sell, for example, for $47 or more.

CHAPTER 3

RETURN AND RISK

Investment success depends on a comprehension of risk and return. Choosing among alternative investment instruments requires that you estimate and evaluate their risk-return tradeoffs. Therefore, you must understand how to accurately measure the return and the risk associated with an investment. We will discuss how to measure both historical and expected rates of return and risk.

WHAT IS RETURN?

Return is the investment reward. You must compare the expected return for an investment with its risk. *Total return on an investment* equals:

1. Periodic cash payments (current income).
2. Appreciation (or depreciation) in value (capital gains or losses).

Current income may be bond interest, cash dividends, rent, and so on. *Capital gains* or *losses* are changes in market value. A capital gain is the excess of selling price over original cost. A capital loss is the opposite.

Return is measured considering the relevant time period (holding period).

$$\text{Holding Period Return (HPR)} = \frac{\text{Current income + Capital gain (or loss)}}{\text{Purchase price}}$$

Example 1—

Assume the following investments in stocks X and Y for a one-year period of ownership:

	Stock	
	X	Y
Purchase price (beginning of year)	$200	$200
Cash dividend received (during the year)	$15	$20
Sales price (end of year)	$217	$186

The current income from the investment in stocks X and Y for a one-year period are $15 and $20, respectively. For stock X, a capital gain of $17 ($217 sales price - $200 purchase price) is realized for the period. In the case of stock Y, a $14 capital loss ($186 sales price - $200 purchase price) arises. The total return on each investment is computed below:

	Stock	
Return	X	Y
Cash dividend	$15	$20
Capital gain (loss)	17	(14)
Total return	$32	$ 6

Then,

$$\text{HPR (stock X)} = \frac{\$15 + \$17}{\$200} = \frac{\$32}{\$200}$$

$$= 16\%$$

$$\text{HPR (stock Y)} = \frac{\$20 - \$14}{\$200} = \frac{\$6}{\$200}$$

$$= 3\%$$

HOW DO YOU MEASURE RETURN OVER TIME?

It is one thing to calculate the return for a single holding period but another to explain a series of returns over time. If you keep an investment for more than one period, you need to understand how to derive the average of the successive rates of return. Two approaches to multiperiod average (mean) returns are arithmetic average return and the compound (geometric) average return. The *arithmetic average return* is the simple mean of successive one-period rates of return, defined as:

$$\text{Arithmetic average return} = 1/n \sum_{t=1}^{n} r_t$$

where n = the number of time periods and r_t = the single holding period return in time t. *Caution:* The arithmetic average return can be misleading in multiperiod return computations.

A more accurate measure of the actual return obtained from an investment over multiple periods is the *compound (or geometric) average return*. The compound return over n periods is derived as follows:

Compound
average return $= n\sqrt{(1 + r_1)(1 + r_2) \ldots (1 + r_n)} - 1$

$= [(1 + r_1)(1 + r_2) \ldots (1 + r_n)]^{1/n} - 1$

Example 2—

Assume the price of a stock doubles in one period and depreciates back to the original price. Dividend income (current income) is nonexistent.

	Time periods		
	t=0	*t=1*	*t=2*
Price (end of period)	$40	$80	$40
HPR	—	100%	-50%

The arithmetic average return is the average of 100% and -50%, or 25%, as indicated below:

$$\frac{100\% + (-50\%)}{2} = 25\%$$

However, the stock bought for $40 and sold for the same price two periods later did not earn 25 percent; it earned zero. This can be illustrated by determining the compound average return.

Note that n = 2, r1 = 100% = 1, and r2 = -50% = -0.5

Then,

Compound return $= 2\sqrt{(1 + 1)(1 - 0.5)} - 1$

$= 2\sqrt{(2)(0.5)} - 1$

$= 2\sqrt{1} - 1 = 0$

Example 3—

Applying the formula to the data below indicates a compound average of 11.63 percent, somewhat less than the arithmetic average of 26.1 percent.

(1)	(2)	(3)	(4)	(5)
Time	Price	Dividend	Total return	Holding period return (HPR)
0	$100	$—	$—	—
1	60	10	-30(a)	-0.300(b)
2	120	10	70	1.167
3	100	10	-10	-0.083

(a) $10 + ($60 - $100) = $-30
(b) HPR = $-30/$100 = -0.300

The arithematic average return is (-0.300 + 1.167 - 0.083)/3 = .261 = 26.1%, but the compound return is $[(1 - 0.300) (1 + 1.167) + (1 - 0.083)]^{1/3} - 1 = 0.1163$, or 11.63%.

WHAT IS THE EFFECTIVE ANNUAL YIELD?

Different kinds of investments use different compounding periods.

For instance, most bonds pay interest semiannually; some banks offer interest quarterly. If you want to compare investments with different compounding periods, you must put them on a relative basis. The effective annual yield, commonly referred to as *annual percentage rate (APR)*, is used for this purpose:

$$APR = (1 + r/m)^m - 1.0$$

where   r = the stated, nominal or quoted rate
         m = the number of compounding periods per year.

Example 4—

If a bank offers 6 percent interest, compounded quarterly, the annual percentage rate is:

$$APR = (1 + .06/4)^4 - 1.0 = (1.015)^4 - 1.0 = 1.0614 - 1.0$$
$$= .0614 = 6.14\%$$

Thus, if one bank offered 6 percent with quarterly compounding, but another offered 6.14 percent with annual compounding, they would both be offering the same yield.

HOW DO YOU COMPUTE THE EXPECTED RATE OF RETURN?

You are interested in forecasting future returns from an investment in a security. You should specify the most probable outcome, called the *expected rate of return*.

Historical (actual) return rates could furnish a useful basis to formulate future expectations. Probabilities (subjective or objective) may be used to evaluate the expected return. The expected rate of return ($\bar{r}$) is the weighted average of possible returns from a particular investment, weights being probabilities.

$$\bar{r} = \Sigma \; r_i \, p_i$$

where r_i is the ith possible return, p_i is the probability of the ith return, and n is the number of possible returns.

Example 5—

Assume the likely rate of return (including dividends and price changes), depending upon the economic climate (i.e., prosperity, normal, and stagflation). What might you earn next year on a $100,000 investment?

State of economy	Return (r_i)	Probability (p_i)
Prosperity	20%	.5
Normal	10	.3
Stagflation	- 5	.2

The expected rate is:

$\bar{r} = (20\%) \; (.5) + (10\%) \; (.3) + (-5\%) \; (.2) = \; 12\%$

On average, your annual return is 12 percent, ranging from a 5 percent loss to a 20 percent gain.

HOW DO YOU MEASURE RISK?

Total risk may be evaluated by the *standard deviation*, a statistical measure of dispersion of the probability distribution of possible returns. The greater the deviation, the wider the distribution, and therefore, the more risky the investment.

Mathematically,

$$\sigma = \Sigma \ (r_i - \bar{r}) \ p_i$$

To calculate σ, we proceed as follows:

Step 1.   Initially calculate the expected rate of return ($\bar{r}$).

Step 2.   Deduct each possible return from $\bar{r}$ to arrive at a set of deviations ($r_i - \bar{r}$).

Step 3.   Square each deviation, multiply the squared deviation by the probability of occurrence for its respective return, and sum these products to determine the variance:

$$\sigma^2 = \Sigma \ (r_i - \bar{r})^2 p$$

Step 4.   Lastly, use the square root of the variance to obtain the standard deviation.

Example 6—

An example of standard deviation computations follows:

		(step 1)	(step 2)		(step 3)
Return (r_i)	Probability (p_i)	$r_i p_i$	$(r_i - r)$	$(r_i - \bar{r})^2$	$(r_i - \bar{r})^2 p_i$
20%	.5	10%	8%	64	32
10	.3	3	-2	4	1.2
-5	.2	-1	-17	289	57.8
		$\bar{r} = 12\%$			$\sigma^2 = 91$

(step 4) $\sigma = \sqrt{91}$

$\sigma = 9.54\%$

The expected annual return has an average variation of 9.54 percent.

Selected return rates and standard deviations appear in Table 1.

Table 1—

Risk and Return 1926-1992

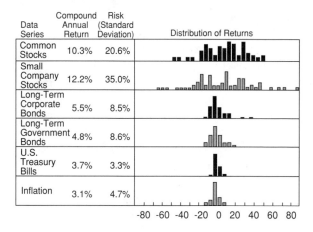

Data Series	Compound Annual Return	Risk (Standard Deviation)	Distribution of Returns
Common Stocks	10.3%	20.6%	
Small Company Stocks	12.2%	35.0%	
Long-Term Corporate Bonds	5.5%	8.5%	
Long-Term Government Bonds	4.8%	8.6%	
U.S. Treasury Bills	3.7%	3.3%	
Inflation	3.1%	4.7%	

-80 -60 -40 -20 0 20 40 60 80

Source: Ibbotson, R., and Rex A. Sinquefield, *Stocks, Bonds, Bills and Inflation 1994 Yearbook*, Ibbotson Associates, Chicago.

Table 1 reveals that the highest return rates and risk are with small company stocks.

WHAT RISKS DO YOU FACE?

Any investment is susceptible to risk (uncertainty). Risk refers to the fluctuation in profit as well as to

the possibility of losing some or all of your investment. You face different types of risks when selecting an investment. The irony is that they could produce unexpected returns. Risks include:

1. *Liquidity risk.* The chance that an asset may not
    be sold on short notice for its market value.

2. *Inflation (purchasing power) risk.* The failure of
    your assets to earn a return to keep up with in-
    creasing price levels. Bonds are exposed to this
    risk because the issuer will be paying back in
    cheaper dollars in inflationary times.

3. *Interest rate risk.* The variability in the value of
    an asset due to changing interest rates and
    money conditions. For example, if interest rates
    increase (decrease), bond (stock) prices decrease
    (increase).

4. *Business risk.* The risk associated with changes
    in firm's sales. This may be due to operating
    difficulties such as strikes and technological ob-
    solescence.

5. *Market risk.* The change in the price of a stock
    arising from changes in the overall stock mar-
    ket, irrespective of the fundamental financial
    condition of the company. For instance, stock
    prices of companies may be affected by bull or
    bear markets.

6. *Default risk.* The risk that the issuing company
    may be unable to pay interest and/or principal
    when due. An example is a financially unsound
    company.

7. *Financial risk.* A type of investment risk associ-
    ated with excessive debt.

8. *Industry risk.* The uncertainty of the inherent na-
    ture of the industry (such as high-technology),
    product liability, and accidents.

9. *International and political risks.* The risks stem-
    ming from foreign operations in politically un-
    stable foreign countries. An example is a U.S.

company with operations located in a hostile country.

10. *Economic risk*. The negative impact on a company from economic slowdowns. For example, airlines have lower business volume in recessions.
11. *Currency exchange risk*. The risk arising from the fluctuation in foreign exchange rates.
12. *Social risk*. Problems facing the company due to ethnic boycott, discrimination cases, and environmental concerns.

Risk levels vary among investments. For example, stocks experience less inflation risk than fixed income securities. Money market investments have less liquidity risk than real estate.

WHAT CAN BE DONE TO REDUCE RISK?

Diversification reduces a portfolio's risk (e.g., stocks, bonds, real estate). The value of each component does not increase or decrease in value in the same amount or at the same time. You are protecting against wide variations. One approach is a mutual fund consisting of a professionally managed portfolio.

Besides diversifying by investments, you can diversify by maturity. For instance, you may buy bonds having different maturity dates so as to minimize interest risk.

WHAT ARE THE CONSIDERATIONS IN DETERMINING HOW MUCH RISK TO TAKE?

In looking at an investment, consider the following:

1.   What types of risk are associated with it?

2.   What risks can or cannot be eliminated or re-
     duced through diversification?

3.   What are the returns for those? Is the return
     sufficient for that risk?

In deciding your risk tolerance, consider:

- *Family status*. If you are single, you can assume
  more risk than if you are married with children.

- *Age*. If you are young, you can assume more
  risk than if you are old.

- *Personality*. If you are a nervous person, invest
  less in stocks or more in cash equivalents such
  as CDs.

- *Financial status*. If your net worth and liquidity
  are healthy, you can assume more investment
  risk.

- *Tax rate*. If your tax bracket is high, you can assume more risk when investing in stocks and
  bonds because the loss for each   year (up to
  $3,000) is tax deductible.

- *Business knowledge*. If you are a sophisticated
  investor, you can take on more risk.

- *Occupation*. Invest defensively if you have an
  uncertain job or fluctuating income.

The risk/return trade-off depends in part upon
your utility preferences and comfort level.

HOW DOES THE RISK/RETURN TRADE-OFF WORK?

Risk and return are the primary ingredients in investment choices. Expected return must be compared to risk. As risk increases, so must the return to compensate for the greater uncertainty. The risk/return trade-off is crucial. A new business may involve a lot of risk. Therefore, a higher return is required. On the other hand, U.S. T-bills have minimal risk, so a low return is appropriate.

Risk (uncertainty) creates potential higher return. You should seek the highest possible return at the risk level you are willing to accept.

Referring back to Table 1, during the period 1926-1992, common stocks produced returns averaging 10.3 percent annually with a 20.6 percent risk. Small company stocks returned 12.2 percent with a higher risk, 35.0 percent. Long-term bonds have averaged 5.5 percent annually with an 8.5 percent risk. Short-term Treasury bills averaged 3.7 percent annually with a meager 3.3 percent risk. These returns illustrate the risk/return trade-off.

The trade-off is on average, not for each case. As an investor, you need to evaluate each investment separately, comparing expected returns with the risks. The trade-off is also a warning flag: Higher potential returns flag higher risks, even if the risks are not apparent at first.

In general, the risk/return characteristics of each of the major investment instruments can be displayed in a risk/return graph, as shown in Figure 1. Although the locations on the diagram are only approximate, it should be apparent that you can pick from a wide variety of vehicles, each having certain risk/return combinations.

Figure 1—

Risk/Return Trade-Offs for Various Investment Vehicles

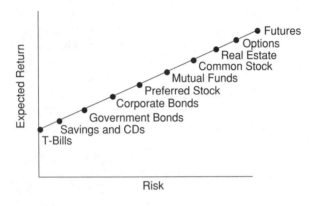

WHAT IS THE MEANING OF BETA?

Total risk of a security equals:

unsystematic risk + systematic risk

Unsystematic risk is specific to the company and is reduced by *diversification*. Examples are union problems and financial difficulties of the firm. When additional securities are added to the portfolio, we spread the risk and the unsystematic risk of the portfolio decreases.

Nondiversifiable risk (systematic) risk emanates from uncontrollable forces and is therefore not unique to the stock. Examples are inflation and interest rate changes. Systematic risk relates to the reaction of specific stocks (or portfolios) to changes in the general market.

In sum, the *total* risk of each stock is irrelevant. It is the systematic component of that total instability that is relevant for valuation. It is the only element of total risk that investors will get paid to assume, and it is measured by *beta*. Beta aids in estimating how much the security will rise or fall if you know which direction the market will go. It assists in determining risk and expected return.

There is a relationship between a security's expected (or required) return and its beta (see Figure 2). The formula to determine a security's expected return is:

$$r_j = r_f + b (r_m - r_f)$$

where r_j = a security's expected (required) return, r_f = risk-free rate, and r_m = market return. Or, stated otherwise:

Expected return = risk-free rate + beta (market return - risk-free rate)

= risk-free rate + beta x market risk premium

where the risk-free rate equals the rate on a security like a T-bill and the risk-free rate *less* expected market return (e.g., Standard & Poor's 500 Stock Composite Index) is called the *market risk premium.*

The market risk premium is the extra return exceeding that offered on a T-bill, to justify taking on certain risk expressed by *beta*. The relevant expression of risk is the risk of the individual security, or its beta. The higher a stock's beta, the greater the return expected (or required) by the investor.

Example 7—

Assume the risk-free rate equals 5.5 percent, and expected market return equals 12 percent. If a beta is 2.0, the risk premium equals: 2.0 x (12% - 5.5%) = 2.0 x 6.5% = 13%

The investor would want an extra 13 percent (risk premium) on the security besides the risk-free return of 5.5 percent. Hence, the expected return is 5.5% + 13% = 18.5%

Figure 2—

Risk and Return

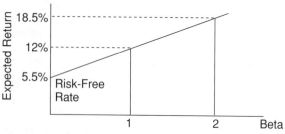

HOW DO YOU READ BETA?

Beta is a security's volatility compared to an average security.

It measures a security's return over time to the overall market. For example, if a company's beta is 1.5, it means that if the stock market rises 10%, the company's common stock increases 15%; if the market falls 10%, the company goes down 15%. A guideline on reading beta follows:

Beta	*Meaning*
0	The security's return is independent of the market. An example is a risk-free security (e.g., T-bill).

0.5   The security is half as volatile as the market.

1.0   The security is as volatile or risky as the market
        (i.e., average risk). This is the beta value of the
        market portfolio (e.g., Standard & Poor's 500).

2.0   The security is twice as volatile or risky, as the
        market.

Betas for stocks are available in investment newsletters and periodicals. Examples are *Value Line Investment Survey* and *S&P's Stock Guide*. Below is a list of some betas:

Companies	Betas
Philip Morris	1.25
Bristol-Meyers	1.05
IBM	.90
Exxon	.80
McDonalds	1.05
Microsoft	1.35
Coca-Cola	1.10

Source: *Value Line Investment Survey* (January 1995), published by Value Line, Inc., 711 3rd Avenue, New York, NY 10017.

Example 8—

XYZ stock returned 10 percent. The risk-free rate on T-bill is 6 percent, market return is 12 percent, and the company's beta is 1.3. What is the expected return?

Expected (required) return = 6% + 1.3 (12% - 6%)

= 6% + 7.8%

= 13.8%

Because the actual return (10 percent) is below the required return (13.8 percent), you would not want to buy the stock.

Example 9—

The higher a stock's beta, the greater the return expected (or demanded) by the investor, as follows:

Stock	Beta	Required return
Mobil	.85	6%+.85(12%-6%)=11.1%
Bristol-Myers	1.0	6%+1.0(12%-6%)=12%
Neiman-Marcus	1.65	6%+1.65(12%-6%)=15.9%

HOW DO INVESTMENT ALTERNATIVES AFFECT THE RISK/RETURN TRADE-OFF?

Investment alternatives differ as to both return and risk. Table 2 summarizes major types of investments and their return/risk characteristics. The rankings are the authors' opinions. The ranking is for a typical investment within the category. However, there are many variations within each class.

Table 2—

Investment Alternatives and Return/Risk Considerations

Investment Type	Total Return	Liquidity Risk	Inflation Risk	Interest Power Risk	Business Rate Risk	Market Risk
Savings accounts, money market accounts, CDs	Low	None	High	High	Very Low or None	None
Savings bonds, Treasury securities	Low	Low	High	High	Very low	None

Investment Type	Total Return	Liquidity Risk	Inflation Risk	Interest Power Risk	Business Rate Risk	Market Risk
High-grade corporate and municipal bonds	Average	Low	Average	Average	Low	Average
Balanced mutual funds, high-grade preferred stock	High	Very low	Low	Average	Low	Average
High-grade common stocks, growth funds	High	Very low	Low	Average	Very low	Average
Real estate	High-Very High	High	Average	High	Low-average	Low
Speculative stocks and bonds	High	Average	High	High	High	High
Options and futures	Very High	Very High	Low-Average	Low-High	Very High	Very High
Collectibles	High-Very High	Aver-age	Aver-age	Aver age	Average-High	Aver-age

CHAPTER **4**

FUNDAMENTAL ANALYSIS

Fundamental analysis concentrates on the future outlook of growth and earnings. The analysis studies such elements as earnings, sales, management, and assets. It looks at three things: The overall economy, the industry, and the company itself. Through the study of these elements, you are trying to determine whether the stock is undervalued or overvalued compared to the current market price.

In other words, for a valuation of a stock, you should be aware of economic conditions, political environment, market status, industry surroundings, and company performance. Ideally, the intelligent investor should obtain answers to at least four basic questions:

1. What is the state of the economy? In view of such conditions, is it a good time to invest? Where are we in the business cycle? Is the boom likely to top out shortly? Is a recession near at hand? Questions in this area will vary with the stage of the business cycle.

2. What is the state of the market? Are we in the early stages of a bull market? Has the low point of a bear market been reached? Is the bull market about to top out? Questions to be asked will vary with the state of the market.

3. What is the state of the industry? If answers to the preceding two questions seem favorable, then there must be an investment selection.

What industries are likely to grow most rapidly? Are there any special factors which favor a particular industry?

4.   What company is desirable? Which company or companies within the industry are likely to be best? Which companies are to be avoided because of poor prospects?

Figure 1 summarizes various factors that will go into your investment decision-making process, ranging from economics and the external environment surrounding the investment vehicle to the company's performance measures.

Figure 1—

```
┌─────────────────────────────────────────┐
│          Economic Analysis               │
│    (Assesing the Future Performance      │
│        of the Overall Economy)           │
├─────────────────────────────────────────┤
│  Business Cycles, Monetary Fiscal Policy,│
│  Economic Indicators, Government Policy,  │
│  World Events and Foreign Trade, Public   │
│  Attitudes of Optimism or Pessimism,      │
│  Domestic Legislation, Inflation, GNP     │
│  Growth, Unemployment, Productivity,      │
│ Capacity Utilization, Interest Rates and More│
└─────────────────────────────────────────┘
                    │
                    ▼
┌─────────────────────────────────────────┐
│           Industry  Analysis             │
│    (Based on the Economic and Market     │
│  Analysis, Determining the Business Cycle's│
│      Impact on Specific Industries and    │
│     Evaluating Industry Characteristics)  │
├─────────────────────────────────────────┤
│    Business Cycle Exposure, Industry      │
│ Structure, Growth of the Industry, Competition,│
│  Product Quality, Cost Elements, Government│
│    Regulations, Labor Position, Technological│
│   Development, Financial Norms and Standards│
└─────────────────────────────────────────┘
                    │
                    ▼
┌─────────────────────────────────────────┐
│           Company Analysis               │
│    (Analyzing how Specfic Companies       │
│    Perform in Terms of their Operating and│
│      Financial Features Given Industry     │
│         Changes and the Economy)          │
├─────────────────────────────────────────┤
│      Growth of Sales, Earnings, Dividends,│
│  Quality of Earnings, Position in the Industry,│
│     Discount Rates, Fundamental Analysis   │
│   (Balance Sheet Analysis, Income Statement│
│    Analysis, Cash Flow Analysis), Analysis of│
│ Accounting Policy and Footnotes, Management,│
│  Research and Development, Return and Risk,│
│  Brands, Patents, Goodwill, and Diversification│
└─────────────────────────────────────────┘
```

FUNDAMENTAL ANALYSIS

Fundamental analysis evaluates a firm's stock based on an examination of the corporation's financial statements. It considers overall financial health, economic and political conditions, industry factors, and future outlook of the company. The analysis attempts to ascertain whether stock is overpriced, underpriced, or priced in proportion to its market value. A stock is valuable to you only if you can predict the future financial performance of the business. Financial statement analysis gives you much of the data you will need to forecast earnings and dividends.

A complete set of financial statements will include the balance sheet, income statement, and statement of cash flows. The first two are vital in financial statement analysis. We will discuss the various financial-statement-analysis tools that you will use in evaluating stocks and bonds. These tools include horizontal, vertical, and ratio analysis, which give a relative measure of the performance and condition of the company.

WHY IS RISK ANALYSIS IMPORTANT?

Before you decide to invest in a company, you should consider that firm's economic and political risk. Economic risk relates to the firm's ability to cope with recession and inflation. To determine this, you should find out if the company's business is cyclical; a cyclical business may not be able to pay fixed expenses in a downward economy. Earnings that are affected by cyclical activity can be unstable. Business cycles arise from three conditions: (1) changes in demand; (2) diversification of customer base; and (3) product diversification. The greater the changes in product demand, the more the company is affected by the business cycle, and thus the greater the profit variability. Diversification of customer base protects the firm because revenue is derived from industries that are affected in different ways by the business cycle. Furthermore, a company with noncyclical or countercyclical business lines has greater stability. Finally, a firm with an inadequately diversified product mix will have high correlation of income between products. The higher this correlation, the more the economic cycle will affect the business. Examples are Eastern Airlines and Chrysler. Can you think of other companies that have a high economic risk?

You should make an analysis of the economy primarily to determine your investment strategy. It is not necessary for you to formulate your own economic forecasts. You can rely on published forecasts in an effort to identify the trends in the economy and adjust your investment position accordingly. You must keep abreast of the economic trend and direction and attempt to see how they affect the security market. Unfortunately, there are too many economic indicators and variables to be analyzed. Each has its own significance. In many cases, these variables could give *mixed* signals about the future of the economy and therefore mislead the investor.

Figure 2 summarizes the types of economic variables and their probable effect on the security market and the economy in general. Figure 3 provides a concise and brief list of the significant economic indicators and how they affect bond yields.

Figure 2—

Economic Variables and Their Impact on the Economy and the Security Market

Economic Variables	*Impact on Security Market*
Real growth in GNP (without inflation)	Positive
Industrial production	Consecutive drops are a sign of recession
Inflation	Detrimental to equity and bond prices
Capacity utilization	A high percentage is positive, but full capacity is inflationary
Durable goods orders	Consecutive drops are a sign of recession
Increase in business investment, consumer confidence, personal income, etc.	Positive
Leading indicators	The rise is bullish for the economy and the market; consecutive drops are a sign of bad times ahead
Housing starts	The rise is positive; vice versa
Corporate profits	Strong corporate earnings are positive for the market; vice versa
Unemployment	Unfavorable for the market and economy

Economic Variables	Impact on Security Market
Increase in business inventories	Positive for the inflationary economy, negative for the stable economy
Federal deficit	Inflationary and negative; positive for the depressed economy
Deficit in trade and balance of payments	Negative
Weak dollar	Negative
Interest rates	Rising rates depress the value of fixed income securities such as bond prices which tend to fall; vice versa

Source: Shim, Jae K., and Joel Siegel, *The Complete Guide to Investment Information* (International Publishing Corporation, 1992).

Figure 3—

*Economic Indicators and Bond Yields**

Indicators**	Effects on Bond Yields***	Reasons
Business Activity		
GNP and industrial production falls	Fall	As economy slows, Fed may ease credit by allowing rates to fall

(continued)

Figure 3—

| | *Effects on* | |
| Indicators** | Bond Yields*** | Reasons |

Business Activity

Unemployment rises	Fall	High unemployment indicates lack of economic expansion; Fed may loosen credit
Inventories rise	Fall	Inventory levels are good indicators of duration of economic slowdown
Trade deficit rises	Fall	Dollar weakens
Leading indicators rise	Rise	Advance signals about economic health; Fed may tighten credit
Housing starts rise	Rise	Growing economy due to increased new housing demand; Fed may tighten; mortgage rates rise
Personal income rises	Rise	Higher income means higher consumer spending, thus inflationary; Fed may tighten

Inflation

| Consumer Price Index rises | Rise | Inflationary |
| Producer Price Index rises | Rise | Early signal for inflation |

Monetary Policy

| Money supply rises | Rise | Excess growth in money supply is inflationary; Fed may tighten |
| Discount rate rises | Rise | Causes increase in business and consumer loan rates; used to slow economic growth and inflation |

Indicators**	Effects on Bond Yields***	Reasons
Monetary Policy		
Fed buys (sells) bills	Rise (fall)	Adds (deducts) money to (from) the economy; interest rates may go down (up)
Required reserve rises	Rise	Depresses banks' lending

---

*This table merely serves as a handy guide and should not be construed as accurate at all time

** Fall in any of these indicators will have the opposite effect on bond yields.

***Note: The effects are based on yield and are therefore opposite of how *bond prices* will be affected.

Source: Shim, Jae K., and Joel Siegel, *The Complete Guide to Investment Information* (International Publishing Corporation, 1992).

Why Are Political Uncertainties Important to Consider?

Political risk relates to foreign operations and governmental regulation. Multinational firms with significant foreign operations face uncertainties applying to the repatriation of funds, currency fluctuations, and foreign customs and regulations. Also, operations in politically unstable regions present risk. You should determine the company's earnings and assets in each foreign country.

You should ascertain whether government regulation—foreign or domestic—is excessively strict. For example, a regulatory agency may try to restrain a utility from passing rate increases on to consumers, or it may refuse to approve construction of a nuclear power plant. Tight environmental and safety regulations may exist, such as stringent safety and pollution control requirements. Also consider the effect of current and proposed tax legislation on the business.

Companies that rely on government contracts and subsidies may lack stability because government spending is susceptible to changing political leadership. You should determine the percent of income a company obtains from government contracts and subsidies.

LOOKING AT THE INDUSTRY

In fundamental analysis, you must appraise trends in the industry of which your chosen company is a part. What is the pattern of expansion or decline in the industry? The profit dollar is worth more if earned in a healthy, expanding industry than a declining one. A firm in a rapidly changing technological industry (computers, for example) faces uncertainty due to obsolescence. A business in a staple industry has more stability because demand for its products does not fluctuate.

Capital-intensive companies usually have a high degree of operating leverage (fixed cost to total cost); examples are airlines and autos. High operating leverage magnifies changes in earnings resulting from small changes in sales leading to earnings instability. Also, risk exists because fixed costs, such as rent, cannot be slashed during a decline in business activity. Earnings will therefore fall off dramatically. Labor-intensive companies are generally more stable because of the variable-cost nature of the business. Variable costs, such as labor, can be reduced when business takes a turn for the worse.

You should examine the past and expected future stability of the industry by examining competitive forces such as ease of entry and price wars. What industries would you avoid, and why? How about industry lifecycles? In the early part of their lives most industries grow at a very rapid rate. After a time the growth rate slows down; while expansion continues, it is at a more moderate pace (mature growth). Finally, they stop growing and either live a relatively stable existence for a long time—or die.

Industries can be categorized as follows:

1. Noncyclical industries—relatively resistant to business cycles (defensive investments), such as food, drugs, or utilities.

2. Cyclical industries—durable goods such as automobiles, heavy equipment, and housing materials.

3. Growth industries—less influenced by business cycles than by investors' expectations that these producers will grow faster than the economy as a whole, including such research-intensive producers as bio-technology firms.

ANALYZING FINANCIAL STATEMENTS

Now you turn to the company. The analysis of financial statements reveals important information to present and prospective investors. Financial statement analysis attempts to answer the following basic questions:

1. How well is the business doing?
2. What are its strengths?
3. What are its weaknesses?
4. How does it fare in the industry?
5. Is the business improving or deteriorating?

What and Why of Financial Statement Analysis?

You, as an investor, are interested in the present and future level of return (earnings) and risk (liquidity, debt, and activity). You, therefore, evaluate a firm's stock based on an examination of its financial statements. This evaluation considers overall financial health, economic and political conditions, industry factors, and future outlook of the company.

What Are Horizontal and Vertical Analyses?

Comparison of two or more years' financial data is known as *horizontal analysis*. Horizontal analysis concentrates on the trend in the accounts in dollar *and* percentage terms over the years. It is typically presented in comparative financial statements (see Biogen, Inc., financial data in Figures 4 and 5). In annual reports, comparative financial data are usually shown for five years.

Through horizontal analysis you can pinpoint areas of wide divergence requiring investigation. For example, in the income statement shown in Figure 4, the significant rise in sales returns taken with the reduction in sales for 19X1-19X2 should cause concern. You might compare these results with those of competitors.

It is essential to present both the dollar amount of change and the percentage of change since the use of one without the other may result in erroneous conclusions. The interest expense from 19X0-19X1 went up by 100.0 percent, but this represented only $1,000 and may not need further investigation. In a similar vein, a large number changes might cause a small percentage change and not be of any great importance.

Key changes and trends can also be highlighted by the use of *common-size statements*. A common-size statement shows the separate items appearing on it in percentage terms. Preparation of common-size statements is known as *vertical analysis*. In vertical analysis, a material financial statement item is used as a base value and all other accounts on the financial statement are compared to it. In the balance sheet in Figure 5, for example, total assets equal 100 percent. Each asset is stated as a percentage of total assets. Similarly, total liabilities and stockholders' equity is assigned 100 percent, with a given liability or equity account stated as a percentage of the total liabilities and stockholders' equity.

Placing all assets in common-size form clearly shows the relative importance of the current assets as compared to the noncurrent assets. It also shows that significant changes have taken place in the composition of the current assets over the last year. Notice, for example, that receivables have increased in relative importance and that cash has declined in relative importance. The deterioration in the cash position may be a result of inability to collect from customers.

For the income statement, 100 percent is assigned to net sales, with all other revenue and expense accounts related to it. It is possible to see at a glance how each dollar of sales is distributed between the various costs, expenses, and profits. For example, notice from Figure 6 that 64.8 cents of every dollar of sales were needed to cover cost of goods sold in 19X2, as compared to only 57.3 cents in the prior year; also notice that only 9.9 cents out of every dollar of sales remained for profits in 19X2—down from 13.6 cents in the prior year.

You should also compare the vertical percentages of the business to those of the competition and
to the industry norms. Then you can determine how
the company fares in the industry.

Figure 6 shows a common-size income statement based on the data provided in Figure 4.

Figure 4—

Biogen, Inc.
Comparative Income Statement (in Thousands of Dollars)
for the Years Ended December 31, 19X2, 19X1, 19X0

	19X2	19X1	19X0	Increase or Decrease 19X2-19X1	Increase or Decrease 19X1-19X0	% Increase or Decrease 19X2-19X1	% Increase or Decrease 19X1-19X0
Sales	$98.3	$120.0	$56.6	($21.7)	$63.4	-18.1%	112.0%
Sales Return & Allowances	$18.0	$10.0	$4.0	$8.0	$6.0	80.0%	150.0%
Net Sales	$80.3	$110.0	$52.6	($29.7)	$57.4	-27.0%	109.1%
Cost of Goods Sold	$52.0	$63.0	$28.0	($11.0)	$35.0	-17.5%	125.0%
Gross Profit	$28.3	$47.0	$24.6	($18.7)	$22.4	-39.8%	91.1%
Operating Expenses							
Selling Expenses	$12.0	$13.0	$11.0	($1.0)	$2.0	-7.7%	18.2%
General Expenses	$5.0	$8.0	$3.0	($3.0)	$5.0	-37.5%	166.7%
Total Operating Expenses	$17.0	$21.0	$14.0	($4.0)	$7.0	-19.0%	50.0%

Figure 4—*continued*

Income from Operations	$11.3	$26.0	$10.6	($14.7)	$15.4	-56.5%	145.3%
Nonoperating Income	$4.0	$1.0	$2.0	$3.0	($1.0)	300.0%	-50.0%
Income before Interest & Taxes	$15.3	$27.0	$12.6	($11.7)	$14.4	-43.3%	114.3%
Interest Expense	$2.0	$2.0	$1.0	$0.0	$1.0	0.0%	100.0%
Income before Taxes	$13.3	$25.0	$11.6	($11.7)	$13.4	-46.8%	115.5%
Income Taxes (40%)	$5.3	$10.0	$4.6	($4.7)	$5.4	-46.8%	115.5%
Net Income	$8.0	$15.0	$7.0	($7.0)	$8.0	-46.8%	115.5%

Figure 5—

Biogen, Inc.
Comparative Balance Sheet (in Thousands of Dollars)
December 31, 19X2, 19X1, 19X0

	19X2	19X1	19X0	Increase or Decrease 19X2-19X1	Increase or Decrease 19X1-19X0	% Increase or Decrease 19X2-19X1	% Increase or Decrease 19X1-19X0
ASSETS							
Current Assets:							
Cash	$28	$36	$36	-8	0	-22.2%	0.0%
Marketable Securities	$22	$15	$7	7	8	46.7%	114.3%
Accounts Receivable	$21	$16	$10	5	6	31.3%	60.0%
Inventory	$53	$46	$49	7	-3	15.2%	-6.1%
Total Current Assets	$124	$113	$102	11	11	9.7%	10.8%
Plant and Equip.	$103	$91	$83	12	8	13.2%	9.6%
Total Assets	$227	$204	$185	23	19	11.3%	10.3%

(continued)

75

Figure 5—continued

LIABILITIES							
Current Liabilities	$56	$50	$51	6	-1	12.0%	-2.0%
Long-Term Debt	$83	$74	$69	9	5	12.2%	7.2%
Total Liabilities	$139	$124	$120	15	4	12.1%	3.3%
STOCKHOLDERS' EQUITY							
Common Stock, $10 par, 4,600 Shares	$46	$46	$46	0	0	0.0%	0.0%
Retained Earnings	$42	$34	$19	8	15	23.5%	78.9%
Total Stockholders' Equity	$88	$80	$65	8	15	10.0%	23.1%
Total Liabilities and Stockholders' Equity	$227	$204	$185	23	19	11.3%	10.3%

Figure 6—

Biogen, Inc.
Income Statement and Common-Size Analysis (in Thousands of Dollars)
for the Years Ended December 31, 19X2 & 19X1

	19X2 Amount	%	19X1 Amount	%
Sales	$98.3	122.4%	$120.0	109.1%
Sales Return & Allowances	$18.0	22.4%	$10.0	9.1%
Net Sales	$80.3	100.0%	$110.0	100.0%
Cost of Goods Sold	$52.0	64.8%	$63.0	57.3%
Gross Profit	$28.3	35.2%	$47.0	42.7%
Operating Expenses				
Selling Expenses	$12.0	14.9%	$13.0	11.8%
General Expenses	$5.0	6.2%	$8.0	7.3%
Total Operating Expenses	$17.0	21.2%	$21.0	19.1%

(continued)

Figure 6—*continued*

Income from Operations	$11.3	14.1%	$26.0	23.6%
Nonoperating Income	$4.0	5.0%	$1.0	0.9%
Income before Interest & Taxes	$15.3	19.1%	$27.0	24.5%
Interest Expense	$2.0	2.5%	$2.0	1.8%
Income before Taxes	$13.3	16.6%	$25.0	22.7%
Income Taxes (40%)	$5.3	6.6%	$10.0	9.1%
Net Income	$8.0	9.9%	$15.0	13.6%

WORKING WITH FINANCIAL RATIOS

Horizontal and vertical analysis compares one figure to another within the same category. It is also
vital to compare two figures applicable to different
categories. This is accomplished by ratio analysis.
In this section, you will learn how to calculate the
various financial ratios and how to interpret them.
The results of the ratio analysis will allow you to:

1. Appraise the position of a business.
2. Identify trouble spots that need attention.
3. Provide the basis for making projections and
   forecasts about the course of future operations.

Think of ratios as measures of the relative health
of a business. Just as a doctor takes readings of a
patient's temperature, blood pressure, heart rate,
and so on, you will take readings of a business's
liquidity, profitability, leverage, efficiency in using
assets, and market value. Where the doctor compares the readings to generally accepted guidelines,
such as a temperature of 98.6 degrees as normal,
you make some comparisons to the norms.

To obtain useful conclusions from the ratios,
you must make two comparisons:

- *Industry comparison.* This will allow you to answer the question, "How does a business fare
  in the industry?" You must compare the
  company's ratios to those of competing companies in the industry or with industry standards (averages). You can obtain industry
  norms from financial services such as *Value Line*,
  Dun and Bradstreet, and *Standard and Poor's*.

- *Trend analysis.* To see how the business is doing over time, you will compare a given ratio
  for one company over several years to see the
  direction of financial health or operational per-

formance. *Note:* It is always advisable to combine these two comparisons, that is, industry comparison and over time, as shown in Figure 7.

Figure 7—

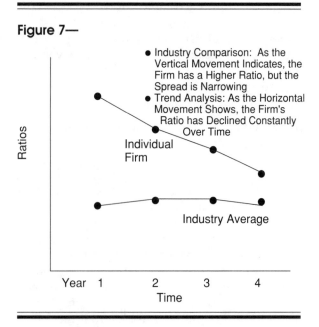

- Industry Comparison: As the Vertical Movement Indicates, the Firm has a Higher Ratio, but the Spread is Narrowing
- Trend Analysis: As the Horizontal Movement Shows, the Firm's Ratio has Declined Constantly Over Time

Individual Firm

Industry Average

Ratios

Year 1   2   3   4

Time

Financial ratios can be grouped into the following types: liquidity, asset utilization (activity), solvency (leverage and debt service), profitability, and market value.

How Do You Evaluate a Company's Liquidity?

Liquidity is the firm's ability to satisfy maturing short-term debt. Liquidity is crucial to carrying out the business, especially during periods of adversity. It relates to the short term, typically a period of one year or less. Poor liquidity might lead to higher cost of financing and inability to pay bills and dividends. The three basic measures of liquidity are (a) net working capital, (b) the current ratio, and (c) the quick (acid-test) ratio.

Throughout our discussion, keep referring to Figures 4 and 5 to make sure you understand where the numbers come from.

Net working capital equals current assets minus current liabilities. Net working capital for 19X2 is:

$$\text{Net working capital} = \text{current assets} - \text{current liabilities}$$
$$= \$124 - \$56$$
$$= \$68$$

In 19X1, net working capital was $63. The rise over the year is favorable.

The current ratio equals current assets divided by current liabilities. The ratio reflects the company's ability to satisfy current debt from current assets.

$$\text{Current ratio} = \frac{\text{current assets}}{\text{current liabilities}}$$

For 19X2, the current ratio is:

$$\frac{\$124}{\$56} = 2.21$$

In 19X1, the current ratio was 2.26. The ratio's decline over the year points to a slight reduction in liquidity.

A more stringent liquidity test can be found in the quick (acid-test) ratio. Inventory and prepaid expenses are excluded from the total of current assets, leaving only the more liquid (or quick) assets to be divided by current liabilities.

$$\text{Quick ratio} = \frac{\text{cash} + \text{marketable securities} + \text{accounts receivable}}{\text{current liabilities}}$$

The quick ratio for 19X2 is:

$$\frac{\$28 + \$21 + \$22}{\$56} = 1.27$$

In 19X1, the ratio was 1.34. A small reduction in the ratio over the period points to less liquidity.

The overall liquidity trend shows a slight deterioration as reflected in the lower current and quick ratios, although it is better than the industry norms (see Figure 8 for industry averages). But a mitigating factor is the increase in net working capital.

How Well Does the Company Utilize Its Assets?

Asset utilization (activity, turnover) ratios reflect the way in which a company uses its assets to obtain revenue and profit. One example is how well receivables are turning into cash. The higher the ratio, the more efficiently the business manages its assets.

Accounts receivable ratios comprise the accounts receivable turnover and the average collection period.

The *accounts receivable turnover* provides the number of times accounts receivable are collected in the year. It is derived by dividing net credit sales by average accounts receivable.

You can calculate average accounts receivable by the average accounts receivable balance during a period.

$$\text{Accounts receivable turnover} = \frac{\text{net credit sales}}{\text{average accounts receivable}}$$

For 19X2, the average accounts receivable is:

$$\frac{\$21 + \$16}{2} = \$18.5$$

The accounts receivable turnover for 19X2 is:

$$\frac{\$80.3}{\$18.5} = 4.34$$

In 19X1, the turnover was 8.46. There is a sharp reduction in the turnover rate pointing to a collection problem.

The *average collection period* is the length of time it takes to collect receivables. It represents the number of days receivables are held.

$$\text{Average collection period} = \frac{365 \text{ days}}{\text{accounts receivable turnover}}$$

In 19X2, the collection period is:

$$\frac{365}{4.34} = 84.1 \text{ days}$$

It takes this firm about 84 days to convert receivables to cash. In 19X1, the collection period was 43.1 days. The significant lengthening of the collection period may be a cause for some concern; it may be a result of the presence of many doubtful accounts, or it may be a result of poor credit management.

Inventory ratios are useful, especially when a buildup in inventory exists. Inventory ties up cash.

Holding large amounts of inventory can result in lost opportunities for profit as well as increased storage costs. Before you extend credit or lend money, you should examine the firm's *inventory turnover* and *average age of inventory*.

$$\text{Inventory turnover} = \frac{\text{cost of goods sold}}{\text{average inventory}}$$

The inventory turnover for 19X2 is:

$$\frac{\$52}{\$49.5} = 1.05$$

For 19X1, the turnover was 1.33.

$$\text{Average age of inventory} = \frac{365}{\text{inventory turnover}}$$

In 19X2, the average age is:

$$\frac{365}{1.05} = 347.6 \text{ days}$$

In the previous year, the average age was 274.4 days.

The reduction in the turnover and increase in inventory age points to a longer holding of inventory. You should ask why the inventory is not selling as quickly.

The *operating cycle* is the number of days it takes to convert inventory and receivables to cash.

$$\text{Operating cycle} = \text{average collection period} + \text{average age of inventory}$$

In 19X2, the operating cycle is:

$$84.1 \text{ days} + 347.6 \text{ days} = 431.7 \text{ days}$$

In the previous year, the operating cycle was 317.5 days. An unfavorable direction is indicated because additional funds are tied up in noncash assets. Cash is being collected more slowly.

By calculating the *total asset turnover*, you can find out whether the company is efficiently employing its total assets to obtain sales revenue. A low ratio may indicate too high an investment in assets in comparison to the sales revenue generated.

$$\text{Total asset turnover} = \frac{\text{net sales}}{\text{average total assets}}$$

In 19X2, the ratio is:

$$\frac{\$80.3}{(\$204 + \$227)/2} = \frac{\$80.3}{\$215.5} = .37$$

In 19X1, the ratio was .57 ($110/$194.5). There has been a sharp reduction in asset utilization.

Biogen, Inc., has suffered a sharp deterioration in activity ratios, pointing to a need for improved credit and inventory management, although the 19X2 ratios are not far out of line with the industry averages (see Figure 8). It appears that problems are inefficient collection and obsolescence of inventory.

Is the Business Solvent?

Solvency is the company's ability to satisfy long-term debt as it becomes due. You should be concerned about the long-term financial and operating structure of any firm in which you have a vested interest. Another important consideration is the size of debt in the firm's capital structure, which is referred to as *financial leverage*. (Capital structure is the mix of the *long-term* sources of funds used by the firm).

Solvency also depends on earning power; in the long run, a company will not satisfy its debts unless it earns profit. A leveraged capital structure subjects the company to fixed interest charges, which contributes to earnings instability. Excessive debt may also make it difficult for the firm to borrow funds at reasonable rates during tight money markets.

The *debt ratio* reveals the amount of money a company owes to its creditors. Excessive debt means greater risk to the investor. (Note that equity holders come after creditors in bankruptcy.) The debt ratio is:

$$\frac{\text{total liabilities}}{\text{total assets}}$$

In 19X2, the ratio is:

$$\frac{\$139}{\$227} = .61$$

The *debt-equity ratio* will show you if the firm has a great amount of debt in its capital structure. Large debts mean that the borrower has to pay significant periodic interest and principal. Also, a heavily indebted firm takes a greater risk of running out of cash in difficult times. The interpretation of this ratio depends on several variables, including the ratios of other firms in the industry, the degree of access to additional debt financing, and stability of operations.

The ratio equals:

$$\frac{\text{total liabilities}}{\text{stockholders' equity}}$$

In 19X2, the ratio is:

$$\frac{\$139}{\$88} = 1.58$$

In the previous year, the ratio was 1.55. The trend is relatively static.

Times interest earned (interest coverage ratio) tells you how many times the firm's before-tax earnings would cover interest. It is a safety margin indicator in that it reflects how much of a reduction in earnings a company can tolerate.

$$\frac{\text{income before interest and taxes}}{\text{interest expense}}$$

For 19X2, the ratio is:

$$\frac{\$15.3}{\$2.0} = 7.65$$

In 19X1, interest was covered 13.5 times. The reduction in coverage during the period is a bad sign. It means that less earnings are available to satisfy interest charges.

You must also note liabilities that have not yet been reported in the balance sheet by closely examining footnote disclosure. For example, you should find out about lawsuits, noncapitalized leases, and future guarantees.

As shown in Figure 8, the company's overall solvency is poor relative to the industry averages, although it has remained fairly constant. There has been no significant change in its ability to satisfy long-term debt. Note that significantly less profit is available to cover interest payments.

Is This a Profitable Company?

A company's ability to earn a good profit and return on investment is an indicator of its financial

well being and the efficiency with which it is managed. Poor earnings have detrimental effects on
market price of stock and dividends. Total dollar
net income has little meaning unless it is compared
to the input required to get that profit.

The *gross profit margin* shows the percentage of
each dollar remaining once the company has paid
for goods acquired. A high margin reflects good
earning potential.

$$\text{Gross profit margin} = \frac{\text{gross profit}}{\text{net sales}}$$

In 19X2, the ratio is:

$$\frac{\$28.3}{\$80.3} = .35$$

The ratio was .43 in 19X1. The reduction shows
that the company now receives less profit on each
dollar of sales. Perhaps higher relative cost of mer-
chandise sold is at fault.

Profit margin shows the earnings generated from
revenue and is a key indicator of operating performance. It gives you an idea of the firm's pricing,
cost structure, and production efficiency.

$$\text{Profit margin} = \frac{\text{net income}}{\text{net sales}}$$

The ratio in 19X2 is:

$$\frac{\$8}{\$80.3} = .10$$

For the previous year, profit margin was .14.
The decline in the ratio shows a downward trend
in earning power. (Note that these percentages are

available in the common-size income statement as given in Figure 4).

Table 1 shows various profit margin ratios.

Table 1—

Profit Margin
(As of 2nd Quarter, 1993)

Burlington Resources	42.8%
Amgen	29.2
H&R Block	22.5
Intel	26.7
Albertson's	2.7
Campbell Soup	6.6

Source: "Industry Scorecard," *Business Week,* McGraw-Hill, August 16, 1993.

Return on investment is a prime indicator because it allows you to evaluate the profit you will earn if you invest in the business. Two key ratios are the *return on total assets* and the *return on equity*.

The return on total assets shows whether management is efficient in using available resources to get profit.

$$\text{Return on total assets} = \frac{\text{net income}}{\text{average total assets}}$$

In 19X2, the return is:

$$\frac{\$8}{(\$227 + \$204)/2} = .037$$

In 19X1, the return was .077. There has been a deterioration in the productivity of assets in generating earnings.

The *return on equity* (ROE) reflects the rate of return earned on the stockholders' investment.

$$\text{Return on common equity} = \frac{\text{net income}}{\text{average stockholders' equity}}$$

The return in 19X2 is:

$$\frac{\$8}{(\$88 + \$80)/2} = 0.095$$

In 19X1, the return was .207. There has been a significant drop in return to the owners.

The overall profitability of the company has decreased considerably, causing a decline in both the return on assets and return on equity. Perhaps lower earnings were due in part to higher costs of short-term financing arising from the decline in liquidity and activity ratios. Moreover, as turnover rates in assets go down, profit will similarly decline because of a lack of sales and higher costs of carrying higher current asset balances. As indicated in Figure 8, industry comparisons reveal that the company is faring very poorly in the industry.

Table 2 shows companies with high return on equity (in excess of 30 percent).

Table 2—

Companies with High Return on Equity (ROE) Rates (in excess of 30%) (12 Months Ending 6/30/93)

Carter Hawley	237.5%
Avon Products	130.3
UST	73.6
Neiman Marcus	64.4
Coca-Cola	52.1
General Mills	41.5
Conseco	40.1
Microsoft	31.7

Source: "Industry Scorecard," *Business Week,* McGraw-Hill, August 16, 1993.

How Are the Company's Earnings and Market Value Related?

Market value ratios relate the company's stock price to its earnings (or book value) per share. Also included are dividend-related ratios.

Earnings per share (EPS) is the ratio most widely watched by investors. EPS shows the net income per common share owned. You must reduce net income by the preferred dividends to obtain the net income available to common stockholders. Where preferred stock is not in the capital structure, you determine EPS by dividing net income by common shares outstanding. EPS is a gauge of corporate operating performance and expected future dividends.

$$EPS = \frac{\text{net income - preferred dividend}}{\text{common shares outstanding}}$$

EPS in 19X2 is:

$$\frac{\$8,000}{4,600 \text{ shares}} = \$1.74$$

For 19X1, EPS was $3.26. The sharp reduction over the year should cause alarm among investors. As you can see in Figure 8, the industry average EPS in 19X2 is much higher than that of Biogen, Inc. ($4.51 per share vs. $1.74 per share).

The *price/earnings (P/E) ratio*, also called *earnings multiple*, reflects the company's relationship to its stockholders. The P/E ratio represents the amount investors are willing to pay for each dollar of the firm's earnings. A high multiple (cost per dollar of earnings) is favored since it shows that investors view the firm positively. On the other hand, investors looking for value would prefer a relatively lower multiple (cost per dollar of earnings) as compared with companies of similar risk and return.

$$\text{P/E ratio} = \frac{\text{market price per share}}{\text{earnings per share}}$$

Assume a market price per share of $12 on December 31, 19X2, and $26 on December 31, 19X1. The P/E ratios are:

$$19X2: \frac{\$12}{\$1.74} = 6.9$$

$$19X1: \frac{\$26}{\$3.26} = 7.98$$

From the lower P/E multiple, you can infer that the stock market now has a lower opinion of the business. However, some investors argue that a low P/E ratio can mean that the stock is undervalued. Nevertheless, the decline over the year in stock price was 54 percent ($14/$26), which should cause deep investor concern.

Table 3 shows price-earnings ratios of certain companies.

Table 3—

P/E Ratios

Company	Industry	As of 7/23/93
Apple	Computer	17
Goodrich	Tire	55
Weyerhauser	Forest Products	15
GTE	Communications	18
Dow Chemical	Chemical	36

Source: "Industry Scorecard," *Business Week*, McGraw-Hill, August 16, 1993.

Book value per share equals the net assets available to common stockholders divided by shares outstanding. By comparing it to market price per share you can get another view of how investors feel about the business.

The book value per share in 19X2 is:

$$\frac{\text{Total stockholders' equity - preferred stock}}{\text{Common shares outstanding}}$$

$$\frac{\$88{,}000 - 0}{4{,}600} = \$19.13$$

In 19X1, book value per share was $17.39.

The increased book value per share is a favorable sign, because it indicates that each share now has a higher book value. However, in 19X2, market price is much less than book value, which means that the stock market does not value the security highly. In 19X1, market price did exceed book value, but there is now some doubt in the minds of stockholders concerning the company. However, some analysts may argue that the stock is underpriced.

The *price/book value ratio* shows the market value of the company in comparison to its historical accounting value. A company with old assets may have a high ratio, whereas one with new assets may have a low ratio. Hence, you should note the changes in the ratio in an effort to appraise the corporate assets.

The ratio equals:

$$\frac{\text{Market price per share}}{\text{Book value per share}}$$

In 19X2, the ratio is:

$$\frac{\$12}{\$19.13} = .63$$

In 19X1, the ratio was 1.5. The significant drop in the ratio may indicate a lower opinion of the company in the eyes of investors. Market price of stock may have dropped because of a deterioration in liquidity, activity, and profitability ratios. The major indicators of a company's performance are intertwined (i.e., one affects the other) so that problems in one area may spill over into another. This appears to have happened to the company in our example.

Dividend ratios help you determine the current income from an investment. Two relevant ratios are:

$$\text{Dividend yield} = \frac{\text{dividends per share}}{\text{market price per share}}$$

$$\text{Dividend payout} = \frac{\text{dividend per share}}{\text{earnings per share}}$$

Table 4 shows the dividend yield and payout ratios of some companies.

Table 4—

Dividend Yield and Payout Ratios—1992

	Yield	Payout
The Limited	1.10%	22%
Texaco	5.08	91
Exxon	4.55	75
Mattel	0.90	14
AT&T	2.34	46

Source: "Industry Scorecard," *Business Week*, McGraw-Hill, August 16, 1993.

There is no such thing as a "right" payout ratio. Stockholders look unfavorably upon reduced dividends because it is a sign of possible deteriorating financial health. However, companies with ample opportunities for growth at high rates of return on assets tend to have low payout ratios.

Overall, Would You Invest in This Company?

As indicated earlier, a single ratio or a single group of ratios is not adequate for assessing all aspects of the firm's financial condition. Figure 8 summarizes the 19X1 and 19X2 ratios calculated in the previous sections, along with the industry average ratios for 19X2. The figure also shows the formula used to calculate each ratio. The last three columns of the figure contain subjective assessments of Biogen's financial condition, based on trend analysis and 19X2 comparisons to the industry norms. (five-year ratios are generally needed for trend analysis to be more meaningful, however.)

By appraising the trend in the company's ratios from 19X1 to 19X2, we see from the drop in the current and quick ratios that there has been a slight decline in short-term liquidity, although they have been above the industry averages. But working capital has improved. A material deterioration in the activity ratios has occurred, indicating that improved credit and inventory policies are required. They are not terribly alarming, however, because these ratios are not way out of line with industry averages. Also, total utilization of assets, as indicated by the total asset turnover, shows a deteriorating trend.

Leverage (amount of debt) has been constant. However, there is less profit available to satisfy interest charges. Biogen's profitability has deteriorated over the year. In 19X2, it is consistently below the industry average in every measure of profitability. In consequence, the return on the owner's investment and the return on total assets have gone down. The earnings decrease may be partly due to the firm's high cost of short-term financing and partly due to operating inefficiency. The higher costs may be due to receivable and inventory difficulties that forced a decline in the liquidity and activity ratios. Furthermore, as receivables and inventory turn over less, profit will fall off from a lack of sales and the costs of carrying more in current asset balances.

The firm's market value, as measured by the price/earnings (P/E) ratio, is respectable as compared with the industry. But it shows a declining trend.

In summary, it appears that the company is doing satisfactorily in the industry in many categories. The 19X1-19X2 period, however, seems to indicate that the company is heading for financial trouble in terms of earnings, activity, and short-term liquidity. The business needs to concentrate on increasing operating efficiency and asset utilization.

Figure 8—

Summary of Financial Ratios—Trend and Industry Comparisons Biogen, Inc., 19X2 and 19X1

Ratios	Definitions	19X1	19X2	Industry Average (a)	Ind. Comp. 19X2	19X1-19X2	Overall (b)
LIQUIDITY							
Net working capital	Current assets - current liabilities	63	68	56	good	good	good
Current ratio	Current assets/current liabilities	2.26	2.21	2.05	OK	OK	OK
Quick (acid-test) ratio	(Cash + marketable securities + accounts receivable)/current liabilities	1.34	1.27	1.11	OK	OK	OK
ASSET UTILIZATION							
Accounts receivable turnover	Net credit sales/average accounts receivable	8.46	4.34	5.5	OK	poor	poor
Average collection period	365 days/accounts receivable turnover	43.1 days	84.1 days	66.4 days	OK	poor	poor
Inventory turnover	Cost of goods sold/average inventory	1.33	1.05	1.2	OK	poor	poor
Average age of inventory	365 days/inventory turnover	274.4 days	347.6 days	N/A	N/A	poor	poor
Operating cycle	Average collection period + average age of inventory	317.5 days	431.7 days	N/A	N/A	poor	poor
Total asset turnover	Net sales/average total assets	0.57	0.37	0.44	OK	poor	poor

Ratios	Definitions	19X1	19X2	Industry Average (a)	Ind. Comp. 19X2	19X1- 19X2	Overall (b)
SOLVENCY							
Debt ratio	Total liabilities/total assets	0.61	0.61	N/A	N/A	OK	OK
Debt-equity ratio	Total liabilities/stockholders' equity	1.55	1.58	1.3	poor	poor	poor
Times interest earned	Income before interest and taxes/interest expense	13.5 times	7.65 times	10 times	OK	poor	poor
PROFITABILITY							
Gross profit margin	Gross profit/net sales	0.43	0.35	0.48	poor	poor	poor
Profit margin	Net income/net sales	0.14	0.1	0.15	poor	poor	poor
Return on total assets	Net income/average total assets	0.077	0.037	0.1	poor	poor	poor
Return on equity (ROE)	Earnings available to common stockholders/average stockholders' equity	0.207	0.095	0.27	poor	poor	poor
MARKET VALUE							
Earnings per share (EPS)	(Net income - preferred dividend)/common shares outstanding	3.26	1.74	4.51	poor	poor	poor

(continued)

Figure 8—*continued*

Ratios	Definitions	19X1	19X2	Industry Average	Ind. Comp. 19X2 (a)	19X1-19X2	Overall (b)
Price/earnings (P/E) ratio	Market price per share/EPS	7.98	6.9	7.12	OK	poor	poor
Book value per share	(Total stockholders' equity - preferred stock)/common shares outstanding	17.39	19.13	N/A	N/A	good	good
Price/book value ratio	Market price per share/book value per share	1.5	0.63	N/A	N/A	poor	poor
Dividend yield	Dividends per share/market price per share						
Dividend payout	Dividends per share/EPS						

(a) Obtained from sources not included in this chapter.
(b) Represent subjective evaluation.

PREDICTING FINANCIAL DISTRESS USING FINANCIAL RATIOS

Will the Company Fail and Your Investment Be Lost?

There has recently been an increasing number of bankruptcies. Will the company of the stock you own be among them? Who will go bankrupt? If you can predict with reasonable accuracy ahead of time, like a year or two, that the company you are interested in is developing financial distress, you would not invest in it. You should avoid or stay out of stocks of potentially troubled companies.

You can identify early warning signs to detect the likelihood of bankruptcy. One popular way is to use the *Z Score* model, which evaluates a combination of several financial ratios to predict the likelihood of future bankruptcy. The model, developed by Edward Altman, uses multiple discriminant analysis to give a relative prediction of whether a firm will go bankrupt within five years.

The model is outlined and described in detail below. Spreadsheet models have been developed to calculate the prediction of bankruptcy using data extracted from *Moody's* and *Standard & Poor's*. Navistar International (formerly International Harvester), the one that continues to struggle in the heavy and medium truck industry, is selected for illustrative purposes. Financial data has been collected for the period 1979 thru 1994 for both companies.

The model is as follows:

$$Z = 1.2\,X_1 + 1.4\,X_2 + 3.3\,X_3 + 0.6\,X_4 + 0.999\,X_5$$

where

X_1 = Working capital/Total assets
X_2 = Retained earnings/Total assets
X_3 = Earnings before interest and taxes (EBIT)/
      Total assets

X_4 = Market value of equity/Book value of debt
         (or Net worth for *private firms*)
X_5 = Sales/Total assets

Altman established the following guidelines for classifying firms:

Z score	Probability of Short-Term Illiquidity
1.8 or less	Very high
1.81 - 2.99	Not sure
3.0 or higher	Unlikely

The Z score is known to be about 90 percent accurate in forecasting business failure one year in the future and about 80 percent accurate in forecasting it two years in the future.

Figure 9 shows a spreadsheet of the 16 year (1979 to 1994) financial history and the Z scores of Navistar International. Figure 10 displays a Z score chart for the company.

The graph shows that Navistar International performed at the edge of the ignorance zone ("unsure area"), for the year 1979. Since 1980, though, the company started signalling a sign of failure. However, by selling stock and assets, the firm managed to survive. Since 1983, the company showed an improvement in its Z scores, although the firm continually scored on the danger zone. Note that the 1994 Z score of 1.19 is in the high probability range of <1.81.

If, however, the 1995 Z score increases over 1993 and 1994, it may be indicating that Navistar is improving its financial position and becoming a more viable investment. As Navistar is a struggling company, its securities might be undervalued. If they are undervalued and an improvement in the Z-score indicates a turning point, this may be a signal to invest in its securities.

Figure 9—

Navistar International - NAV (NYSE)

Z SCORE - PREDICTION OF FINANCIAL DISTRESS

	Balance Sheet						Income Statement	Stock Data		Calculations					Misc. Graph Values			
Year	Curr. Assts. (CA)	Tot. Assts. (TA)	Current Liab. (CL)	Tot. Liab. (TL)	Retn. Earn. (RE)	Wking. Cap. (WC)	SALES	EBIT	MV or Net worth (MKT-NW)	WC/TA (X1)	RE/TA (X2)	EBIT/TA (X3)	MKT-NW/TL (X4)	SALES/TA (X5)	Z Score	Top Gray Gray	Btm. Gray Gray	Year
1979	3266	5247	1873	3048	1505	1393	8426	719	1122	0.2655	0.2868	0.1370	0.3681	1.6059	3.00	2.99	1.81	1979
1980	3427	5843	2433	3947	1024	994	6000	-402	1147	0.1701	0.1753	-0.0688	0.2906	1.0269	1.42	2.99	1.81	1980
1981	2672	5346	1808	3864	600	864	7018	-16	376	0.1616	0.1122	-0.0030	0.0973	1.3128	1.71	2.99	1.81	1981
1982	1656	3699	1135	3665	-1078	521	4322	-1274	151	0.1408	-0.2914	-0.3444	0.0412	1.1684	-0.18	2.99	1.81	1982
1983	1388	3362	1367	3119	-1487	21	3600	-231	835	0.0062	-0.4423	-0.0687	0.2677	1.0708	0.39	2.99	1.81	1983
1984	1412	3249	1257	2947	-1537	155	4861	120	575	0.0477	-0.4731	0.0369	0.1951	1.4962	1.13	2.99	1.81	1984
1985	1101	2406	988	2364	-1894	113	3508	247	570	0.0470	-0.7872	0.1027	0.2411	1.4580	0.89	2.99	1.81	1985
1986	698	1925	797	1809	-1889	-99	3357	163	441	-0.0514	-0.9813	0.0847	0.2438	1.7439	0.73	2.99	1.81	1986
1987	785	1902	836	1259	-1743	-51	3530	219	1011	-0.0268	-0.9164	0.1151	0.8030	1.8559	1.40	2.99	1.81	1987
1988	1280	4037	1126	1580	150	154	4082	451	1016	0.0381	0.0372	0.1117	0.6430	1.0111	1.86	2.99	1.81	1988
1989	986	3609	761	1257	175	225	4241	303	1269	0.0623	0.0485	0.0840	1.0095	1.1751	2.20	2.99	1.81	1989
1990	2663	3795	1579	2980	81	1084	3854	111	563	0.2856	0.0213	0.0292	0.1889	1.0155	1.60	2.99	1.81	1990
1991	2286	3443	1145	2866	332	1141	3259	232	667	0.3314	0.0964	0.0674	0.2326	0.9466	1.84	2.99	1.81	1991

(continued)

Figure 9—continued

	Balance Sheet				Income Statement			Stock Data		Calculations					Misc Graph Values			
Year	Curr. Assts. (CA)	Tot. Assts. (TA)	Current Liab. (CL)	Tot. Liab. (TL)	Retn. Earn. (RE)	Wking. Cap. (WC)	SALES	EBIT	MV or Net worth (MKT-NW)	WC/ TA (X1)	RE/ TA (X2)	EBIT/ TA (X3)	MKT-NW/ TL (X4)	SALES/ TA (X5)	Z Score	Top Gray	Btm. Gray	Year
1992	2472	3627	1152	3289	93	1320	3875	-145	572	0.3639	0.0256	-0.0400	0.1738	1.0684	1.51	2.99	1.81	1992
1993	2672	5060	1338	4285	-1588	1334	4694	-441	1765	0.2636	-0.3138	-0.0872	0.4119	0.9277	0.76	2.99	1.81	1993
1994	2870	5056	1810	4239	-1532	1060	5337	158	1469	0.2097	-0.3030	0.0313	0.3466	1.0556	1.19	2.99	1.81	1994

Notes: (1) To calculate Z score for private firms, enter Net Worth in the MKT - NW column. (For publicly held companies, enter Market Value of Equity.)

(2) EBIT = Earnings before Interest and Taxes.

Figure 10—

Z Score

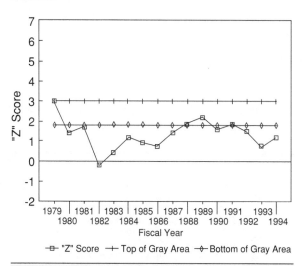

A SYSTEMATIC APPROACH FOR STOCK PICKING

Fundamental stock analysis can be broken down into two categories—*screening* and *valuation*. Screening refers to the act of searching through a large universe of securities to locate a few that might hold promise and warrant further analysis. Valuation (to be discussed in detail in Chapter 7), on the other hand, refers to taking one company and applying a series of valuation methods to determine if the current price can be considered fair.

A more practical, systematic approach to stock picking would start with building a list of potential candidates through screening. Screening would be based on some predetermined criteria, such as your investment objectives, philosophy, risk tolerance level, and return needs. The next step is a narrowing down. You want to investigate a list of serious candidates using techniques such as financial ratio analysis in hopes of forming future earnings expectations and determining the appreciation potential of a company. Next, determine what you feel the stock is worth, applying a series of valuation models. Finally, you come to a decision based on your determination of the stock's worth relative to the current market price.

Figure 11 is a flowchart representation of a systematic approach for picking a stock.

Figure 11—

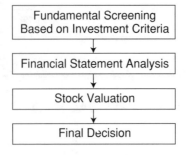

FUNDAMENTAL SCREENING BY PC

Screening represents the first step in fundamental analysis. Below is a list of popular screening software, on-line and disk-based.

Disk-Based Screening

Wealthbuilder, by *Money* magazine (DOS, Mac)
Reality Technologies, Inc., (800) 346-2024 or (215) 277-7600

Stock Investor (DOS, Windows)
American Association of Individual Investors, (312)
280-0170

Value/Screen III (DOS, Mac)
Value Line Publishing, (800) 654-0508 or (212)
687-3965

Fundamental Investor (DOS)
Savant Software, Inc., (800) 231-9900 or (603) 471-
0400

On-Line Screening

CompuServe—Fundwatch Online, by *Money* magazine
CompuServe, Inc., (800) 543-4616 or (212) 227-3881

Prodigy—Strategic Investor (DOS, Mac)
Prodigy Services Company, (800) 776-3449 or (914)
993-8000

Telescan—Telescan Analyzer, Telescan Edge,
Telescan Mutual Fund Edge, ProSearch 4.0 (DOS)
Telescan, Inc., (800) 324-8246 or (713) 952-1060

CHAPTER **5**

TECHNICAL ANALYSIS

Fundamental analysis is used primarily to select *what* to invest in, while technical analysis is used to help decide *when* to invest in it. Technical analysts attempt to offer guidelines on investment timing. They look at price (and volume) movements in the market for clues as to when to buy or sell. They pay particular attention to market indexes and averages and to "charting" price movements of individual stocks.

WHAT IS TECHNICAL ANALYSIS?

Will it go up? Will it go down? Does history really repeat it self? Every investor is searching for the answers to these questions. Technical analysts believe that history repeats itself. Technical analysis concentrates on changes of a security, on a daily, weekly, monthly, and yearly basis. There are a number of primary assumptions underlying technical analysis:

1. Market action discounts everything.
2. History repeats itself.
3. Supply and demand determine market price.
4. Prices move in trends.

Supply and demand have a lot to do with the price of the security. The direction of the market is very important. If demand is greater than supply, prices will go up. If demand is less than supply, then

prices will fall. There is no purpose in trying to fore-
tell which way the market will go, because there
are too many circumstances that sway the market,
and by the time you discover the reason the market
will change again. It is an advantage to know the
reason behind fluctuations in the economy, but it is
not essential.

The stock market is dictated 85 percent by psychology and only 15 percent by economics. Investors and traders will react the same way each time
there is a rise or a fall in the market. It is reasonable
to conclude, that as price go up, investors and traders will buy, and as prices drop, investors and traders will sell. This cycle will continue due to the vast
majority that will behave in this predetermined
manner.

Technicians believe that a stock will continue
in the same direction until it is interrupted by an
outside source. A price trend does not change its
direction until it is influenced by the market action.

WHAT ARE THE TOOLS OF TECHNICAL ANALYSIS?

Technical analysts believe the market can be predicted in terms of direction and magnitude. They
study the stock market by way of *charting* and using various *indicators* to project future market movements. Stock prices of companies tend to move with
the market because they react to various demand
and supply forces. The technical analysts try to
predict short-term price changes and then recom-
mend the timing of a purchase and sale. They attempt to uncover a consistent pattern in prices or a
relationship between stock price changes and other
market data. Technical analysts also look at charts
and graphs of internal market data, including prices
and volume.

Figure 1 reflects the movement in the price of a company's stock.

You should be familiar with some of the terms used in technical analysis:

- *Momentum*: The rate of change of a stock price or market index over a period of time.

- *Accumulation*: A price rise on a large volume of stock that is moving from "weak hands" to "strong hands."

Figure 1—

Sample Company Stock Chart
ACME Motor Co. Stock

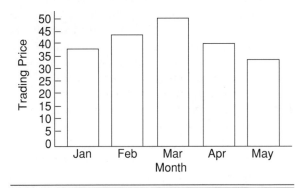

- *Distribution*: A price decline on a large volume of stock that is moving from "strong hands" to "weak hands."

- *Consolidating phases*: Time periods during which prices move within a narrow band.

- *Resistance phases*: Time periods during which prices move with difficulty.

- *Bellwether stocks*: Stocks that accurately reflect the condition of the market (GE, for example).

The Dow Theory

The foundation for technical analysis is the Dow Theory. The theory claims that stock market direction must be confirmed by both averages—the *Dow Jones Industrial Average* and the *Dow Jones Transportation Average*. A strong market—bullish or bearish—is one in which both averages are moving in the same direction.

The market is assumed to have three movements at the same time: day-to-day fluctuations, secondary movements (3 weeks to 3 months), and primary trends (28 weeks to 33 months). According to the theory, secondary movements and daily fluctuations are only important to the extent that they reflect a long-term primary trend in the market. Primary trends may be characterized as either bullish or bearish. Figure 2 displays the Dow Theory to analyze a market trend. It is seen that the primary movement in the market is positive despite two secondary movements that are downward. The point is that each low of the secondary movement is higher than the previous low and each high is higher than the previous high. This tends to confirm the primary trend, which is bullish.

In a nutshell, the Dow Theory implies a strategy:

1. Buy when the market goes higher than the last peak.
2. Sell when it goes below the preceding valley.

Here is the rationale of the Dow Theory: the market is up when the cyclical movements of the market averages increase over time and the successive market lows get higher; the market is down when the successive highs and successive lows in the stock market are lower than the previous highs and lows.

It applies to individual stocks and to the overall market. One limitation of this theory is that it is an after measure having no forecasting ability.   It does not predict when a reversal will take place but merely confirms that the reversal has occurred.

Figure 2—

Dow Theory Chart

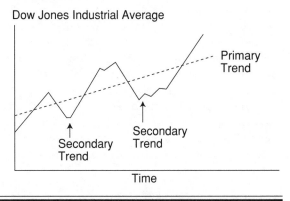

Dow Jones Industrial Average

Primary Trend

Secondary Trend

Secondary Trend

Time

Many Dow believers contend that the action of the Dow Jones Transportation Average must confirm the action of the Dow Jones Industrial Average before a true bull or bear market signal is posted. Others believe the use of the Transportation Average in this manner has lost much of its validity, since these two averages will not usually follow the same pattern.

There are two primary tools of technical analysts. They are *charting* and *key indicators*.

WHAT IS CHARTING?

In deciding whether to buy a particular security or when evaluating market conditions, a technical ana-

lyst, often called a *chartist*, usually turns to charting. Charting means plotting the stock's price movement over time on a graph. For example, if the security has moved up and down in price, but has
remained within a band bounded by the lower limit
(support level) and the higher limit (resistance
level). Chartists think that once a stock breaks
through such a level (e.g., falls below the support
level), then it is likely to decline considerably further. Similarly, if the price were to penetrate above
the resistance level, it would be an indication that
the price will continue to rise. Some chartists think
a "head and shoulders" formation indicates that a
stock has peaked (top form) and will start to fall; an
inversion of this pattern would indicate that a stock
has bottomed out and is ready to rise. In order to
interpret charts you must be able to analyze forma-
tions and spot buy and sell indicators. Note, however, that different analysts looking at the same chart
pattern may come up with different interpretations.

What Types of Charts May Be Used?

The two basic types of charts are *bar* and *point-and-
figure*. Bar charts record the high and low, the close,
and volume over time. The vertical line shows price
and the horizontal line shows time. Vertical lines
appear at each time period, and the top and bottom
of each bar shows the high and low prices. A horizontal line across the bar marks the ending price
(see Figure 3).

   While bar charts plot transactions according to
time (that is, hourly, daily, weekly, monthly), point-
and-figure charts plot price changes only and are independent of time. The focus of point- and-figure
charts is on reversal patterns. They consider just the
closing prices of significant price moves, and attempt
to show emerging price patterns in the market in
general or for specific stocks. A rise in price is de-

noted by an X while a decrease is shown as an O. The chart will only show that the stock moved up one point and does not tell you how long it takes the stock to move up one point. The purpose of this chart is to clarify a trend without regard to how long that trend will be, or has been, in effect.

In point-and-figure charts, there is a vertical price scale. Plots on the chart are made when a price changes by a predetermined amount. Significant price changes and their reversals are depicted. What is significant is up to the individual technical analyst. The analyst can use either ending prices or interday prices, depending on time constraints. The usual predetermined figures are 1 or 2 points for medium-priced stocks, 3 or 5 points for high-priced stocks, and 1/2 point for low-priced stocks. Most charts contain specific volume information. Analysts should plot prices representing a trend in a single column, moving to the next column only when the trend is reversed. They will usually round a price to the nearest dollar and start by plotting a beginning rounded price. Nothing new appears on the chart if the rounded price does not change. If a different rounded price occurs, the analysts plot it. If new prices continue in the same direction, they will appear in the same column. A new column begins when there is a reversal. Notice there is no time dimension. A column of X's shows an upward price trend while a column of O's reveals a downward price trend. One simple rule with point-and-figure charts is:

1.   A buy signal when an up (x) column goes above a previous up (X) column.

2.   A sell signal is when a down (O) column goes below a previous down (O) column.

Figure 4 shows simple point-and-figure chart signals.

Note: There is another form of charting, known as *candlesticks*, which has been used in Japan.

Figure 3—
Bar Chart

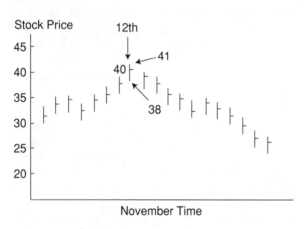

Figure 4—
Point-and-Figure Chart Signals

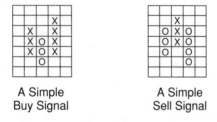

You can use these charts to determine whether the market is in a major upturn or downturn and whether the trend will reverse. You can also see

what price may be accomplished by a given stock
or market average. Further, these charts can help
you predict the magnitude of a price swing.

What Are Moving Averages?

You can use moving averages to evaluate interme-
diate- and long-term stock movements by averaging a portion of the series and then adding the following number to the numbers already averaged,
omitting the first number, and obtaining a new average, as shown in Table 1. A moving average shows
the underlying direction and magnitude of change
of very volatile numbers.

Table 1—

Moving Average

Day	Index	Three-Day Moving Total	Three-Day Moving Average
1	111		
2	132		
3	123	366 (Days 1-3)	122 (366/3)
4	108	363 (Days 2-4)	121 (363/3)

By examining the movement of short-term average prices compared to the long-term moving
average of prices, you can foresee a reversal in a
major uptrend in price of a particular security or
the general market. A 200-day moving average is a
standard measure for a long-term moving average.
A short-term moving average may be 1, 2, or 5 days.

The general rule says:

1. Buy when the short moving average rises above
    the long term.

2. Stay in the market until the short-term average
    falls below the long-term average; and then ei-
    ther move out of the market or sell short.

What Do Support and Resistance Levels Show?

Point-and-figure charts provide data about substance and resistance levels (points). Breakouts from
resistance levels indicate market direction. The
longer the sideways movement before a break, the
more the stock can increase in price.

Support and resistance levels are the most important building blocks in practical technical analysis. A support level (a price "floor") is the lower
end of a trading range; a resistance level (a price
"ceiling") is the upper end. The "channel" is the
area of the chart between the support level and resistance level. Figure 5 shows an example of a typical channel. Support may occur when a stock goes
to a lower level of trading because new investors
may now want to purchase it. If so, new demand
will occur in the market. Resistance may take place
when a security goes to the high side of the normal
trading range. Investors who purchased on an earlier high may view this as a chance to sell the stocks
at a profit. When market price goes above a resistance point or below a support point (in a "trading
range breakout") investors assume the stock is trading in a new range and that higher or lower trading
values are imminent.

Some basic rules suggest:

1. Buy when a stock is trading in a channel run-
    ning sharply upward and currently trading near
    the low end of that channel, or when a stock
    has been trading in a sideway channel and fi-
    nally trades over its resistance level.

2.   Sell when a stock is trading in a downward channel or a stock's price goes below a support level.

   Note: There is strong statistical evidence showing that simple trading rules—moving averages and support and resistance levels—have the power to predict future price changes.

Figure 5—

Support and Resistance

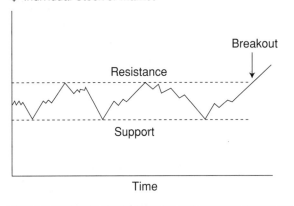

$ Individual Stock or Market

What Is Relative Strength Analysis?

Evaluating relative strength—a measure of price trend to an overall market and/or industry index—helps you predict individual stock prices. Here you buy and hold those stocks that are acting well, that is, outperforming the general market and/or industry indices in the recent past. By the same token, the stocks that act poorly relative to the market should be averted or even sold short.

Relative strength for a security may be computed:

$$\frac{\text{Monthly average stock price}}{\text{Monthly average market (or industry group) index}}$$

An increase in this ratio means that the company's stock is performing better than the overall market or industry.

A relative strength index (RSI) may be computed as follows:

$$RSI = 100 - \frac{100}{1 + RS}$$

where

$$RS = \frac{\text{Average of up closing prices}}{\text{Average of down closing prices}}$$

Example 1—

Assume that you are interested in the relative strength for the period of one month, which has 20 exchange days. The trading data follow (the U stands for an increase and D stands for a decrease):

Day:	1	2	3	4	5	6	7	8	9	10
Price:	10U	3D	4D	5U	2U	4D	6U	1D	6D	7U

Day:	11	12	13	14	15	16	17	18	19	20
Price:	8U	3D	5U	6D	1D	3D	4U	1D	3U	2U

$$RS = \frac{52U/10}{32D/10} = \frac{5.2}{3.2} = 1.625$$

$$RSI = 100 - \frac{100}{1 + RS} = 100 - 38.10 = 61.90$$

In general, you look to be invested in stocks with improving relative strength.

Note: Investment reports, such as the *Value Line Investment Survey,* provide relative strength information on companies.

PUBLISHED VERSUS COMPUTER CHARTING

There are several hundred software products offering some variation of technical analysis, including charting. On-line services and computer charting are increasingly popular at a more and more affordable cost. Furthermore, there exist many printed (or published) chart services that cover a wide variety of securities traded on the major exchanges, available at many libraries and brokerage houses. Examples of published sources are *Standard and Poor's Trendline* (Standard & Poor's, (212) 208-8792) and *Daily Graphs* (William O'Neil and Co., (310) 820-2583). Published services are mostly dated to a certain degree and limited in their coverage of stocks. They offer one important advantage, however. They allow you to quickly scan a broad number of issues and interpret developing trends.

WHAT DO YOU DO WITH KEY INDICATORS?

Key indicators of market and stock performance include trading volume, market breadth, *Barron's* Confidence Index, mutual fund cash position, short

selling, odd-lot theory, and the Index of Bearish
Sentiment.

Why Is Price-Trading Volume Important?

Significant price increases and decreases are often
accompanied by heavy trading volume. Tracking
volume indicates the health of the security. Price
follows volume. For example, we expect to have
increased price on increased volume. You may have
a buying opportunity when a security's price begins to rise with increasing volume. This may indicate that the investment community looks favorably
upon the stock.

Increasing price of a stock on heavy volume is
considered to be a much more positive sign than
increasing price on light volume. The idea is that
low volume means an absence of buyers, as sellers
are always present. By the same token, decreasing
price on heavy volume is a more ominous sign than
decreasing price on low volume. Trading volume
of the overall market and individual stocks can be
found in the financial pages of daily newspapers as
well as financial newspapers (e.g., *Barron's*).

Why Is Market Breadth Relevant?

Market breadth is an indicator which takes into account the number of issues which are higher versus the number of issues which are lower. It can be
useful as an advance indicator of major stock price
declines and advances. The Breadth Index is determined as follows:

$$\frac{\text{Number of net advances or declines in the stock market}}{\text{Number of securities traded}}$$

Relevant data can be found in *The Wall Street Journal.* If, over time, the figure is positive (advances exceed declines), the situation is bullish. A strong market is one that shows net advances. The degree of strength is based on the spread between the number of advances and the number of declines.

Example 2—

Assume on Monday the following market diary:

Issues traded	1,425
Advances	920
Declines	312
Unchanged	75
New highs	94
New lows	26

The net advancing issues is 608 (920 - 312). The index is 608/1425 = .427

The higher the plus percentage, the more positive the market. Breadth analysis focuses on change rather than level. Once you have determined the Breadth Index, you should chart it against a market average such as the Dow Jones Industrial. Typically, they will move together. The Breadth Index for the current year may also be compared to that of a base year.

You can also use market breadth to examine individual securities. Net volume (rises in price minus decreases in price) is determined.

Example 3—

Assume IBM trades 110,000 shares for the day, with 70,000 on the upside (rising in

price), 30,000 on the downside (falling in
price), and 10,000 showing no change. The
net volume difference at day's end is 40,000
between the price trend and the net volume
of IBM. When a divergence takes place, we
can expect a reversal of the price trend.
When price decreases and net volume increases, we know that accumulation is oc-
curring.

What Is Barron's *Confidence Index* and How Is It Used?

Barron's Confidence Index analyzes the trading
trend of investors in bonds. You can use it to ascertain when to purchase and sell stocks. This index
presumes that bond traders are more knowledgeable than stock traders and recognize trends sooner.
If we know what bond traders are doing today, we
can predict what stock traders will be doing next.
Many believe that there is a lead time of several
months between the Confidence Index and what
happens with the stock market. The index is published weekly in *Barron's*. The index is computed
as follows:

$$\frac{\text{Yield on } Barron's \text{ 10 top-grade corporate bonds}}{\text{Yield on Dow Jones 40 bond average}}$$

Example 4—

If the Dow Jones yield is 15 percent while
the *Barron's* yield is 14 percent, the Confidence Index is 93.3 percent (14%/15%).
   The numerator has a lower yield compared to the denominator since it consists

of higher-quality bonds. Less risk means less return. Because top-grade bonds have lower yields than lower-grade bonds, the index will be less than 100 percent. The trading range is typically between 75 and 95 percent. If bond investors are bullish, yield difference between the high-grade and low-grade bonds will be minimal; in this case the index may approach 95 percent.

If markets are bearish, bond investors will desire high-quality issues. Some investors who desire a high yield for the greater risk. The Confidence Index will now decline, because the denominator will be getting larger. If much confidence exists, investors are likely to buy lower-quality bonds. In consequence, the yield on high-grade bonds will decrease while the yield on low-grade bonds will increase.

WHAT ARE THE CONTRARIAN INDICATORS?

A "contrarian" is an investor who buys when the majority sells, and who sells when the majority buys. Indicators reflecting a contrarian view include mutual fund cash positions, the short interest ratio, the odd-lot trading indicator, and the index of bearish sentiment.

Why Is the Amount of Cash Held by the Mutual Funds Revealing?

The purchasing pattern of mutual funds is often an indicator of the purchasing potential of large institutional investors. It is measured by the ratio of mutual fund cash and cash equivalents to total assets provided monthly by the Investment Company Institute. Changes in the figures show institutional portfolio management thinking. The ratio usually hovers between 5 and 25 percent. When a mutual fund's cash position is large, you would think mutual fund managers must have a bearish outlook on the market. However, it is a contrarian indicator. To a technical analyst, the higher the cash percentage, the more bullish the general market outlook. When this cash is invested in the market, stock prices will increase. In other words, high mutual fund cash positions represent pent-up demand. A low cash balance is a bearish sign.

What Is the Short Interest Ratio?

Short selling takes place when investors believe stock prices will decline. Some analysts believe that an increase in the number of short sellers indicates a bullish market. It is believed that short sellers get emotional and overreact. Also, the short seller will later purchase the short-sold stock. Increased short sales and increased market activity will create additional market supply. Then, when the market goes down, the short sellers will buy back their shares, and this will produce increased market demand.

The short-interest ratio is:

$$\frac{\text{Number of stocks sold short for the month}}{\text{Daily average volume for the month}}$$

A high ratio is bullish and a low ratio is bearish. In the past, the ratio for all stocks on the New York Stock Exchange has hovered between 1.0 and 1.65. A short-interest ratio of 2.0 or greater would indicate a market low. *Note:* The short interest is reported weekly in *The Wall Street Journal* and *Barron's*.

Why Look at Short Sales by Specialists?

Watch short sales positions of specialists, measured by the ratio:

$$\frac{\text{Specialists' short sales}}{\text{Total short sales on an exchange}}$$

Example 5—

If specialists sell 100,000 shares short in a week and the total number of short sales is 400,000, the specialists' sales constitute 25 percent. Specialists keep a book of limit orders on their securities, so they are knowledgeable as to market activity at a particular time. However, if most of their short sales are covered, this is a bullish sign.

A normal ratio is approximately 55 percent. A ratio of 65 percent or more is bearish. A ratio less than 40 percent is bullish.

What Is the Odd-Lot Trading Indicator?

The odd-lot theory operates on the same premise — the rule of contrary opinion. Odd-lot trading reflects popular opinion. In other words, you will determine what losers are doing and then you will do the opposite. In other words, knowledgeable investors should sell when the small traders (odd-lot sellers) are buying and buy when they are selling, since they believe that the small investor is usually wrong.

Odd-lot trading data are published in *The Wall Street Journal* and *Barron's*. Volume is usually expressed in number of shares rather than dollars. Some technical analysts use the *SEC Statistical Bulletin*, however, in which volume is given in dollars.

An odd-lot index is:

$$\frac{\text{Odd-lot buys}}{\text{Odd-lot sales}}$$

This ratio usually fluctuates between .40 and 1.60 (see Figure 7).

Example 6—

Assume that on a particular day, 186,526 odd-lot shares are bought and 382,020 shares are sold. The odd-lot index is .488 (186,526/382,020).

You should also examine odd-lot short sales. Many odd-lotters are uninformed. An odd-lotter short sale ratio of around .5 percent indicates optimism; a ratio of 3.0 or more reflects pessimism.

Note: Stock market research does not fully support the odd-lot theory. In fact, studies showed that the small investor was correct more frequently than institutional investors.

Figure 7—

Ratio of Odd-Lot Purchases to Sales (Plotted Inversely)

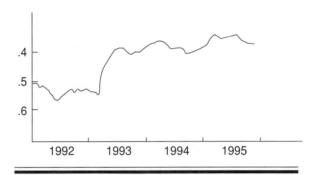

What Is the Index of Bearish Sentiment?

This index is based on a reversal of the recommendations of investment advisory services as contained in their newsletters.   The Index of Bearish Sentiment is:

$$\frac{\text{Number of bearish services}}{\text{Number of services giving an opinion}}$$

This index operates according to the contrary opinion rule: Whatever the investment advisory service recommends, you should do the opposite. The reasoning of Investors Intelligence is that the advisory services are trend followers rather than anticipators. Therefore, the services' least bearish reports mean the market will drop, and their most bearish reports mean the market will increase.

The general rule is: When 42 percent or more of the advisory services are bearish, the market in fact will increase. If 17 percent or less of the services are bearish, the market will decrease. This index is found in *Barron's*.

Example 7—

Of 350 investment advisory services, 225 of them are bearish on the stock market, the index equals 64 percent (225/350). Since 64 percent are pessimistic about the market, or more than the 42 percent benchmark, you should buy securities.

Are Puts and Calls Revealing?

A put is the right to sell a stock at a fixed price by a specified date. One put is for 100 shares. A call is the right to buy a stock at a fixed price by a certain date. The investor expects the stock's price to appreciate. A sizable gain is possible from a minimal investment, but the entire investment amount is lost if the stock price does not go up.

Option trading activity may help you predict market trends. The put-call ratio equals put volume divided by call volume. The ratio increases due to more put activity from pessimism around the market bottom. The ratio decreases due to more call activity from investor optimism around the market peak.

The option buy (initial option transaction establishing a long position) call percentage looks at open buy call transactions to total call volume. Investor optimism is reflected in a high ratio, while trader caution is indicated in a low ratio.

A CAVEAT

Technical analysis deals with charts, strengths, different patterns of trends, and a good number of indicators. However, the main thing to remember with
technical analysis is that one indicator is never
enough; a conclusion should be confirmed by other
indicators, because:

1. There are many disagreements and contradic-
    tions in charting interpretations.
2. The use of a technical indicator has produced
    mixed results in predicting future performance.

> *Note:* There are many other technical indi-
> cators, such as the *Arms Index*, the *McCellan Os-
> cillator*, *Fibonnaci stochastics*, and the *Summation
> Index*. They are not discussed here because they
> are usually beyond the needs of average inves-
> tors.

TECHNICAL ANALYSIS BY PC

Technical analysis is well suited to computerization,
since it involves the manipulation of a large amount
of data. Technical analysis software allows you to
quickly obtain data, plot it, and apply various technical indicators, such as *moving averages.*

Technical analysis programs vary widely in the
types of indicators they provide. They may emphasize the analysis of a particular market or security
type and provide those indicators most suited for
that type of analysis. For example, the *Technician*,
by Equis, is geared for the analysis of the overall
direction of the market and contains a different set
of indicators than its sister program *MetaStock*,
which is a more general technical analysis tool.

WHAT ARE THE SOURCES OF
TECHNICAL ANALYSIS SOFTWARE AND
PUBLISHED CHARTING?

The following are major published charting services:

Daily Action Charts
Current Market Perspectives
Trendline, Standard & Poor's, (212) 208-8792

Red Book of 5-Trend Security Charts
Blue Book of 5-Trend Cycli-Graphs
Securities Research Co., (617) 235-0900

Daily Graphs
Log Term Values
William O'Neil and Co., (310) 448-6843

Chartcraft Point & Figure Charts
Chartcraft Inc., (914) 632-0422

Mansfield Charts
Mansfield Stock Chart Service, (201) 795-0629

The following is a list of popular technical software.

Behold! (Mac)
Investor's Technical Services, (512) 328-8000

Omni Trader (DOS)
NIRVANA Systems Inc., (800) 880-0338 for a free
demo or (512) 345-2566

MegaTech Chart System (DOS)
Ret-Tech Software, Inc., (708) 382-3903

Technician, MetaStock, and MetaStock RT (DOS)
EQUIS International, (800) 882-3040 or (801)
265-8886

Metastock (DOS)
EQUIS International, (800) 882-3040 or (801) 265-
8886

Dow Jones Market Analyzer (DOS)
Dow Jones & Co., (800) 522-3567 for free demo

Ensign 6 (DOS, Windows)
BMI, (800) 255-0655

Parity Plus (Windows)
ParTech Software Systems, (415) 546-9316

Personal Hotline and Professional Analyst (Mac)
Trendsetter Software, (800) 825-1852 or (714)
547-5005

SuperCharts 2.1 (Windows)
Omega Research, Inc., (800) 556-2022 ext. 225c for a
free demo, (800) 422-8587 ext. 225c or (305) 270-1095

Technifilter Plus (DOS)
RTR Software, Inc., (919) 829-0789

Telechart 2000 System (DOS)
Worden Brothers, Inc., (800) 776-4940 or (919)
408-0542

Telescan Analyzer and Telescan ProSearch (DOS)
Telescan, Inc., (800) 324-8246 or (713) 952-1060

TradingExpert (DOS)
AIQ Systems, Inc., (800) 332-2999 or (702) 831-2999

Wall Street Watcher (Mac)
Micros Trading Software, Inc., (203) 762-7820

Technical Investor (DOS)
Savant Corp., (800) 231-9900 or (603) 471-0400

Windows on WallStreet (Windows)
MarketArts Inc., (800) 998-VIEW for a free demo or
(214) 235-9594

CHAPTER 6

COMMON STOCKS AND PREFERRED STOCKS

Securities cover a broad range of investment instruments, including common stocks, preferred stocks, bonds, and options.

There are two broad categories of securities available to investors: Equity securities, which represent ownership of a company, and debt securities, which represent a loan from the investor to a company or government. Each type of security has not only distinct characteristics, but also advantages and disadvantages which vary by investor.

WHAT IS COMMON STOCK?

Common stock is a security that represents an ownership interest in a corporation. This ownership interest is evidenced by a transferable stock certificate. For example, if you hold 5,000 shares of ABC Corporation, which has 100,000 shares outstanding, your ownership interest is 5 percent. Each share is a fractional ownership interest in a corporation. You acquire an equity interest in the corporation by buying its stock. As a stockholder, you can vote for the board of directors of the corporation. The equity investment has no maturity date. Common stock return comes in the form of dividend income and appreciation in the market price of stock.

The corporation's stockholders have certain rights and privileges including:

1. *Control of the firm.* The stockholders elect the firm's directors, who in turn select officers to manage the business.

2. *Preemptive right.* This is the right to purchase new stock.

   A preemptive right entitles a common stockholder to maintain his or her proportional ownership by offering the stockholder an opportunity to purchase, on a pro rata basis, any new stock being offered or any securities convertible into common stock.

(a) Value of right "cum rights"

$$\text{Value of a right} = \frac{\text{Market price(M) - Subscription price(S)}}{\text{\# of rights required(N) + 1}}$$

(b) Value of right "ex-rights"

$$\frac{\text{Adjusted M - S}}{N}$$

Example 1—

If a stock is selling for $60 and two rights are required to purchase a single share at the subscription price of $51, the value of a single right would be ($60 - $51)/ (2 + 1) = $3. If the stock is now "ex-rights" its market value should reflect that and be $60-$3, or $57. Thus, we have ($57 - $51)/ 2 = $3.

3. *Voting rights*. Shareholders have rights to vote on all important matters affecting them:

    *   alterations to the corporate charter
    *   mergers and acquisitions
    *   recapitalization (e.g., an exchange of bond for stock)
    *   financial reorganization
    *   election of the board of directors

WHAT ARE THE CHARACTERISTICS OF COMMON STOCK ?

The characteristics that make common stock an attractive investment alternative can be summarized as follows:

1. Common stocks provide an ownership feature, as compared with fixed income securities, such as bonds, which do not.

2. Common stocks provide an income potential not only in terms of current income in the form of dividends but also future capital gain (or loss).

3. Common shareholders can participate in the firm's earnings and lay claim to all the residual profits of the entity.

4. Common stock can be a good inflation hedge, if the total return from investment in common stock exceeds the rate of inflation.

5. Because there are a variety of stocks available, as discussed above, the investor may choose from a broad spectrum of risk/return combinations from common stock investment.

Table 1 summarizes characteristics of common stock.

Table 1—

Characteristics of Common Stock

Voting rights	One vote per share
Income	Dividends; not fixed
Capital gain/loss potential	Yes
Price stability	No
Inflation hedge	Yes
Preemptive right	Yes
Priority of claim	Residual after all other claims paid
Unit of purchase	Usually in units of 100 shares

Some key terms regarding common stock are:

1. *Par value.* Traditionally set at a low price partly for tax purposes; a corporation may also issue no-par stock.

2. *Book value.* The net worth (assets minus liabilities) of the corporation divided by the number of shares outstanding:

$$\text{Book Value} = \frac{\text{Assets - Liabilities}}{\text{Number of shares outstanding}}$$

3. *Market value.* Currently quoted price of a share of stock in the market. The market value or capitalization of a firm is its stock price times the number of shares outstanding. The ratio of a stock's market price to its book value (*price/ book ratio*) gives an indication of how investors regard the company. Dividing the share price by the book value gives a market/book ratio, and thus the higher the ratio, the more expensive the stock price (compared with its book value).

4. *Cash dividends*. Cash dividends are paid to investors if and when declared by the Board of Directors. Important dates to remember:

    (a) Declared date—the date on which the Board declares the dividend.
    (b) Record Date—investors registered on the corporate books on the record date (set by the Board) will receive the dividend.
    (c) Ex-dividend date—the date that a stock will begin trading without the value of the pending dividend factored into its market value; the ex-dividend date is *three business days before the record date*.

Example 2—

Sun	Mon	Tue	Wed	Thurs	Fri	Sat
	1	2	3	4	5	6
7	8	9	10	11	12	13

Assume that the 10th day of the month is the record date for a dividend. The shareholders registered by the close of business on the 10th day are entitled to the dividend. Suppose that you buy the stock on the 8th day of the month (trade date). You are entitled to the dividend.

    (d) Payable date—the date on which investors on record will receive dividends.

5. *Stock dividends*. For example, if XYZ Corp. declares a 5 percent stock dividend, a holder of 200 shares would receive a stock certificate for 10 additional shares. Most often, firms redeem fractional shares for cash.

6. *Stock splits.* Each old share is equal to some number of new shares. Stock splits do not change the value of the underlying corporation and so the other values are changed proportionately.

7. *Reverse splits.* Each old share is equal to some fraction of a new share.

Example 3—

A stock with a par value of $1 and a market value of $20 which had a two-for-one stock split would now have twice as many authorized shares. But both the par and market values would be halved. In a one-for-two reverse split, 200 shares of old stock would be 100 shares of the new stock. Both the par and market values would be doubled.

WHAT TYPES OF STOCKS ARE THERE?

The stock you buy should be best for your particular circumstances and goals. The types of stock include:

1. *Income stocks.* These stocks are issued by companies having high dividends and a fairly stable stream of earnings. They are desirable if you seek high current income instead of capital growth and desire less risk. An example is utility companies. Income stocks give you the highest stable income to satisfy your present living needs.

2. *Cyclical stocks.* They are stocks whose price movements follow the business cycle. Firms'

prices increase in expansion and decline in recession. These stocks are thus somewhat risky. Examples include construction and airlines.

3. *Defensive stocks.* Often called countercyclical stocks, they are stocks that remain stable during periods of contraction. They are safe and consistent but have a lower return. However, the return earned is lower. An example is consumer goods stocks.

4. *Growth stocks.* Growth stocks are companies evidencing higher rates of growth in operations and earnings than other firms. An example is high-technology firms. These stocks normally pay little or no dividends. Growth stocks usually increase in price faster than others, but they may fluctuate more. They appeal to investors seeking capital appreciation rather than dividend income.

5. *Blue chips.* Blue chips are common stocks that provide uninterrupted streams of dividends and strong long-term growth prospects, such as General Electric. These stocks have low risk but are less susceptible to cyclical market changes than other stocks.

6. *Penny stocks.* Penny stocks are stocks which usually have market prices below $1 a share. Penny stocks are issued by financially weak and risky companies.

7. *Speculative stocks.* These stocks have the potential for large profits, with uncertainty in earnings. You buy a speculative stock if you are willing to take a high risk for a very high return. Speculative stocks have high price fluctuations and price/earnings ratios. Examples of speculative stocks include mining and biotechnology company stocks.

WHAT IS THE YIELD ON COMMON STOCK INVESTMENTS?

Yield is the return for a common stock at its initial cost or present market value. Typically, both yields are computed.

$$\text{Yield} = \frac{\text{Dividend per share}}{\text{Market price per share}}$$

Example 4—

You paid $80 for a stock currently worth $100. The dividends per share is $4. The yield on your investment is:

$$\frac{\$4}{\$80} = .05 = 5\% \text{ or } \frac{\$4}{\$100} = .04 = 4\%$$

(based on original investment)   (based on market value)

You can use the yield as an indication of the reasonableness of the price of the stock, particularly when dividends are stable (e.g., utilities). Yield on stock is also helpful if you are an income-oriented investor that wishes to compare equity dividend returns with those of fixed income securities.

More exactly, the yield on your stock investment for a single period can be calculated using the formula:

$$r = \frac{D_1}{P_o} + \frac{(P_1 - P_o)}{P_o}$$

where r = expected return for a single period
D_1 = dividend at the end of the period
P_1 = price per share at the end of the period
P_0 = price per share at the beginning of the period

Translated,

$$r = \frac{\text{Dividends}}{\text{Beginning price}} + \frac{\text{Capital gain}}{\text{Beginning price}}$$
$$= \text{Dividend yield} + \text{capital gain yield}$$

Note: This formula is derived from the *Gordon's dividend growth model.* To repeat, if a company's dividends are expected to grow at a constant rate, then:

$$P_0 = \frac{D_1}{r - g}$$

Solving for r gives:

$$r = \frac{D_1}{P_0} + g \text{ , where } g = \frac{(P_1 - P_0)}{P_0} \text{ for a single period.}$$

Example 5—

Consider a stock selling for $50. The company is expected to pay a $3 cash dividend at the end of the year, and the stock's market price at the end of the year is expected to be $55 a share. Thus, the expected return would be:

$$r = \frac{D_1}{P_0} + \frac{(P_1 - P_0)}{P_0} = \frac{\$3}{\$50} + \frac{(\$55 - \$50)}{\$50} = \frac{(\$3 + \$5)}{\$50} = 6\% + 10\%$$

Or,

$$\text{Dividend yield} = \$3/\$50 = 6\%$$
$$\text{Capital gain yield} = \$5/\$50 = 10\%$$
$$\text{Total yield} = \text{dividend yield} + \text{capital gain yield}$$
$$= 6\% + 10\% = 16\%$$

WHAT IS PREFERRED STOCK?

Preferred stock is paid quarterly and carries a fixed dividend. The dividend is stated as a percentage of par value of the stock, or in dollar terms per share. Preferred stock is viewed as a hybrid security because it possesses features of both corporate bonds and common stocks. It is similar to common stock in that:

- It pays dividends.
- It represents owners' equity.
- It is issued without stated maturity dates.

Preferred stock is also similar to corporate bonds in that:

- Its dividends are fixed for the life of the issue.
- It provides for prior claims on assets and earnings.
- It can carry convertible and call characteristics and sinking fund provisions.

Preferred stocks are traded on the basis of the yield offered to investors. They are viewed as fixed income securities and, as a result, are in direct competition with bonds in the marketplace. *Note*: Corporate bonds, however, occupy a position senior to preferred stocks.

Advantages of owning preferred stock are:

- Relatively higher yields than comparably rated fixed income securities.

- Quarterly dividend payments. Bonds pay interest every six months.

- Safety. Preferred stocks take precedence over common stocks. The preferred stock dividend must be paid before *any* dividends on common stock can be paid. *Note:* Most preferreds are cumulative.

- Lower per-share cost, which even small investors can afford.

- Call protection for the first five to ten years of issuance.

- Active—both listed and OTC—and fairly liquid.

    Disadvantages include:

- Their vulnerability to interest rates and price level changes.

- They have restricted capital gains except for convertible preferreds.

Note: Convertible preferreds allow the holder to exchange your preferred shares for a fixed number of common shares.

Table 2 presents major features of preferred stock.

Table 2—

Characteristics of Preferred Stock

Voting rights	No unless dividend not paid
Income	Fixed as long as dividend paid
Capital gain/loss potential	Only if interest rates change or company's preferred stock rating changes

(continued)

Table 2—*continued*

Inflation hedge	No, except for adjustable
Preemptive right	No
Priority of claim	Prior to common stock
Unit of purchase	Usually 100 shares

HOW IS PREFERRED STOCK RATED?

Like bond ratings, Standard & Poor's and Moody's rate the quality of preferred stocks. S&P has basically a similar rating scheme as bonds, but triple A ratings are not assigned to preferred stocks. Moody's scheme is somewhat different (see Table 3); these ratings are based on the financial soundness of the issuing company and its ability to meet its payment obligations in a timely manner. Preferred stockholders come after bondholders in the event of bankruptcy.

Table 3—

Description of Preferred Stock Ratings

Standard & Poor's	*Quality Indication*
*	Highest quality
AA	High quality
A	Upper medium grade
BBB	Medium grade
BB	Contains speculative elements
B	Outright speculative
CCC & CC	Default definitely possible
C	Default, only partial recovery likely
D	Default, little recovery likely

*Triple A rating is not given.

Moody's

aaa	Top quality
aa	High grade
a	Upper medium grade
baa	Lower medium grade
ba	Speculative type
b	Little assurance of future dividends
caa	Likely to be already in arrears

HOW DO YOU CALCULATE EXPECTED RETURN FROM PREFERRED STOCK?

Return on preferred stock is computed in the same manner as that on bonds. The calculations depend upon whether the preferred stock is issued in perpetuity or if it has a call that is likely to be exercised.

A Perpetuity

Since preferred stock usually has no maturity date when the company must redeem it, you cannot calculate a yield to maturity. You can calculate a current yield, as follows:

$$\text{Current yield} = D/P$$

where D= annual dividend and P= the market price of the preferred stock.

Example 6—

A preferred stock paying $2.00 per annum in dividends with a market price of $20 would have a current yield of 10% ($2/$20).

Yield to Call

If a call is likely, a more appropriate return measure is *yield to call (YTC)*. Theoretically, YTC is the rate that equates the present value of the future dividends and the call price with the current market price of the preferred stock. Two examples are given below.

Example 7—

Consider the following two preferreds:

Preferreds	Market price	Call Price	Dividends	Term to call	YTC
A	$8/share	$9	$1/year	3 years	16.06%
B	10	9	$1	3	6.89

Comparison to Bond Yields

The example shows that yields on straight preferreds are closely correlated to bond yields, since both are fixed income securities. However, yields on preferreds are often below bond yields, which seems unusual because preferreds have a position junior to bonds. The reason is that corporate investors favor preferreds over bonds because of a dividend exclusion allowed in determining corporate taxable income.

WHAT ARE THE TYPES OF PREFERRED STOCK?

There are many types of preferred stock. They are:

Perpetual preferreds. Tthe most common type of preferred stock. Its dividend can be either fixed or floating and is paid quarterly. It has no maturity date. Most issues, however, are callable at the option of the issuer after a specified period of time. Perpetual preferreds typically offer the highest current yields.

Convertible preferreds. Convertible into common shares, thus offering growth potential plus fixed income; tend to behave differently in the marketplace than straight preferred. The market price of a convertible preferred should equal the common stock price times the conversion rate.

Cumulative preferreds. Any dividend due that is not declared accumulates and must be paid before any common stock dividend can be declared. Most preferreds are cumulative.

Non-cumulative preferreds. Left over from the heyday of the railroads; rare today. Dividends, if unpaid, do not accumulate.

Participating preferreds. Usually and typically issued by firms desperate for capital. Preferred shareholders share in profits with common holders by way of extra dividends declared after regular dividends are paid. This type may have voting rights.

Prior preferred stock (or preference shares). This type has a priority claim on assets and earnings over other preferred shares.

Callable preferreds. This type carries a provision that permits the company to call in the issue and pay it off at full value, plus a premium of perhaps 5 percent.

Adjustable-rate preferreds (ARPs). Also called floating- or variable-rate preferreds, these are perpetual preferreds with a floating dividend rate that resets each quarter. The rate is determined by using the highest of the three benchmark rates: the 3-month T-bill, 10-year T-note, and 20- or 30-year T-bond. Thus, you are assured of a favorable dividend regardless of the shape of the yield curve.

Foreign bank preferreds, American depository receipt (ADR). Shares issued by foreign banks. They are SEC-registered, U.S.-dollar-denominated perpetual preferreds. They offer the following advantages:

- Higher fixed dividend rates than domestic preferreds.

- A special tax advantage on a portion of the dividend income in the form of a 15 to 25 percent tax credit. This means a higher after-tax yield than many comparable tax-exempt municipal bonds. *Note:* Tax-deferred retirement accounts such as IRAs do not qualify, however.

- Opportunity to diversify globally without foreign currency exposure.

WHAT ABOUT INVESTING IN MONEY MARKET PREFERRED STOCK?

Money market preferred stock (MMPS), also known as auction-rate preferred stock, is the newest and most popular member of the preferred stock group, attractive to many investors because it offers the following advantages:

- Low market risk in the event of price decline
- Competitive yield
- Liquidity

MMPS pay dividends and adjust rates up or down, depending on the current market, every seven weeks. Unlike other adjustable-rate preferreds, the market, not the issuer, sets the rate at the auction. If no bids are placed for a stock, MMPS' dividend rate is automatically set at the 60-day AA commercial paper rate quoted by the Federal Reserve Bank. There is a possibility, however, of a failed auction if no buyers show up at the auction. You must take into account the credit quality of a money market preferred stock.

Money market preferreds include:

- Short-term auction-rate stock (STARS)
- Dutch-auction-rate transferable securities (DARTS)
- Market-auction preferred stock (MAPS)
- Auction-market preferred stock (AMPS)
- Cumulative auction-market preferred stock (CAMPS)

Note: If you are looking to supplement your monthly cash flow, you may do so with a diversified portfolio of preferred stocks discussed above.

CHAPTER 7

HOW MUCH ARE YOU WILLING TO PAY FOR A COMMON STOCK?

The purpose of valuing a stock is to determine if the market price makes sense considering expected future earnings and dividends. Is the stock appropriately valued?

A number of approaches exist to determine a fundamental value for a security investment. They are, among others, time value, multiplier of earnings, and dividend-oriented. Time value is a basic cornerstone for stock valuation.

WHAT IS TIME VALUE OF MONEY?

A dollar is worth more today than tomorrow because you earn interest on the money. A time value problem can be viewed in one of two ways: future value and present value. *Future value* computations, which involve compounding, are necessary to appraise the future value of an investment. *Present value* computations, which involve discounting, are used to determine the present worth of expected future cash flows from an investment. Each is discussed below.

Future Value of $1

Compound interest means interest is received on interest. Future value of a single receipt shows the

value of an investment in the future (see Table 1).
Multiply the beginning amount invested by the
Table 1 value for the appropriate number of years
and interest rate.

Example 1—

What is the future value in 12 years of
$5,000 invested today at 10%?

Multiply the beginning amount invested by the Table 1 value for the appropriate number of years and interest rate.

$5,000 x 3.139 = $15,695

Future Value of an Annuity of $1

An annuity is equal cash flows received per period,
such as constant dividends from a stock or interest
payments from a bond. Compounding is involved
because the payments earn interest (see Table 2).
Multiply the amount of an annuity invested by the
Table 2 value for the appropriate number of years
and interest rate.

Example 2—

What is the future value of $5,000 invested
today at 10 percent *annually* after 12 years?

$5,000 x 21.385 = $106,925

Present Value of $1

Present value determines the worth today of un-equal future cash flows from an investment (see Table 3). Multiply the beginning amount invested by the Table 3 value for the appropriate number of years and interest rate.

Example 3—

> You have an opportunity to receive $50,000 five years from now. You earn 12 percent on your investment. What is the most you would be willing to pay for this invest-ment?
>
> $50,000 x .567 = $28,350

Present Value of an Annuity of $1

This determines the worth today of receiving equal annual future cash flows from an investment. Mul-tiply the amount of the annuity to be received by the Table 4 value for the appropriate number of years and interest rate.

Example 4—

> You will receive $5,000 a year for 10 years at 10 percent. What is the present worth?
>
> $5,000 x 6.145 = $30,725

Table 1—
Future Value of $1

PERIODS	4%	6%	8%	10%	12%	14%	20%
1	1.040	1.060	1.080	1.100	1.120	1.140	1.200
2	1.082	1.124	1.166	1.210	1.254	1.300	1.440
3	1.125	1.191	1.260	1.331	1.405	1.482	1.728
4	1.170	1.263	1.361	1.464	1.574	1.689	2.074
5	1.217	1.338	1.469	1.611	1.762	1.925	2.488
6	1.265	1.419	1.587	1.772	1.974	2.195	2.986
7	1.316	1.504	1.714	1.949	2.211	2.502	3.583
8	1.369	1.594	1.851	2.144	2.476	2.853	4.300
9	1.423	1.690	1.999	2.359	2.773	3.252	5.160
10	1.480	1.791	2.159	2.594	3.106	3.707	6.192
11	1.540	1.898	2.332	2.853	3.479	4.226	7.430
12	1.601	2.012	2.518	3.139	3.896	4.818	8.916
13	1.665	2.133	2.720	3.452	4.364	5.492	10.699
14	1.732	2.261	2.937	3.798	4.887	6.261	12.839
15	1.801	2.397	3.172	4.177	5.474	7.138	15.407
16	1.873	2.540	3.426	4.595	6.130	8.137	18.488
17	1.948	2.693	3.700	5.055	6.866	9.277	22.186
18	2.026	2.854	3.996	5.560	7.690	10.575	26.623
19	2.107	3.026	4.316	6.116	8.613	12.056	31.948
20	2.191	3.207	4.661	6.728	9.646	13.743	38.338
30	3.243	5.744	10.063	17.450	29.960	50.950	237.380
40	4.801	10.286	21.725	45.260	93.051	188.880	1469.800

Table 2—

Future Value of an Annuity of $1

PERIODS	4%	6%	8%	10%	12%	14%	20%
1	1.000	1.000	1.000	1.000	1.000	1.000	1.000
2	2.040	2.060	2.080	2.100	2.120	2.140	2.200
3	3.122	3.194	3.246	3.310	3.374	3.440	3.640
4	4.247	4.375	4.506	4.641	4.779	4.921	5.368
5	5.416	5.637	5.867	6.105	6.353	6.610	7.442
6	6.633	6.975	7.336	7.716	8.115	8.536	9.930
7	7.898	8.394	8.923	9.487	10.089	10.730	12.916
8	9.214	9.898	10.637	11.436	12.300	13.233	16.499
9	10.583	11.491	12.488	13.580	14.776	16.085	20.799
10	12.006	13.181	14.487	15.938	17.549	19.337	25.959
11	13.486	14.972	16.646	18.531	20.655	23.045	32.150
12	15.026	16.870	18.977	21.385	24.133	27.271	39.580
13	16.627	18.882	21.495	24.523	28.029	32.089	48.497
14	18.292	21.015	24.215	27.976	32.393	37.581	59.196
15	20.024	23.276	27.152	31.773	37.280	43.842	72.035
16	21.825	25.673	30.324	35.950	42.753	50.980	87.442
17	23.698	28.213	33.750	40.546	48.884	59.118	105.930
18	25.645	30.906	37.450	45.600	55.750	68.394	128.120
19	27.671	33.760	41.446	51.160	63.440	78.969	154.740
20	29.778	36.778	45.762	57.276	75.052	91.025	186.690
30	56.085	79.058	113.283	164.496	241.330	356.790	1181.900
40	95.026	154.762	259.057	442.597	767.090	1342.000	7343.900

*Payments (or receipts) at the *end* of each period.

Table 3—
Present Value of $1

PERIODS	4%	6%	8%	10%	12%	14%	16%	18%	20%	22%	24%	26%	28%	30%
1	.962	.943	.926	.909	.893	.877	.862	.847	.833	.820	.806	.794	.781	.769
2	.925	.890	.857	.826	.797	.769	.743	.718	.694	.672	.650	.630	.610	.592
3	.889	.840	.794	.751	.712	.675	.641	.609	.579	.551	.524	.500	.477	.455
4	.855	.792	.735	.683	.636	.592	.552	.516	.482	.451	.423	.397	.373	.350
5	.822	.747	.681	.621	.567	.519	.476	.437	.402	.370	.341	.315	.291	.269
6	.790	.705	.630	.564	.507	.456	.410	.370	.335	.303	.275	.250	.227	.207
7	.760	.665	.583	.513	.452	.400	.354	.314	.279	.249	.222	.198	.178	.159
8	.731	.627	.540	.467	.404	.351	.305	.266	.233	.204	.179	.157	.139	.123
9	.703	.592	.500	.424	.361	.308	.263	.225	.194	.167	.144	.125	.108	.094
10	.676	.558	.463	.386	.322	.270	.227	.191	.162	.137	.116	.099	.085	.073
11	.650	.527	.429	.350	.287	.237	.195	.162	.135	.112	.094	.079	.066	.056
12	.625	.497	.397	.319	.257	.208	.168	.137	.112	.092	.076	.062	.052	.043
13	.601	.469	.368	.290	.229	.182	.145	.116	.093	.075	.061	.050	.040	.033
14	.577	.442	.340	.263	.205	.160	.125	.099	.078	.062	.049	.039	.032	.025
15	.555	.417	.315	.239	.183	.140	.108	.084	.065	.051	.040	.031	.025	.020

PERIODS	4%	6%	8%	10%	12%	14%	16%	18%	20%	22%	24%	26%	28%	30%
16	.534	.394	.292	.218	.163	.123	.093	.071	.054	.042	.032	.025	.019	.015
17	.513	.371	.270	.198	.146	.108	.080	.060	.045	.034	.026	.020	.015	.012
18	.494	.350	.250	.180	.130	.095	.069	.051	.038	.028	.021	.016	.012	.009
19	.475	.331	.232	.164	.116	.083	.060	.043	.031	.023	.017	.012	.009	.007
20	.456	.3t2	.215	.149	.104	.073	.051	.037	.026	.019	.014	.010	.007	.005
21	.439	.294	.199	.135	.093	.064	.044	.031	.022	.015	.011	.008	.006	.004
22	.422	.278	.184	.123	.083	.056	.038	.026	.018	.013	.009	.006	.004	.003
23	.406	.262	.170	.112	.074	.049	.033	.022	.015	.010	.007	.005	.003	.002
24	.390	.247	.158	.102	.066	.043	.028	.019	.013	.008	.006	.004	.003	.002
25	.375	.233	.146	.092	.059	.038	.024	.016	.010	.007	.005	.003	.002	.001
26	.361	.220	.135	.084	.053	.033	.021	.014	.009	.006	.004	.002	.002	.001
27	.347	.207	.125	.076	.047	.029	.018	.011	.007	.005	.003	.002	.001	.001
28	.333	.196	.116	.069	.042	.026	.016	.010	.006	.004	.002	.002	.001	.001
29	.321	.185	.107	.063	.037	.022	.014	.008	.005	.003	.002	.001	.001	.001
30	.308	.174	.099	.057	.033	.020	.012	.007	.004	.003	.002	.001	.001	.001
40	.208	.097	.046	.022	.011	.005	.003	.001	.001					

Table 4—

Present Value of an Annuity of $1

n	1%	2%	3%	4%	5%	6%	7%	8%	9%	10%
1	.990	.980	.971	.962	.952	.943	.935	.926	.917	.909
2	1.970	1.942	1.913	1.886	1.859	1.833	1.808	1.783	1.759	1.736
3	2.941	2.884	2.829	2.775	2.723	2.673	2.624	2.577	2.531	2.487
4	3.902	3.808	3.717	3.630	3.546	3.465	3.387	3.312	3.240	3.170
5	4.853	4.713	4.580	4.452	4.329	4.212	4.100	3.993	3.890	3.791
6	5.795	5.601	5.417	5.242	5.076	4.917	4.767	4.623	4.486	4.355
7	6.728	6.472	6.230	6.002	5.786	5.582	5.389	5.206	5.033	4.868
8	7.652	7.326	7.020	6.733	6.463	6.210	5.971	5.747	5.535	5.335
9	8.566	8.162	7.786	7.435	7.108	6.802	6.515	6.247	5.995	5.759
10	9.471	8.983	8.530	8.111	7.722	7.360	7.024	6.710	6.418	6.145
11	10.368	9.787	9.253	9.760	8.306	7.887	7.499	7.139	6.805	6.495
12	11.255	10.575	9.954	9.385	8.863	8.384	7.943	7.536	7.161	6.814
13	12.134	11.348	10.635	9.996	9.394	8.853	8.358	7.904	7.487	7.103
14	13.004	12.106	11.296	10.563	9.899	9.295	8.746	8.244	7.786	7.367
15	13.865	12.849	11.938	11.118	10.380	9.712	9.108	8.500	8.061	7.606
16	14.718	13.578	12.561	11.652	10.838	10.106	9.447	8.851	8.313	7.824
17	15.562	14.292	13.166	12.166	11.274	10.477	9.763	9.122	8.544	8.022
18	16.398	14.992	13.754	12.659	11.690	10.828	10.059	9.372	8.756	8.201
19	17.226	15.679	14.324	13.134	12.085	11.158	10.336	9.604	8.950	8.365
20	18.046	16.352	14.878	13.590	12.462	11.470	10.594	9.818	9.129	8.514

n	1%	2%	3%	4%	5%	6%	7%	8%	9%	10%
21	18.857	17.011	15.415	14.029	12.8-11	11.764	10.836	10.017	9.292	8.649
22	19.661	17.658	15.937	14.451	13.163	12.042	11.061	10.201	9.442	8.772
23	20.456	18.292	16.444	14.857	13.489	12.303	11.272	10.371	9.580	8.883
24	21.244	18.914	16.936	15.247	13.799	12.550	11.469	10.529	9.707	8.985
25	22.023	19.524	17.413	15.622	14.094	12.783	11.654	10.675	9.823	9.077
30	25.808	22.397	19.601	17.292	15.373	13.765	12.409	11.258	10.274	9.47
40	32.835	27.356	23.115	19.793	17.159	15.046	13.332	11.925	10.757	9.779
50	39.197	31.424	25.730	21.482	18.256	15.762	13.801	12.234	10.962	9.915

WHAT IS THE FUNDAMENTAL VALUE OF COMMON STOCK?

A stock's value equals the present value of a security's expected cash flows, using your desired rate of return as the discount rate. The calculation follows.

Value of common stock =   Present value of
                          future dividends

                          + Present value of
                          selling price

For example, for an investor holding a common stock for only one year, the value of the stock would be the present value of both the expected cash dividend to be received in one year (D_1) and the expected market price per share of the stock at year-end (P_1). If r represents an investor's required rate of return, the value of common stock (P_0) would be:

$$P_0 = \frac{D_1}{(1+r)^1} + \frac{P_1}{(1+r)^1}$$

$$= (D_1 \times \text{Table 3 value}) + (P_1 \times \text{Table 3 value})$$

Example 5—

You are thinking about buying stock A at the beginning of the year. The year-end dividend is expected to be $1.50, and the market price by the end of the year is expected to be $40. If the investor's required rate of return is 10 percent, the value of the stock would be:

$$P_0 = \frac{D_1}{(1+r)^1} + \frac{P_1}{(1+r)^1} = \frac{\$1.50}{(1+0.10)} + \frac{\$40}{(1+0.10)}$$

$$= (D_1 \times \text{Table 3 value}) + (P_1 \times \text{Table 3 value})$$
$$= \$1.50(.909) + \$40(.909)$$
$$= \$1.36 + \$36.36 = \$37.72$$

Since common stock has no maturity date and is held for many years, a more general, multiperiod model is needed. The general common stock valuation model is defined as follows:

$$P_0 = \sum_{t=1}^{n} \frac{D_t}{(1 + r)^t}$$

where D_t = dividend in period t.

Three cases of growth in dividends are explained below. They are: (a) zero growth, (b) constant growth, and (c) modified constant growth. We will explain each of these cases.

(a) Zero Growth Case

In the case of zero growth (i.e., $D_0 = D_1 = \ldots = D_n$), then the valuation model reduces to the formula:

$$P_0 = \frac{D}{r}$$

This is the case with a perpetuity. This model is most applicable to the valuation of preferred stocks, or the common stocks of very mature companies, such as large utilities.

Example 6—

Assuming dividends (D) equals $2.50 and r equals 10 percent, then the value of the stock is:

$$P_0 = \frac{\$2.50}{0.1} = \$25$$

(b) Constant Growth Case

In the case of constant growth, if we assume that dividends grow at a constant rate of g every year [i.e., $D_t = D_0(1 + g)^t$], then the general model is simplified to:

$$P_0 = \frac{D_1}{r - g}$$

where D_1 = expected next annual dividend

g = expected long-term growth rate of the dividend (and earnings, assuming the dividend payout is as constant as the growth rate)

r = total return required on the stock considering the risk of the future earnings and dividend stream; includes dividend yield and the growth in stock price. r must be greater than g. *Note:* by rearranging the equation, you arrive at r - g = D/P, which is the dividend yield.

Written out,

$$\text{Common stock value} = \frac{\text{dividend in year 1}}{(\text{required rate of return}) - (\text{growth rate})}$$

This formula is known as the *Gordon's dividend valuation model.* This model is most applicable to the valuation of the common stocks of very large or broadly diversified firms and best suited for those companies that are at the expansion or maturity stage of their lifecycle.

Example 6—

Consider a common stock that paid a $.78 dividend per share at the end of the last year and is expected to pay a cash dividend every year at a growth rate of 15 percent. Assume the investor's required rate of return is 16.5 percent. The value of the stock would be:

$$D_1 = D_0(1 + g) = \$.78(1 + 0.15) = \$.90$$

$$P_0 = \frac{D_1}{r - g} = \frac{\$.90}{0.165 - 0.150} = \$60$$

(c) Modified Constant Growth Case

We modify the constant growth case as follows:

$$P_0 = E_1 \times \frac{D_1/E_1}{r - g}$$

where E_1 = expected next earnings per share

D/E= dividend payout ratio, the percentage of earnings per share paid out in dividends

Note: By rearranging the equation, you arrive at $(D/E) \div (r - g) = P/E$, which is the price-earnings (P/E) ratio.

Example 7—

In Example 6, assume further that $E_0 = \$2.00$ and $D/P = 1.5\% = 0.015$. Then, $E_1 = E_0 (1 + g) = \$2.00(1 + 0.15) = \$2.30$

$$P_o = E_1 \times \frac{D_1/E_1}{r-g} = \$2.30 \times \frac{\$.90/\$2.30}{0.165 - 0.15}$$

$$= \$2.30 \times 26.1$$

$$= \$60$$

Note: Neither model would work if the long-term expected dividend yield was zero and, consequently, the dividend payout ratio was zero. Dividend valuation would be impossible and the price-earnings ratio would have to be estimated by other means.

HOW DO YOU DETERMINE THE REQUIRED RATE OF RETURN?

There are several ways to determine an investor's required rate of return (r) used in the Gordon's model. One is to use the beta-based model discussed in Chapter 3.

$$r_j = r_f + b(r_m - r_f)$$

where r_j =a security's required return, r_f =risk-free rate, and r_m = market return.

Thus:

Required return = risk-free rate + beta (market return - risk-free rate)

Example 8—

Coca-Cola's beta is 1.1. Assume that the risk-free rate (for example, return on a T-bill) = 5.5 percent and market return (for example, return on the S&P 500) = 10 percent. Then the return on Coca-Cola stock required by investors would be:

Expected (required) return = 5.5% + 1.1 (10% - 5.5%)

$$= 5.5\% + 4.95\%$$

$$= 10.45\%$$

Another approach is to add the stock's dividend yield and growth rate in dividends together:

$$r = \frac{D_1}{P_0} + g$$

Example 9—

Using the data in Example 8, r = 15% + 1.5% = 16.5%

WHAT ARE SOME PRICE/EARNINGS RATIO APPROACHES?

A more popular, pragmatic approach to valuing a common stock is to use the P/E ratio (or multiple). You may use the simple formula:

Expected stock price = a selected P/E ratio
x projected EPS (E_1)

Comparing the current price against the computed expected value price could help indicate if the stock is under- or overvalued.

Example 10—

The XYZ Corporation had EPS of $5. The EPS is expected to grow at 20 percent. The company's normal P/E ratio is estimated to be 7, which is used as the multiplier. Estimated EPS =$5(1 + .20) = $6.00. The value of the stock is:

7 x $6.00 = $42

It is important to realize that for the P/E method to be effective in forecasting the future value of a stock, (a) earnings need to be correctly projected and (b) the appropriate P/E multiple must be applied. Forecasting EPS is not an easy task. Furthermore, there is no agreed-upon method of picking a meaningful P/E ratio. Some analysts use an average of historical earnings; some normalize earnings; some come up with a P/E ratio relative to the market's P/E ratio; and so on. A discussion of the various approaches follows.

1. The first approach is simply to look at historical P/E ratios. A 5- or 10-year average price-earnings ratio is a useful benchmark because it will smooth out fluctuating earnings and prices during both economic expansions and recessions. Table 5 illustrates this approach. It shows the calculated high, low, and average P/E ratios of each of the last 5 years. You can estimate a range of stock values by using these five-year average high, low, and average P/Es with an earnings estimate.

Table 5—

Normalized Price-Earnings Ratio Example Using Coca-Cola

STOCK PRICE ($)

	1990	1991	1992	1993	1994	1995
High	24.50	40.90	45.40	45.00	51.30	—
Low	16.30	21.30	35.60	37.50	38.90	—

EARNINGS PER SHARE ($)

1990	1991	1992	1993	1994	1995
—	1.22	1.43	1.68	2.00*	2.30*

NORMALIZED PRICE-EARNINGS RATIO
(STOCK PRICE ÷ NEXT YEAR'S EARNINGS PER SHARE)

	1990	1991	1992	1993	1994	1995
High	20.1	28.6	27.0	22.5	22.3	—
Low	13.4	14.9	21.2	18.8	16.9	—

Average normalized price-earnings ratios:

24.1 = Five-year high
17.0 = Five-year low
20.6 = Five-year average

Stock Valuation

High $2.30 x 24.1 = $55.4
Low $2.30 x 17.0 = $39.1
Average $2.30 x 20.6 = $47.4

*Value Line estimated earnings.

This approach, however, does not account for market factors, and we should adjust for them.

2. The second approach gets around this problem by looking at market-relative P/E ratios. The relative price-earnings ratio examines the relative relationship of the price-earnings ratio of a

stock to the price-earnings ratio of the overall market or the stock's industry. It simply compares them with the overall market's price-earnings ratio by dividing a company's price-earnings ratio by the market's (S&P 500 or Value Line Index), as shown below. *Note:* A relative price-earnings ratio of 1.0 would indicate a price-earnings ratio that is equal to the market's. A relative price-earnings ratio above 1.0 would indicate that a company's price-earnings ratio is above the market's. By tracking the relative price-earnings over a number of years, you can estimate a relative price-earnings that a stock tends to follow.

$$\text{Relative P/E ratio} = \frac{\text{company P/E}}{\text{market P/E}}$$

Company P/E = relative P/E ratio x current market P/E

Table 6 illustrates this approach.

Table 6—

Relative Price-Earnings Ratio Example

In this example, the relative ratio is based upon the most recent 12 months of earnings divided by the year-end market price-earnings ratio.

TRAILING PRICE-EARNINGS RATIO
(STOCK PRICE ÷ EARNINGS PER SHARE)

	1990	1991	1992	1993	1994	1995
High	24.0	33.5	31.7	26.8	25.7	—
Low	16.0	17.5	24.9	22.3	19.5	—

S&P TRAILING PRICE-EARNINGS RATIO
(STOCK PRICE ÷ EARNINGS PER SHARE)

	1990	1991	1992	1993	1994	1995
High	17.3	26.1	21.1	21.5	17.6	—
Low	13.9	19.5	18.0	19.6	16.1	—

RELATIVE PRICE-EARNINGS RATIO
(COMPANY P/E ÷ S&P 500 P/E)

	1990	1991	1992	1993	1994	1995
High	1.4	1.3	1.5	1.2	1.5	—
Low	1.1	0.9	1.4	1.1	1.2	—

Average relative price-earnings ratios:

    1.4 = Five-year high
    1.2 = Five-year low
    1.3 = Five-year average

Also note:

    24.9 = Current price-earnings ratio of market
    $2.30 = Expected next annual earnings per share

Price-earnings ratio, based on a relative ratio and current market ratio:

High:	1.4 x 24.9 = 34.9
Low:	1.2 x 24.9 = 30.0
Average:	1.3 x 24.9 = 32.4

Stock Valuation:

High:	34.9 x $2.30 = $80.3
Low:	30.0 x $2.30 = $69.0
Average:	32.4 x $2.30 = $74.5

Note: All the computational results are somewhat different from the spreadsheet figures due to rounding.

3. The third approach, developed by Graham and Dodd, is another market-adjusted P/E approach. The adjustment is based on (1) a statistical relationship between P/Es and growth, (that is, P/E = 8.5 + 2g) and (2) an interest adjustment (that is 4.4%/Y, where Y = corporate AAA bond yield). The adjusted P/E ratio is:

$$\text{P/E} \times \frac{4.4\%}{Y}$$

$$(8.5 + 2g) \times \frac{4.4\%}{Y}$$

Example 11—

Assume:
E = $2.30, expected next annual earnings per share
g = 15%, annual growth in earnings per share
Y = 8%, current AAA corporate bond yield

Price-earnings ratio:

$$[8.5 + (2 \times 15\%)] \times \frac{4.4\%}{8\%} = 21.2$$

Expected stock price = a P/E ratio x projected EPS (E_1)

$$= 21.2 \times \$2.30 = \$48.76$$

WHAT OTHER PRAGMATIC APPROACHES EXIST?

In valuing a stock investment, there are several pragmatic techniques you may employ: price-sales (P/S), price-dividends, and price-book (P/B) value ratios.

The Price-Sales (P/S) Ratio

This is an increasingly popular tool for determining underlying stock value. It is computed as:

$$\frac{\text{Market price per share}}{\text{Sales per share}}$$

A P/S of, say, 0.83 means you are paying 83 cents for every dollar of sales. The P/S ratio reflects a company's underlying strength. A company with a low P/S ratio is more attractive, one with a high ratio is less attractive. *Note:* As a rule of thumb, you should avoid stocks with a P/S ratio of 1.5 or more. Further, you should sell a stock when the ratio is between 3 and 6.

You may use the simple formula:

Expected price = projected sales per share
x average P/S ratio

Example 12—

The XYZ corporation projects sales to be $3.5 per share. The company's five-year average P/S ratio is 14.4, which is used as the multiplier. The value of the stock is $50.40 ($3.5 x 14.4)

The Price-Dividends (P/D) Ratio

This is another popular tool for determining underlying stock value. It is computed as:

$$\frac{\text{Market price per share}}{\text{Dividends per share}}$$

You may use the simple formula:

Expected price = projected dividends per share
x average P/D ratio

Example 13—

The XYZ corporation projects dividends to
be $0.88 per share. The company's 5-year
average P/S ratio is 61.3, which is used as
the multiplier. The value of the stock is
$53.94 ($0.88 x 61.3)

The Price-Book (P/B) Ratio

Book value (net asset, liquidation value) per share
is the amount of corporate assets for each share of
common stock. You may benefit by uncovering
stock that is selling below book value or whose assets are significantly undervalued. A stock may represent a good value when its market price is below
or close to book value because the security is undervalued. Companies with lower ratios of market
price to book value have historically earned better
returns than those with higher ratios.

$$\frac{\text{Market price per share}}{\text{Book value per share}}$$

where book value per share = total stockholders' equity/total shares outstanding.

Example 14—

You are thinking of investing in a company
that has a market price per share of $40. The
book value per share is = $50. This may be
a buying opportunity, as market price ($40)

is well below book value ($50)—P/B ratio of .9 ($40/$50)—and an upward movement in prices may occur.

You may use the simple formula:

Expected price = projected book value per share x average P/B ratio

Example 15—

The XYZ corporation projects sales to be $5.50 per share. The company's five-year average P/S ratio is 10.4, which is used as the multiplier. The value of the stock is $57.20 ($5.50 x 10.4)

Note: Various financial services track industries and companies. They offer expectations as to future earnings, sales, dividends, book value, and even market prices of stock. For example, reference may be made to Standard and Poor's *Stock Reports* and Value Line's *Investment Survey. Institutional Brokers Estimate System* (I/B/E/S) is a database available on CompuServe that provides consensus earnings estimates on over 3,400 publicly traded corporations. *Zack's* performs a similar service and is available through Dow Jones News/Retrieval. These provide a thorough analysis of companies and provide clues as to future expectations and a source of earnings estimates.

Figures 1, 2, and 3 presents a computer spreadsheet model illustrating for a selected company various valuation approaches discussed in this chapter.

Figure 1—

Earnings-Based and Dividends-Based Valuations

STOCK VALUATION SPREADSHEET

| Company: Coca-Cola
Ticker: KO (NYSE) | Current Price $51.00
Current P/E 24.9 | Dividend Yld. 1.5%
Relative P/E 1.72 | | | Beta 1.1
Date (12/31/94) | | |

Per Share Data and Financial Ratio Analysis

	1990	1991	1992	1993	1994	1995**	5-year Avg.
Price: High	24.5	40.9	45.4	45.0	51.3		
Low	16.3	21.3	35.6	37.5	38.9		
Earnings per Share (EPS)	1.02	1.22	1.43	1.68	2.00 *	2.30	18.5%
Dividends per Share (DPS)	0.40	0.48	0.56	0.68	0.78 *	0.88	15.5%
Book Value per Share (BV)	2.82	3.33	2.98	3.53	4.40 *		8.5%
Long-term Debt	536	985	1120	1428	1480 *		
Equity	3849	4426	3888	4584	5600 *		

Financial Ratios

	1990	1991	1992	1993	1994	1995**	5-year Avg.
(1) Normalized P/E Ratio:							
Average: (High+Low)/2	16.7	21.7	24.1	20.6	19.6		20.6
High (High Price/EPS)	20.1	28.6	27.0	22.5	22.3		24.1
Low (Low Price/EPS)	13.4	14.9	21.2	18.8	16.9		17.0

	1990	1991	1992	1993	1994	1995**	5-year Avg.
(2)Trailing P/E Ratio:							
Average: (High+Low)/2	20.0	25.5	28.3	24.6	22.6		24.2
High (High Price/EPS)	24.0	33.5	31.7	26.8	25.7		28.3
Low (Low Price/EPS)	16.0	17.5	24.9	22.3	19.5		20.0
Dividend Yield % (DY): Avg.	2.0%	1.7%	1.4%	1.7%	1.8%		1.7%
High (DPS/Low Price)%	2.5%	2.3%	1.6%	1.8%	2.0%		2.0%
Low (DPS/High Price)%	1.6%	1.2%	1.2%	1.5%	1.5%		1.4%
Payout Ratio % (DPS/EPS)	39.2%	39.3%	39.2%	40.5%	39.0%		39.4%
Return on Equity (EPS/BV)%	36.2%	36.6%	48.0%	47.6%	45.5%		42.8%
Long-term debt/Equity %	13.9%	22.3%	28.8%	31.2%	26.4%		24.5%

VALUATION ESTIMATES

Earnings-Based Valuation:

(1) Normalized P/E Ratio Approach:

5-year high P/E x estimated 1995 EPS:	24.1	x	2.30	= $55.4	(High valuation)
5-year low P/E x estimated 1995 EPS:	17.0	x	2.30	= $39.1	(Low valuation)
5-year avg. P/E x estimated 1995 EPS:	20.6	x	2.30	= $47.4	(Avg. valuation)

(continued)

Figure 1—*continued*

(2) Trailing P/E Ratio Approach:

5-year high P/E x estimated 1995 EPS:	28.3	×	2.30	=	$65.1	(High valuation)
5-year low P/E x estimated 1995 EPS:	20.0	×	2.30	=	$46.0	(Low valuation)
5-year avg. P/E x estimated 1995 EPS:	24.2	×	2.30	=	$55.7	(Avg. valuation)

Dividends-Based Valuation:

Estimated 1995 annual DPS 5-year low DY:	0.88	/	0.014	=	$62.9	(High valuation)
Estimated 1995 annual DPS 5-year high DY:	0.88	/	0.020	=	$44.0	(Low valuation)
Estimated 1995 annual DPS 5-year avg. DY:	0.88	/	0.017	=	$51.8	(Avg. valuation)

*Value Line's 1994 estimates.
**Value Line's 1995 estimates.

Figure 2—

Relative Price-Earnings Ratio and Graham-Dodd Approaches

STOCK VALUATION SPREADSHEET

Company: Coca-Cola Ticker: KO (NYSE)	Current Price $51.00 Current P/E 24.9	Dividend Yld. 1.5% Relative P/E 1.72	Beta 1.1 Date (12/31/94)

COMPANY AND MARKET DATA

Per Share and Financial Data	1990	1991	1992	1993	1994	1995	5-year Avg.
Company Data:							
Price: High	24.5	40.9	45.4	45.0	51.3		
Low	16.3	21.3	35.6	37.5	38.9		
Earnings per Share (EPS)	1.02	1.22	1.43	1.68	2.00	* 2.30**	18.5
Price-Earnings Ratio (P/E): Avg.	20.0	25.5	28.3	24.6	22.6		24.2
High (High Price/EPS)	24.0	33.5	31.7	26.8	25.7		28.3
Low (Low Price/EPS)	16.0	17.5	24.9	22.3	19.5		20.0
S&P Data:***							
Price-Earnings Ratio (P/E): Avg	15.6	22.8	19.6	20.6	16.9		19.1
High (High Price/EPS)	17.3	26.1	21.1	21.5	17.6		20.7
Low (Low Price/EPS)	13.9	19.5	18.0	19.6	16.1		17.4
Relative P/E Ratio (Company P/E Divided by S&P P/E): Avg.	1.3	1.1	1.4	1.2	1.3		1.3
High (High Price/EPS)	1.4	1.3	1.5	1.2	1.5		1.4
Low (Low Price/EPS)	1.1	0.9	1.4	1.1	1.2		1.2
Corporate AAA Bond Yield:						8.00***	

(continued)

Figure 2—*continued*

VALUATION ESTIMATES

Relative Price-Earnings Ratio Approach

First, compute P/E ratio, based on relative ratio and current company P/E ratio:

High	1.4	×	24.9	=	34.3
Low	1.2	×	24.9	=	28.8
Average	1.3	×	24.9	=	31.5

Then, multiply them by estimated 1995 EPS:

5-year high P/E x estimated 1995 EPS:34.3	×	2.30	=	$78.9	(High valuation)
5-year low P/E x estimated 1995 EPS: 28.8	×	2.30	=	$66.2	(Low valuation)
5-year avg. P/E x estimated 1995 EPS: 31.5	×	2.30	=	$72.5	(Avg. valuation)

Graham-Dodd Approach

The formula is:

(8.5 + 2G) x (4.4%/ AAA Bond Yield)]   x   estimated   1995 EPS = 25.0   x   2.30 = $57.5

*Value Line's 1994 estimates.
**Value Line's 1995 estimates.
***Source of S&P data: S&P Outlook

Figure 3—

Price-to-Book-Sales Ratio, Price-to-Dividends Ratio, and Price-to-Book-Value Ratio Approaches

STOCK VALUATION SPREADSHEET

Per Share Data and Financial Ratio Analysis

	1990	1991	1992	1993	1994	1995**	5-year Avg.
Price: Average	20.4	31.1	40.5	41.25	45.1		
High	24.5	40.9	45.4	45.0	51.3		
Low	16.3	21.3	35.6	37.5	38.9		
Sales per Share (SPS)	7.66	8.71	10.00	10.76	12.60	14.40 *	
Dividends per Share (DPS)	0.40	0.48	0.56	0.68	0.78	0.88 *	
Book Value per Share (BV)	2.82	3.33	2.98	3.53	4.40	5.50 *	
Financial Ratios							
(1) Price-to-Sales (P/S) Ratio	2.7	3.6	4.1	3.8	3.6		3.5
(2) Price-to-Dividends (P/D) Ratio	51.0	64.8	72.3	60.7	57.8		61.3
(3) Price-to-Book (P/B) Ratio	7.2	9.3	13.6	11.7	10.3		10.4

VALUATION ESTIMATES

(1) Price-to-Sales (P/S) Ratio Approach
Projected Sales per share x Avg. P/S Ratio: 14.4 × 3.5 = $50.4

(continued)

181

Figure 3—*continued*

(2) Price-to-Dividends (P/D) Ratio Approach
Projected Dividends per Share x Avg. P/D Ratio: 0.88 x 61.3 = $53.9

(3) Price-to-Book (P/B) Ratio Approach
Projected Book Value per Share x Avg. P/B Ratio: 5.50 x 10.4 = $57.2

*Value Line's 1994 estimates.
**Value Line's 1995 estimates.

WHAT IS THE BOTTOM LINE?

Several valuations have been presented so far. The key is to decide which valuation model(s) is best suit the company you are interested in. For example, if your company is a mature, dividend-paying stock, such as a public utility, which is generally a low-growth stock, the dividend-based models make sense. If your company is a growth-oriented company, you should use a earnings-based model since the stock's price will be driven by earnings potential rather than dividends. Nonetheless, it is a good idea to perform sensitivity analysis and obtain a range of estimates. Any final decision on your valuation estimates should, however, be based on a better understanding of the company, its management, and its competitive environment.

STOCK VALUATION BY PC

Computers are well suited to fundamental screening, but weak when it comes to assisting in stock valuation. This is because so much of the valuation rests on your personal growth forecasts for the economy, a company's industry, and the company itself. There are, however, a few programs that can assist investors with fundamental stock valuation. Some programs that have compiled a series of valuation models that examine factors such as price-earnings ratios, dividend yields, earnings, and sales growth rates and apply models such as the dividend discount or relative price-earnings ratio model. Entering the appropriate historical information along with your projected growth rates will enable these programs to return valuation estimates. These programs are typically spreadsheet templates, such as the one illustrated in the previous section. Below is a list of popular valuation software.

Fin Val/Finstock (DOS)
PC Solutions, Inc., (718) 275-7930

Take Stock (Windows, Mac)
Triple-I, (305) 829-2892

Macro*World Investor (DOS)
Black River Systems Corp., (800) 841-5398

CHAPTER **8**

FIXED INCOME SECURITIES

Fixed income securities generally emphasize current fixed income with minimal capital appreciation potential. They are typically marketable, with low risk. They do better during low inflation and economic stability. As interest rates drop, the price of fixed income investments increases. Examples of fixed income securities include: Corporate bonds, convertible bonds, government bonds, tax-exempt bonds, and short-term debt securities. Bonds have interest rate and default risk.

WHAT IS A BOND?

A bond is a certificate evidencing a loan by you to a business or to government. You will receive for your investment interest and principal repayment. Advantages of bonds include:

- Periodic annual interest income.
- Bonds are safer than stock because bondholders come before common stockholders in profit distribution and in bankruptcy.

  Disadvantages of bonds include:
- Do not share in incremental profit.
- No voting rights.

WHAT ARE THE CHARACTERISTICS OF BONDS?

The terms and features of bonds include:

1. *Indenture.* A legal document of the issuer's duties related to the bond issue. It includes the terms of the bond issue and the restrictive provisions referred to as *restrictive covenants*. An independent trustee is assigned. A restrictive covenant includes maintenance of minimum ratio percentages and working capital amounts.

2. *Trustee.* A third party responsible for insuring that indenture provisions are satisfied.

3. *Maturity date.* The date the last principal payment is due.

4. *Par value.* The face value of a bond is typically $1,000.

5. *Coupon rate.* The periodic interest payment you will receive. It is based on the interest rate multiplied by face value.

6. *Yield.* Yield differs from the coupon interest rate (see Example 1). It is the effective interest rate you earn on the bond investment. If a bond is purchased below its face value (discount), the yield is higher than the coupon rate. If a bond is bought above face value (premium), the yield is below the coupon rate. Computations of alternative yield measures on a bond are presented later in this chapter.

Example 1—

A bond with an 8% coupon rate	*Annual Interest*	*Yield*
If you buy it at par—$1,000	$80.00	8%

A bond with an 8% coupon rate	*Annual Interest*	*Yield*
If you buy it at a discount price of $800	80.00	10%
If you buy it at a premium price of $1,200	80.00	6 2/3%

7. *Call feature.* Most bonds may be redeemed early by the issuing company, at face or at a premium. An issuer may opt to call a bond early if market interest rates decline. The issuer can issue bonds to replace the old bonds at a lower interest rate. Investors are insulated from calls for a specified time subsequent to the bonds' issuance (usually 10 years).

8. *Sinking fund provision.* The issuing company may have to put money aside periodically (e.g., annually) into a "sinking fund." The funds will be used to retire the bonds at maturity or to retire part of the issue each year after a particular date. Such a stipulation may exist to protect investors.

BOND YIELDS, INTEREST RATES, AND BOND PRICES

Keep in mind adaily fact of financial life: Bond yields move in the opposite direction of bond prices. Again, a bond's current yield is different from its interest rate (coupon rate). While your rate of return holds steady, the yield (real return) moves up and down as interest rates change. When interest rates rise, the price of your bond goes down, because its interest rate becomes less attractive than the high rates of newly issued bonds of similar quality. Because the payments promised by the bond issuer don't change, the market adjusts the yield by raising or lowering the value of the bonds.

WHAT IS THE YIELD CURVE?

The yield curve graphically depicts the relationship between length of time to maturity and yields of bonds. Other factors, such as default risk and tax treatment, are held constant. It helps you decide whether to buy long- or short-term bonds. Analysts frequently investigate the yield curve carefully in order to make judgments about the direction of interest rates. Remember, the interest rate is a critical factor in determining a bond's yield and price. A yield curve is simply a graphical presentation of the term structure of interest rates.

WHAT ARE THE TYPES OF BONDS?

Table 1 summarizes the various features of bonds.

Table 1—

The World of Bonds

	Maturity	Denomination	Pricing	Call Provision
Corporate bonds	20 - 30 yrs.	$1,000	% of par	Often callable
Municipal bonds	1 month - 30 yrs.	$5,000 -$10,000 (usually $5,000)	Quoted on yield-to-maturity basis	Often callable
Agency bonds	30 days - 20 yrs.	$1,000 - $25,000 and up	Quoted on yield-to-maturity basis	No
Marketable government securities				
Treasury bills	13, 26, or 52 wks	$10,000 - $1m in increments of $5,000	Issued at discount; priced in basis points	No
Treasury notes	2-10 yrs.	$1,000 - $1m	Issued at par; priced at % of par	Usually not callable
Treasury bonds	Over 10 yrs.	$1,000 - $1m (usually $10,000)	Priced at % of par	Usually not callable

(continued)

Table 1—*continued*

	Maturity	Denomination	Pricing	Call Provision
Non-marketable government securities				
Series EE	Adjustable	$50 - $10,000	Issued at 50% discount	No
Series HH	10 yrs.	$500 - $10,000	Issued at par	No

*Government securities are priced in 1/32's of a percentage point, corporate bonds in 1/8ths.

Bonds may be categorized as follows:

1. *Secured bonds.* Specific collateral is pledged to back the bond issue.

    (a) *Mortgage bonds,* backed by collateralized property which may be sold if the bonds are defaulted on. In case of default, the bondholders may foreclose on the secured property and sell it to satisfy their claims. They take various forms. First mortgage bonds (senior lien bonds) have claim against the corporation's fixed assets, and second mortgage bonds (junior liens) are backed by real property, but second in priority.

    (b) *Collateral trust bonds,* backed by marketable securities deposited with the trustees.

    (c) *Equipment trust certificates,* issued generally by transportation corporations (railroads or airlines). The trustee holds title to the equipment until the certificate is paid.

2. *Unsecured bonds.*

    (a) *Debentures* are backed by the issuing corporation's *good faith and credit.* The issuing company must be financially sound. High credit ratings are essential. Government bonds are examples.

    (b) *Subordinated debentures,* honored after debentures in the case of liquidation or reorganization (though still before stocks). Junior debentures are sometimes issued by finance companies.

3. *Income bonds.* The bonds pay interest only if there is profit.

4. *Convertible bonds.* These bonds may be converted to common stock at a later date at a specified conversion price. They have features of both bonds and common stock in that they gen-

erate constant interest income and capital appreciation through related common stock. Relevant formulas are:

Conversion ratio = Par value of a bond/Conversion price

Parity price of a bond = Common stock price x conversion ratio

Parity price of a stock = Price of the bond/conversion
ratio

Example 2—

If a $1,000 par value bond had a conver-
sion price of $40 this would imply a con-
version ratio of 25:1 ($1,000/$40=25, or
$40x25=$1,000). If the bond was selling at
$1,150, then the parity price of the stock
would be $1,150/ 25 = $46.

---

5.   *Zero-coupon bonds.* Zeros are purchased at a discount and mature at par. Each year, the portion
of the discount that is earned is taken as interest income on the tax return. Tax must be paid
on the "earned" portion of the discount every
year, even though no payment is made by the
issuer. Zero coupon bonds involve a lower initial investment. *Note:* Many corporations, municipalities, Federal agencies (such as Fannie
Mae and Freddie Mac), and the U.S. Treasury
issue zero coupon bonds. Zero coupon Treasury
bonds are also called *Treasury STRIPs.*

6.   *Tax-exempt bonds.* Municipal bonds are free of
tax on interest. They have a lower interest rate
than comparable corporate bonds. The after-
tax yield is usually higher than an equivalent
taxable bond.

7. *U.S. government securities.* These include bills, notes, bonds, and mortgages (e.g., "Ginnie Maes"). Treasury bills are used for near-term government financing and have a maturity of 12 months or less. U.S. Treasury notes mature in 1 to 10 years. Treasury bonds mature in 10 to 25 years. They can be bought in denominations of $1,000. Interest earned on U.S. government securities is tax-free for state and local returns. "Ginnie Maes" are guaranteed pools of 25- to 30-year Federal Housing Administration (FHA) or Veterans Administration (VA) mortgages.

8. *Deep discount bonds.* They are bought at a substantial discount from face value. The bonds may be risky and/or have a long maturity date.

9. *Junk bonds.* They are bonds with low credit ratings from Moody's and Standard & Poor's. They are issued by financially unsound companies. They offer high return but have high risk.

10. *Serial bonds.* They are bonds that mature in installments over time rather than at one maturity date. Some serial bonds have *balloon maturity* where most mature in one year.

11. *Series bonds.* They are issued over a period but with the same maturity date.

HOW TO SELECT A BOND?

When selecting a bond, you should take into consideration basically five factors:

1. Quality
2. Maturity
3. Features
4. Tax treatment
5. Effective interest rate

Quality

Quality of a bond is indicated by its bond rating, which reflects risk and considers interest rate, price, maturity period, and financial health. Bond investors tend to place more emphasis on independent analysis of quality than do common stock investors. Bond analysis and evaluation are performed by Standard & Poor's and Moody's. A listing of the classifications of these independent agencies is shown below. For original versions of descriptions, refer to Moody's *Bond Record* and Standard & Poor's *Bond Guide* (see Table 2).

Table 2—

Description of Bond Ratings*

Moody's	Standard & Poor's	Quality Indication
Aaa	AAA	Highest quality
Aa	AA	High quality
A	A	Upper medium grade
Baa	BBB	Medium grade
Ba	BB	Contains speculative elements
B	B	Outright speculative
Caa	CCC & CC	Default definitely possible
Ca	C	Default, only partial recovery likely
C	D	Default, little recovery likely
	R	Risky applied to *derivatives*.

*Ratings may have + or - signs to indicate relative class standings.

A higher bond rating means a lower yield. Because ratings change over time, rating agencies provide "credit watch lists."

Maturity

Longer maturities mean more risk because of greater volatility in price with interest rate changes. Shorter maturities translate to lower yields. A "safe" investor should not choose bonds maturing in more than 10 years.

Features

Is there a call feature allowing the issuing company to buy back its bonds after a specified time if it so selects, instead of waiting to maturity?   In such a case, you will likely receive a slight premium above par. Bonds are typically called if their interest rates exceed prevailing market rates. Stay away from bonds of companies with call provisions involved in "event risk" (e.g., leveraged buyouts).

Is there a conversion feature into stock? A convertible bond allows for periodic interest income and appreciation value of the underlying common stock. Bond (income) mutual funds offer professional management.

Taxes

Do you have a high tax rate? If so, tax-exempt bonds may be suitable. You may buy them directly or through a mutual fund.

Yield

Yield (effective interest rate) depends on bond rating, and is discussed later.

Note: A bond may be bought at a discount (below face value) when:

1. There is a long maturity period.
2. It is a risky company.
3. The interest rate on the bond is less than the "current market interest rate."

A bond may be bought at a premium when the aforementioned circumstances are reversed.

HOW DO YOU DETERMINE INTEREST RATE RISK?

Interest rate risk can be determined in two ways. One way is to look at the term structure of a debt security by measuring its average term to maturity—a duration. The other way is to measure the sensitivity of changes in a debt security's price associated with changes in its yield to maturity (YTM). We will discuss two measurement approaches: Macaulay's duration coefficient and interest rate elasticity.

Macaulay's Duration Coefficient

Macaulay's duration (D) is an attempt to measure risk in a bond by considering the maturity and the time pattern of cash inflows (i.e., interest payments and principal). It is defined as the number of years until a bond pays back its principal. A simple example illustrates the duration calculations.

Example 3—

A bond pays a 7 percent coupon rate annually on its $1,000 face value if it has 3 years until its maturity and has a YTM of 6 percent. The computation of duration involves the following three steps:

Step 1   Calculate the present value of the bond for each year.

Step 2   Express present values as proportions of the price of the bond.

Step 3   Multiply proportions by years' digits to obtain the weighted average time.

(1)	(2)	(3)	(Step 1) (4)	(Step 2) (5)	(Step 3) (6)
Year	Cash Flow	PV Factor @ 6%	PV of Cash Flow	PV as Propor-tion of Bond Price	Column (1) x Column (5)
1	$70	.9434	$66.04	.0643	.0643
2	70	.8900	62.30	.0607	.1214
3	1,070	.8396	898.37	.8750	2.6250
			$1,026.71	1.0000	2.8107

This 3-year bond's duration is a little over 2.8 years. Although duration is expressed in years, think of it as a percentage change. Thus, 2.8 years means this particular bond will gain (lose) 2.8 percent of its value for each 1 percentage drop (rise) in interest rates.

Note: (1) In all cases, a bond's duration is less than or equal to its term to maturity. Only a pure discount bond—that is, one with no coupon or sinking-fund payments—has duration equal to the maturity.

(2) The higher the D value, the greater the interest rate risk, as it implies a longer recovery period.

(3) Duration will not tell you anything about the credit quality or yield of your bonds, although some bonds (or bond funds) manage to produce top returns without undue risk. For example, Harbor Bond Fund has returned a respectable annualized

11.5 percent over the past five years. Yet its duration is a middle-of-road 5.3 years.

Interest Rate Elasticity

A bond's interest rate elasticity (E) is defined as

$$E = \frac{\text{Percentage change in bond price}}{\text{Percentage change in YTM}}$$

Since bond prices and YTMs move inversely,
the elasticity will always be a negative number. Any
bond's elasticity can be determined directly with
the above formula. Knowing the duration coefficient (D), we can calculate E using the following
simple formula:

$$(-1)\ E = D\ \frac{\text{YTM}}{(1+\text{YTM})}$$

Example 4—

Using the same date in Example 3, the elasticity is calculated as follows:

$$(-1)\ E = 2.8107\ [.06/(1.06)] = .1591$$

which means that bonds (and bond
funds) will lose or gain 15.91 percent of
principal value for each 1 percentage point
move in interest rates.

HOW DO YOU COMPUTE THE EFFECTIVE INTEREST RATE (YIELD) ON A BOND?

Bonds are appraised using many different kinds of
returns, such as current yield, yield to maturity,
yield to call, and realized yield.

1. *Current yield*. It equals annual interest divided by the current market price of the bond. It is published in *Barron's*.

$$\text{Current Yield} = \frac{\text{Annual interest payment}}{\text{Current price}}$$

Example 5—

A 10 percent coupon rate, $1,000 face value bond sells for $920. Current yield equals $100/$920 = 10.9%

This measure of return is deficient because it does not consider the maturity date. A bond having a 2-year maturity and another with a 20-year maturity would have identical current yields assuming interest payments of $100 and a price of $920. Obviously, the 2-year bond is better because you not only obtain $100 in interest, but also a capital gain of $80 ($1,000 - $920) with a year time period. You could reinvest the money earned for a return.

---

2. *Yield to maturity (YTM)*. It considers the maturity date. It is the real return received from interest plus capital gain if the bond is kept to maturity.

$$\text{Yield to maturity} = \frac{I + (\$1,000 - V)/n}{(\$1,000 + V)/2}$$

where V= market value of bond
I= dollar interest per annum
n= number of years to maturity

Example 6—

You were considering a 5-year, 10 percent coupon, $1,000 face value bond at a price of $850.

$$\text{Yield to maturity} = \frac{\$100 + (\$1000 - \$850)/5}{(\$1,000 + \$850)/2} = \frac{\$130}{\$925} = 14\%$$

Because the bond is purchased at a discount, the yield (14 percent) exceeds the coupon rate (10 percent).

3. *Yield to call (YTC).* If the bond may be called before maturity, the yield to maturity formula will have the call price instead of the face value of $1,000.

Example 7—

A 20-year bond was issued at a 13.5 percent nominal interest rate, and after two years, rates have declined. The bond is now selling for $1,180, the yield to maturity is 11.15 percent, and the bond can be called in five years after issue at $1,090. Therefore, if you buy the bond two years after issue, your bond may be called back after three more years at $1,090. The YTC is calculated below:

$$\frac{\$135 + (\$1,090 - \$1,180)/3}{(\$1,090 + \$1,180)/2} = \frac{\$135 + (-\$90/3)}{\$1,135} = \frac{\$105}{\$1,135}$$

$$= 9.25\%$$

Note: The yield to call figure of 9.25 percent is 190 basis points less than the yield to maturity of 11.15 percent. Obviously, you must be aware of the differential since a lower return is earned.

---

4. *Realized yield*. You may trade in and out of a bond before it matures. You need a return measure to appraise the attractiveness of any bonds you expect to buy and sell. Realized yield is a variation of yield to maturity. There are two variables changed in the yield to maturity formula. Future price is substituted for face value ($1,000) and the holding period is substituted for the number of years to maturity.

Example 8—

In Example 6, assume you expect to hold the bond for just four years. You estimate interest rates will change in the future so that the price of the bond will move to approximately $960 from its current amount of $850. Therefore, you will purchase the bond today for $850 and sell it four years later for $960.

$$\text{Realized yield} = \frac{\$100 + (\$960 - \$850)/4}{(\$960 + \$850)/2} = \frac{\$128}{\$905} = 14.1\%$$

You can refer to a bond table to determine the value for various yield measures. A reference is *The Thorndike Encyclopedia of Banking and Financial Tables* by Warren, Gorham & Lamont, Boston (See Table 3).

Table 3—

A Bond Value Table

Yield	15 yr	16 yr	17 yr	18 yr	19 yr	20 yr	21 yr	22 yr	23 yr	24 yr	25 yr	26 yr	27 yr	28 yr
6.50	152.20	154.21	156.09	157.86	159.52	161.07	162.53	163.90	165.18	166.39	167.52	168.58	169.57	170.50
6.60	150.93	152.87	154.69	156.39	157.99	159.49	160.89	162.21	163.44	164.60	165.68	166.70	167.65	168.54
6.70	149.67	151.55	153.30	154.95	156.49	157.93	159.28	160.55	161.73	162.84	163.88	164.85	165.76	166.61
6.80	148.42	150.24	151.94	153.52	155.01	156.39	157.69	158.91	160.04	161.11	162.10	163.03	163.90	164.71
6.90	147.19	148.95	150.58	152.11	153.54	154.88	156.13	157.30	158.38	159.40	160.36	161.24	162.08	162.85
7.00	145.98	147.67	149.25	150.73	152.10	153.39	154.59	155.71	156.75	157.73	158.64	159.49	160.28	161.02
7.10	144.78	146.41	147.94	149.36	150.68	151.92	153.07	154.14	155.15	156.08	156.95	157.76	158.52	159.23
7.20	143.59	145.17	146.64	148.00	149.28	150.47	151.57	152.60	153.56	154.46	155.29	156.07	156.79	157.47
7.30	142.42	143.94	145.35	146.57	147.90	149.04	150.10	151.09	152.01	152.86	153.66	154.40	155.09	155.74
7.40	141.26	142.73	144.09	145.36	146.53	147.63	148.65	149.59	150.48	151.29	152.06	152.76	153.42	154.04
7.50	140.12	141.53	142.84	144.06	145.19	146.24	147.22	148.12	148.97	149.75	150.48	151.15	151.78	152.36
7.60	138.98	140.34	141.60	142.70	143.86	144.87	145.81	146.68	147.48	148.23	148.93	149.57	150.17	150.72
7.70	137.86	139.17	140.39	141.51	142.55	143.52	144.42	145.25	146.02	146.74	147.40	148.01	148.58	149.11
7.80	136.76	138.02	139.18	140.26	141.26	142.19	143.05	143.84	144.58	145.26	145.90	146.48	147.02	147.53
7.90	135.66	136.88	138.00	139.03	139.99	140.88	141.70	142.46	143.16	143.82	144.42	144.98	145.49	145.97
8.00	134.58	135.75	136.82	137.82	138.74	139.59	140.37	141.10	141.77	142.39	142.96	143.50	143.99	144.44
8.10	133.52	134.63	135.66	136.62	137.50	138.31	139.06	139.75	140.40	140.99	141.53	142.04	142.51	142.94
8.20	132.46	133.53	134.52	135.43	136.28	137.05	137.77	138.43	139.04	139.61	140.13	140.61	141.05	141.46
8.30	131.42	132.44	133.39	134.27	135.07	135.81	136.50	137.13	137.71	138.25	138.74	139.20	139.62	140.01
8.40	130.38	131.37	132.28	133.11	133.88	134.59	135.24	135.85	136.40	136.91	137.38	137.81	138.21	138.58

Yield	15 yr	16 yr	17 yr	18 yr	19 yr	20 yr	21 yr	22 yr	23 yr	24 yr	25 yr	26 yr	27 yr	28 yr
8.50	129.36	130.31	131.18	131.97	132.71	133.39	134.01	134.58	135.11	135.59	136.04	136.45	136.83	137.17
8.60	128.35	129.26	130.09	130.85	131.55	132.20	132.79	133.33	133.83	134.29	134.72	135.11	135.46	135.79
8.70	127.36	128.22	129.01	129.74	130.41	131.02	131.59	132.11	132.58	133.02	133.42	133.79	134.13	134.44
8.80	126.37	127.20	127.95	128.65	129.28	129.87	130.40	130.90	131.35	131.76	132.14	132.49	132.81	133.10
8.90	125.40	126.18	126.90	127.57	128.17	128.73	129.24	129.70	130.13	130.52	130.88	131.21	131.51	131.79
9.00	124.43	125.18	125.87	126.50	127.07	127.60	128.09	128.53	128.93	129.30	129.64	129.95	130.24	130.50
9.10	123.48	124.19	124.85	125.45	125.99	126.49	126.95	127.37	127.75	128.10	128.42	128.72	128.99	129.23
9.20	122.54	123.22	123.84	124.41	124.92	125.40	125.83	126.23	126.59	126.92	127.22	127.50	127.75	127.98
9.30	121.61	122.25	122.84	123.39	123.87	124.32	124.73	125.10	125.44	125.76	126.04	126.30	126.54	126.75
9.40	120.69	121.30	121.86	122.37	122.83	123.25	123.64	123.99	124.32	124.61	124.88	125.12	125.34	125.55
9.50	119.78	120.36	120.88	121.37	121.80	122.20	122.57	122.90	123.20	123.48	123.73	123.96	124.17	124.36
9.60	118.88	119.42	119.92	120.33	120.79	121.17	121.51	121.82	122.11	122.37	122.60	122.82	123.01	123.19
9.70	117.98	118.50	118.97	119.40	119.80	120.15	120.47	120.76	121.03	121.27	121.49	121.69	121.87	122.04
9.80	117.10	117.59	118.04	118.44	118.80	119.14	119.44	119.71	119.96	120.19	120.40	120.58	120.75	120.91
9.90	116.23	116.69	117.11	117.49	117.83	118.14	118.42	118.68	118.91	119.13	119.32	119.49	119.65	119.79
10.00	115.37	115.80	116.19	116.55	116.87	117.16	117.42	117.66	117.88	118.08	118.26	118.42	118.57	118.70
10.10	114.52	114.92	115.29	115.62	115.92	116.19	116.44	116.66	116.86	117.04	117.21	117.36	117.50	117.62
10.20	113.68	114.05	114.39	114.70	114.98	115.23	115.46	115.67	115.86	116.03	116.18	116.32	116.44	116.56
10.30	112.85	113.20	113.51	113.80	114.06	114.29	114.50	114.69	114.87	115.02	115.16	115.29	115.41	115.51
10.40	112.02	112.35	112.64	112.90	113.14	113.36	113.55	113.73	113.89	114.03	114.16	114.28	114.39	114.48

(continued)

Table 3—*continued*

Yield	15 yr	16 yr	17 yr	18 yr	19 yr	20 yr	21 yr	22 yr	23 yr	24 yr	25 yr	26 yr	27 yr	28 yr
10.50	111.21	111.51	111.78	112.02	112.24	112.44	112.62	112.78	112.93	113.06	113.18	113.29	113.38	113.47
10.60	110.40	110.68	110.93	111.15	111.35	111.53	111.70	111.85	111.98	112.10	112.21	112.31	112.40	112.48
10.70	109.61	109.86	110.08	110.29	110.47	110.64	110.79	110.92	111.04	111.15	111.25	111.34	111.42	111.49
10.80	108.82	109.05	109.25	109.44	109.61	109.76	109.89	110.01	110.12	110.22	110.31	110.39	110.46	110.53
10.90	108.04	108.24	108.43	108.60	108.75	108.88	109.01	109.11	109.21	109.30	109.38	109.45	109.52	109.57
11.00	107.27	107.45	107.62	107.77	107.90	108.02	108.13	108.23	108.32	108.40	108.47	108.53	108.59	108.64
11.10	106.50	106.67	106.82	106.95	107.07	107.17	107.27	107.36	107.43	107.50	107.56	107.62	107.67	107.71
11.20	105.75	105.89	106.02	106.14	106.24	106.34	106.42	106.49	106.56	106.62	106.67	106.72	106.77	106.81
11.30	105.00	105.13	105.24	105.34	105.43	105.51	105.58	105.64	105.70	105.75	105.80	105.84	105.88	105.91
11.40	104.27	104.37	104.46	104.55	104.62	104.69	104.75	104.80	104.85	104.90	104.93	104.97	105.00	105.03
11.50	103.54	103.62	103.70	103.77	103.83	103.88	103.93	103.98	104.02	104.05	104.08	104.11	104.14	104.16
11.60	102.81	102.88	102.94	103.00	103.04	103.09	103.13	103.16	103.19	103.22	103.24	103.26	103.28	103.30
11.70	102.10	102.15	102.19	102.23	102.27	102.30	102.33	102.35	102.38	102.40	102.41	102.43	102.45	102.46
11.80	101.39	101.42	101.45	101.48	101.50	101.52	101.54	101.56	101.57	101.59	101.60	101.61	101.62	101.63
11.90	100.69	100.71	100.72	100.74	100.75	100.76	100.77	100.77	100.78	100.79	100.79	100.80	100.80	100.81
12.00	100.00	100.00	100.00	100.00	100.00	100.00	100.00	100.00	100.00	100.00	100.00	100.00	100.00	100.00
13.00	93.47	93.33	93.21	93.10	93.01	92.93	92.85	92.79	92.73	92.68	92.64	92.60	92.56	92.53
14.00	87.59	87.35	87.15	86.96	86.81	86.67	86.55	86.44	86.35	86.27	86.20	86.14	86.08	86.04
15.00	82.28	81.98	81.71	81.48	81.28	81.11	80.96	80.83	80.72	80.62	80.54	80.47	80.40	80.35
16.00	77.48	77.13	76.83	76.57	76.34	76.15	75.99	75.85	75.73	75.62	75.53	75.46	75.39	75.34

Yield	15 yr	16 yr	17 yr	18 yr	19 yr	20 yr	21 yr	22 yr	23 yr	24 yr	25 yr	26 yr	27 yr	28 yr
17.00	73.13	72.75	72.42	72.15	71.91	71.71	71.54	71.40	71.28	71.17	71.09	71.01	70.95	70.89
18.00	69.18	68.78	68.45	63.16	67.93	67.73	67.56	67.42	67.30	67.20	67.11	67.04	66.98	66.93
19.00	65.58	65.18	64.84	64.56	64.33	64.13	63.97	63.84	63.72	63.63	63.55	63.49	63.43	63.39
20.00	62.29	61.89	61.57	61.29	61.07	60.88	60.73	60.60	60.50	60.41	60.34	60.28	60.23	60.19
21.00	59.29	58.90	58.58	58.32	53.11	57.93	57.79	57.67	57.58	57.50	57.43	57.38	57.34	57.30

Source: *Bond Value Tables*, Publication No. 183, 1981 (Boston: Financial Publishing Company).

5. *Tax-equivalent yield.* Yield on a municipal bond may be appraised on an equivalent prior-tax yield basis because of the tax-free interest. Thus, munis might make the most sense for people whose tax-equivalent yield on a tax-free bond or bond fund would be greater than the yield from a similar taxable alternative. Here are two equations to determine whether tax-exempt yields are right for you.

For tax-equivalent yields:

$$\frac{\text{tax-free yield}}{(1 - \text{tax rate})} = \text{tax-equivalent yield}$$

For combined effective federal/state tax rates (if you're considering buying bonds or funds with bonds issued in your home state):

State rate x (1- federal) = effective state rate

$$\frac{\text{effective}}{\text{state rate}} + \frac{\text{federal}}{\text{rate}} = \frac{\text{combined effective}}{\text{federal/state tax rate}}$$

Example 9—

If your marginal *federal* tax rate is 36 percent and your municipal bond investment earns 7 percent interest, the tax-equivalent yield on a taxable investment is:

7%/(1 - .36) = 10.94%

You could select from a taxable investment of 10.94 percent and a tax-exempt bond of 7 percent and be indifferent between the two.

Refer to Table 4 for tax-equivalent yields if free from (a) federal taxes and (b) combined federal and state taxes in selected states.

Table 4—

Tax-Equivalent Yields

Tax-Equivalent

Tax-free yield	yield free from fed. tax	Tax-equivalent yield if free from state/federal taxes in the following states*					
		CA	CT	FL	MA	NJ	NY
4.00%	6.25%	7.02	6.54	6.25	7.10	6.72	7.13
5.00	7.81	8.78	8.18	7.81	8.88	8.40	8.91
6.00	9.38	10.53	9.82	9.38	10.65	10.0	10.69
7.00	10.94	12.29	11.45	10.94	12.43	11.76	12.48

*Tax-equivalent yields in the table are based on a federal tax rate of 36%. Based on the combined effective federal/state rate:CA-43.04%; CT-38.88%; FL-36.00%; MA-43.68%; NJ-40.48%; NY-43.89% (includes New York City rate).

WHAT ARE MUNICIPAL BONDS?

Municipal bonds are issued by state or local governments or by any political subdivision or public agency that is not federal. *Interest income from municipal bonds is exempt from federal tax.* Bonds issued by a state and purchased by residents of that state are exempt from state income taxes. For this reason, munis will pay the lowest rate of interest compared to other taxable bond issues. The minimum investment in munis is $5,000 principal. Any capital gain realized in the purchase and sale of a municipal bond is subject to capital gain tax. (When municipals are issued at a discount, however, the difference between the discount and par is considered interest income.)

Munis may be categorized either as *general obligation (G.O.) bonds* or *revenue bonds.*

1. General obligation (G.O.) bonds are backed by
    the full faith and credit (and by the taxing
    power) of the issuer. Local governments have
    the ability to collect property taxes, known as
    "ad valorem" taxes, while most state govern-
    ments collect income and sales taxes. In the
    event of a default, G.O. bondholders have the
    right to compel a tax levy or legislative appro-
    priation to make payment on the debt.

2. Revenue bonds are backed by revenues from
    the facilities built with the proceeds of the bond
    issue. Sewer bonds, stadium bonds, solid waste
    disposal bonds, or toll bridge bonds are ex-
    amples of revenue bonds. Since only the speci-
    fied revenues back a revenue bond, this is a self-
    supporting debt. *Note:* Because revenue bonds
    are backed by a single source of funds, they
    have greater credit risk than G.O. bonds. Be-
    cause of this, most revenue bonds are issued
    under a "Trust Indenture."

HOW ABOUT TRADING IN MUNICIPAL BONDS?

Municipal bonds are *not* traded on national exchanges but in the over-the-counter market. Generally, this confines investor interest in municipal
issues to residents of the state of issuance. *Note:* Be
sure to ask your broker if he or she has access to
any on-line services, such as *J.J. Kennedy Information Systems,* which provide a comprehensive database of most munis outstanding and is necessary
for accurate portfolio analysis and prompt answers
to credit questions. Another factor that limits municipal trading is that most issues are "serial"
maturities: Within a bond offering there are multiple maturities, each having a relatively small principal amount. The small amount of each maturity
available limits trading.

WHAT ARE GOVERNMENT BONDS?

Government bonds are the most liquid issues traded on any market, are extremely safe, have some tax advantages (returns are not usually subject to state and local taxes), and can be used as loan collateral.

Treasury Bills

Treasury bills have a maximum maturity of one year and common maturities of three months (91 days, or 13 weeks), six months (182 days, or 26 weeks), or one year (52 weeks). They trade in minimum units of $10,000. They do not pay interest in the traditional sense; they are sold at a discount and redeemed when the maturity date arrives at face value. T-bills are extremely liquid in that there is an active secondary or resale market for these securities. T-bills have an extremely low risk because they are backed by the U.S. government. Another reason for the popularity of Treasuries is that the interest income they produce is exempt from state and local income taxes.

The price is *quoted in terms of the discount yield*. For example, "March 4, bid 4.30%, asked 4.20%"; or offering to buy the bill at 95.70 percent of par (an offer to pay $9,570 for the bill since par value of T-bills is usually $10,000) and offering to sell at 95.80 percent of par.

The yield on discount securities such as T-bills, called the *discount yield* (d), is calculated using the formula:

$$d = \frac{\$10{,}000 - P}{P} \times \frac{365}{\text{days-to-maturity}}$$

where P = purchase price. The formula simply states that the yield on the discount security is equal to the gain on the bill relative to its face value of

$10,000, ($10,000 - P)/$10,000, *times* a factor which annualizes this gain, 365/days-to-maturity.

Example 10—

Assume that P = $9,800. The T-bill yield is:

$$\frac{\$10,000 - \$9,800}{\$9,800} \times \frac{365}{90} = \frac{\$200}{\$9,800} \times 4.06 = 0.0829 = 8.29\%$$

The so-called *equivalent bond yield (EBY)* allows you to compare the yields on discount securities with other kinds of bonds. It makes discount instruments comparable to bonds. The idea is to compute a yield that reflects the opportunity that bond market investors have to receive and reinvest semi-annual coupon payments. The formula is:

$$EBY = \frac{365 \times d}{360 - (d \times days\text{-}to\text{-}maturity)}$$

Example 11—

For the 90-day instrument used in the previous example, the EBY would be:

$$EBY = \frac{365 \times 0.0829}{360 - (0.0829 \times 90)} = 0.0858 = 8.58\%$$

Auctions for 3- and 6-month T-bills take place weekly, and 12-month bills are auctioned monthly.

Treasury Notes

Treasury notes have maturities of 2 to 10 years, available in registered form. They are not callable. They are quoted in 1/32's of a percentage point: "Maturing 11/10/90 - Bid: 99.16; Ask: 99.24" means bid at 99 16/32 (or $995); ask at 99 24/32 (or $997.50).

Treasury Bonds

Treasury bonds have maturities ranging from 10 to 30 years. Some *have optional call dates*, as in "Due 6/30 1992/97," where the first date shown is the call date and the second is the maturity date. They are quoted like T-notes.

Treasury STRIPS (Separate Trading of Registered Interest and Principal of Securities)

Also called zero coupon Treasuries, Treasury STRIPS are designated Treasury notes and bonds that can be stripped directly by dealers in order to create zero-coupon securities. The bonds are "stripped" of their coupons and units are sold representing only the repayment of principal at the maturity date. Each of the interest payments on the bonds is grouped into a unit and sold as a separate "zero-coupon" issue. All new Treasury notes and bonds of 10 years or longer are eligible for the STRIP program. Investors are attracted to STRIPS because of their predictability, fixed rate of interest, and maturity at a known value. One chief drawback: Although they do not pay interest until maturity, the IRS requires you to pay taxes on each year's accrued value as though you had received a check in the mail. *Note:* They typically outperform straight Treasuries by 15 to 50 basis points.

HOW DO YOU BUY TREASURIES?

You can buy Treasuries for as little as $1,000 and up to $10,000 (depending on the type of security), with no commission cost, through a program called Treasury Direct. Or, you can pay $50 or $60 per transaction and buy through a broker. Each of these purchasing methods has its pros and cons.

Treasury securities are sold in a variety of maturities at regularly scheduled auctions. The dates for nonweekly auctions are announced about a week in advance. Table 5 compares Treasuries. To learn the exact dates, call the nearest Federal Reserve Bank. For example, in New York City, the telephone number is (212) 720-6619. You can either speak directly with a service representative or listen to a recording of relevant information. The office will mail you the proper investment forms to fill out and mail back.

Table 5—

U.S. Treasury Securities

Treasury bills

What: 13-week and 26-week.
When: Every Monday, except holidays.
How much: $10,000 minimum, then $1,000 increments.

What: 52-week.
When: Every four weeks, generally on a Thursday.
How much: $10,000 minimum, then $1,000 increments.

Treasury notes

What: 2-year.
When: Monthly, generally on a Tuesday late in the month.
How much: $5,000 minimum, then $1,000 increments.

What: 3-year.
When: Quarterly, in early February, May, August, and November.
How much: $5,000 minimum, then $1,000 increments.

What: 5-year.
When: Monthly, generally on a Wednesday late in the month.
How much: $1,000 minimum, then $1,000 increments.

What: 10-year.
When: Quarterly, in early February, May, August, and November.
How much: $1,000 minimum, then $1,000 increments.

Treasury bonds

What: 30-year.
When: Twice a year, in February and in August.
How much: $1,000 minimum, then $1,000 increments.

Zero coupon treasuries—treasury strips

What: Three months to 30-year
When: Quarterly, in early February, May, August, and November.
How much: $1,000 minimum, then $1,000 increments.

WHAT ARE GOVERNMENT AGENCY BONDS?

The next area of fixed income bonds is that of government agency bonds. The U.S. Government promotes home ownership through the activities of the Federal Home Loan Banks, the Federal National Mortgage Association (FNMA, or "Fannie Mae"), the Government National Mortgage Association (GNMA, or "Ginnie Mae"), and the Federal Home Loan Mortgage Corporation (FHLMC, or "Freddie Mac"). These agencies make a secondary market in home mortgages. Their function is to add liquidity and safety to investing in the mortgage market. They purchase mortgages from the local banks that originated the loans. The agencies obtain the funds to buy the mortgages by selling bonds to the public. The U.S. Government does not directly back these issues, with the exception of the Government National Mortgage Association.

The Government National Mortgage Association (GNMA) is described as a mortgage pass-through agency. It buys, from conventional lenders, pools (or groups) of a large number of home mortgages insured by the Veterans Administration and Federal Housing Administration, and then reissues new certificates of these mortgage pools to GNMA investors (*"pass through" certificates*). GNMAs are offered with a minimum $25,000 face amount and $5,000 increments thereafter. They pay interest and part principal monthly. In this sense, you, as a GNMA investor, are in a similar position to that of a mortgage lender. *Note:* There are many mutual funds available which invest primarily, or exclusively, in GNMAs. GNMA funds enjoy the same advantages as regular mutual funds—diversification and professional management.

Fannie Mae also issues mortgage-backed pass-through certificates. But they are not limited to FHA- or VA-approved loans. FHLMC, or "Freddie Mac," offers *collateralized mortgage obligations (CMOs)*. Note that Fannie Mae and Freddie Mac are not truly government agencies, but "privatized" companies whose stocks are listed on the NYSE and are legally owned by the shareholders.

Pass-through certificates have problems because mortgage pools have a long fixed life and mortgage prepayment risk is high. CMOs were developed to eliminate or minimize these risks.

On the basis of expected cash flows to be received over the life of the pool, separate classes of securities called "tranches" are created. For example, a 15-year mortgage pool may be broken up into 5 tranches, as follows:

Tranch 1	1 - 3 years
Tranch 2	4 - 6 years
Tranch 3	7 - 9 years
Tranch 4	10 - 12 years
Tranch 5	13 - 15 years

As mortgages are prepaid, the payments are applied to Tranch 1 securities. After Tranch 1 is retired, prepayments then are used to retire Tranch 2 starting in the 4th year, and so on. Thus, *prepayment risk is reduced*. Investors can buy a mortgage backed securities with a wide range of maturities. Even though prepayment risk is reduced, CMO pricing can be volatile. The most volatile are so-called "zero-Tranch" portions of CMOs, which receive no interest payments until the preceding tranches are retired.

WHAT ARE OTHER FIXED INCOME SECURITIES?

They are available very secure debt obligations whose maturities are less than one year, characterized by their short term, high quality, and marketability. They may be held temporarily, and include:

- *Certificates of deposit (CDs)*. High-quality instruments of banks, usually from $2,000 and up. The maturity period is usually three months or more. A penalty is assessed for early redemption. However, the penalty on early withdrawal is treated for tax purposes as a deduction of gross income.

- *Banker's acceptances (BAs)*. A banker's acceptance is a time draft (an order to pay a specified amount to the holder on a specified date), drawn on and "accepted" by a bank. By accepting the draft, a bank assumes the responsibility to make payment at maturity of the draft, thereby making the draft more readily marketable. It is usually used in foreign trade. BAs are bearer securities, and can be held to maturity or can be traded. The maturity is nine months or less and the security trades at a discount to face value. Only the highest quality BAs are eligible for Fed trading, known as "prime BAs."

- *Eurodollars.* These are deposit liabilities, denominated in U.S. dollars, of banks located outside the U.S. Since the Eurodollar market is relatively free of regulation, banks in the Eurodollar market can operate on narrower margins or spreads between dollar borrowing and lending rates than banks in the U.S.

- *Commercial paper.* A short-term financial instrument issued by high-quality, large companies on an unsecured discount basis. It is typically for $100,000 or more.

- *Money market fund.* A safe class of mutual fund investing in high-quality near-term, liquid securities (e.g., Treasury bills). It is a conservative investment usually stated on a $1 per share basis.

Table 6 ranks various short-term investment vehicles in terms of their default risk.

Table 6—

Default Risk among Short-Term Investment Vehicles

Higher	
Degree of Risk	Eurodollar time deposits and CDs Commercial paper (top quality) Bank CDs (uninsured) Bankers' acceptances (BAs) U.S. Treasury repos U.S. government agency obligations U.S. Treasury obligations
Lower	

HOW DO YOU INVEST IN SAVINGS BONDS?

U.S. savings bonds are nontransferable instruments. They can only be redeemed by the purchaser, and can neither be marketed nor used as collateral for loans. There are two types of U.S. savings bonds: Series EE and Series HH.

Series EE is a bond purchased for 50 percent of its face value. It pays no periodic interest, since the interest accumulates between the purchase price and the bond's maturity value. For example, a Series EE bond can be purchased for $100 and redeemed at maturity for $200. Series EE bonds can be purchased in denominations from $25 to $5,000, with a maximum purchase limit of $15,000 annually. The early redemption is penalized with a lower interest rate than stated on the bond.

When held for at least five years, Series EE bonds earn the higher of either a guaranteed 4 percent return or market-based interest. Bonds held for less than five years earn a lower rate of return. The market-based rate, announced each May and November, is 85 percent of the market average on five-year Treasury securities. *Note:* Since yields are adjusted every six months, the bonds offer unique opportunities in times of rising interest rates.

Any bonds purchased *after* May 1, 1995, however, will be based on two methods to compute market-based interest:

1. A short-term rate for bonds held less than five years. It will be 85% of the average of six-month Treasury security yields.

2. A long-term rate for those bonds held 5 to 17 years. This rate will be 85 percent of the 5-year treasury security yields.

Series HH is a bond issued only in exchange for Series EE savings bonds. They are purchased at face value and pay interest semiannually until maturity five years later. Early redemption will be penalized at slightly less than face value. It can be redeemed after six months and has a maturity period of 10 years. Maximum purchase in one year is $20,000 face value, but they can be purchased only by trading EE bonds. Interest on HH series bonds is taxable each year.

Example 12—

George Lee decided to invest $5,000 in a Series EE savings bond for his retirement. If the interest averages 8% after 10 years, how much will he have after 10 years? (Assume a semiannual interest accrual.)

The future value of $1 (Table 1 in Chapter 7) for 20 periods at a semiannual rate of 4 percent is 2.191 is $10,955 ($5,000 x 2.191).

Advantages

- The interest earned on savings bonds is free from state and local taxes. Federal income taxes can be deferred on Series EE bonds until they are redeemed. It can be deferred even beyond this point by rolling over the EE bonds into Series HH bonds. *Note:* Parents who sell EE bonds to pay for their children's college tuition don't have to pay federal income taxes on the interest earned if their income is under a certain amount (for example, if 1995 income is under $63,450 for couples or $42,300 for single parents) and if the bonds are in the parents' names.
- There are no service charges when one purchases or redeems savings bonds, as there are with many other investments.
- Safety and complete security backed by the U.S. government.

Disadvantages

- Lack of liquidity. You are barred from cashing them in for at least six months.
- Relatively lower yield. *Note:* Instead of exchanging all the bonds, you might be better off selling the EE bonds paying the low rates and putting the proceeds in a high-yielding investment vehicle.

U.S. savings bonds can be purchased without fees at most banks and other financial institutions or through payroll thrift plans. They can be replaced if lost, stolen, or destroyed. Both series must be held at least 6 months before redeeming.

Note: 1. To find out what a particular savings bond is worth, go to any bank that sells the bonds or the Treasury to obtain a redemption value table.

Send request to *Savings Bond Marketing Office*, 800
K. St., NW, Suite 800, Washington D.C., 20226.

2. For details involving mistakes and anxieties
regarding U.S. savings bonds, refer to a new book
by Daniel Pederson, *U.S. Savings Bonds: A Comprehensive Guide for Bond Owners and Financial Profes-
sions*, TSBI, Detroit, Michigan, (800) 927-1901.

SHOULD YOU INVEST IN A BOND FUND?

It is possible that an investor may decide to invest in
a bond fund. There are three key facts about the
bonds in any portfolio:

- *Quality*. Check the credit rating of the typical
  bond in the fund. Ratings by Standard & Poor's
  and Moody's show the relative danger that an
  issuer will default on interest or principal payments. AAA is the best grade. A rating of BB or
  lower signifies a junk bond.

- *Maturity*. The average maturity of your fund's
  bonds indicates how much you stand to lose if
  interest rates rise. The longer the term of the
  bonds, the more volatile the price. For example,
  a 20-year bond may fluctuate in price four times
  as much as a 4-year issue.

- *Premium or discount*. Some funds with high current yields hold bonds that trade for more than
  their face value or at a premium. Such funds
  are less vulnerable to losses if rates go up. Funds
  that hold bonds trading at a discount to face
  value can lose the most.

You must keep in mind the following guidelines:

- Rising interest rates drive down the value of all bond funds. For this reason, rather than focusing only on current yield, you should look primarily at total return (yield plus capital gains from falling interest rates or minus capital losses if rates climb).

- All bond funds do not benefit equally from tumbling interest rates. If you think interest rates will decline and you want to increase total return, you should buy funds that invest in U.S. Treasuries or top-rated corporate bonds. You should consider high-yield corporate bonds (junk bonds) if you believe interest rates are stabilizing.

- Unlike bonds, bond funds do not allow the investor to lock in a yield. A mutual fund with a constantly changing portfolio is not like an individual bond, which can be kept to maturity. If you want steady, secure income over several years or more, you should consider, as alternatives to funds, buying individual top-quality bonds or investing in a municipal bond *unit trust*, which maintains a fixed portfolio.

HOW ABOUT CONSIDERING UNIT INVESTMENT TRUSTS?

Like a mutual fund, a unit investment trust (UIT) offers to investors the advantages of a large, professionally selected and diversified portfolio. Unlike a mutual fund, however, its portfolio is fixed; once structured, it is not actively managed. Unit investment trusts are available with tax-exempt bonds, money market securities, corporate bonds of different grades, mortgage-backed securities, preferred stocks, utility common stocks, and other investments. Unit trusts are most suitable for investors who need a fixed income and a guaranteed return of capital. They disband and pay off investors after the majority of their investments have been redeemed.

INVESTING IN MUNICIPAL BONDS— THREE APPROACHES

As discussed earlier, you may consider municipal bonds for tax or income reasons. If you do, you face three investment choices for diversification: (1) buying them on your own, (2) muni unit investment trust (UIT), and (3) muni mutual funds. If the preservation of capital is of primary importance, the UIT may be a better investment than a mutual fund. Table 7 compares aspects of the three approaches.

Table 7—

Investing in Municipal Bonds—Three Choices

	Direct Purchase	*UIT*	*Mutual Fund*
Portfolio policy and management	Your own selection	Passive; no management	Active management
Payments	Twice a year	Monthly	Monthly or automatic reinvestment
Commissions	Usually some percent buy-sell spread	Some percent buy-sell spread plus front-end load	Load or no-load
Investor profile	Experienced with sizable funds	Long-term (10 years)	Smaller and short-term
Interest rate risk	High	Low	Medium
Capital gain /loss potential	High	Low	Medium

WHAT ABOUT INVESTING IN MORTGAGE-BACKED SECURITIES?

A mortgage-backed security is a share in an organized pool of residential mortgages. Some are pass-through securities where the principal and interest payments are passed through to shareholders, usually monthly. There are several kinds of mortgage-backed securities. They include:

(a) *Government National Mortgage Association (GNMA - Ginnie Mae)* securities. GNMA primarily issues pass-through securities. These securities pass through all payments of interest and principal received on a pool of federally insured mortgage loans. GNMA guarantees that all payments of principal and interest will be made on the mortgages on a timely basis. Since many mortgages are repaid before maturity, investors in GNMA pools usually recover most of their principal investment well ahead of schedule. Ginnie Mae is considered an excellent investment. The higher yields, coupled with the U.S. government guarantee, provide a competitive edge over other intermediate to long-term securities issued by the U.S. government and other agencies.

(b) *Federal Home Loan Mortgage Corporation (FHLMC - Freddie Mac)* securities. Freddie Mac was established to provide a secondary market for conventional mortgages. It can purchase conventional mortgages for its own portfolio. Freddie Mac also issues pass-through securities—called participation certificates (PCs)—and guaranteed mortgage certificates (GMCs) that resemble bonds. Freddie Mac securities do not carry direct government guarantees and are subject to state and federal income tax.

(c) *Federal National Mortgage Association (FNMA - Fannie Mae)* securities. FNMA is a publicly held corporation whose goal is to provide a secondary market for government-guaranteed mortgages. It does so by financing its purchase by selling debentures with maturities of several years and short-term discount notes from 30 to 360 days to private investors. FNMA securities are not government guaranteed and are an unsecured obligation of the issuer. For this reason, they often provide considerably higher yields than Treasury securities.

(d) *Collaterized mortgage obligations (CMOs)*. CMOs are mortgage-backed securities that separate mortgage pools into short-, medium-, and long-term portions. You can choose between short-term (such as 5-year) and long-term (such as 20-year). CMOs offer high current income from a mortgage security that gets around the problem of uncertainty regarding the timing of principal return. They offer, however, a slightly lower yield than other pass-through securities in exchange for easing that uncertainty. CMOs typically sell in minimum denominations ranging between $1,000 and $12,000.

Note: In general, mortgage-backed securities enjoy liquidity and a high degree of safety because they are either government-sponsored or otherwise insured.

SOFTWARE FOR BOND AND FIXED INCOME SECURITIES ANALYSIS

Fixed income analysis software analyzes the quality and maturity structures of bond and other fixed income securities. Below is a list of popular fixed income analysis software.

Bondeye (DOS)
Ergo, Inc., (805) 969-9366

Bonspec (DOS)
Interactive Data Corp., (617) 863-8295

Bondcalc (DOS, Windows, OS/2)
Bondcalc Corp., (212) 587-0097

Bond Calculator and MBS/ABS Calculator (DOS)
Bond-Tech, Inc., (513) 836-3991

Bond Portfolio and Bond Pricing (Windows, Mac)
Baarns Publishing, (800) 377-9235 or (818) 837-1441

Bonds and Interest Rates Software (DOS)
Programmed Press, (516) 599-6527

CHAPTER 9

GLOBAL INVESTING

As you learn more about portfolio management and mutual funds, it becomes increasingly clear that there are advantages to holding a broad range of investment vehicles. In this chapter, you will see that risk can further be reduced by holding securities issued in foreign markets.

Global investing involves the direct or indirect acquisition of foreign securities by individuals or institutions without any control over or participation in the management of the foreign companies. Interest in overseas equities has increased notably in recent years, spurred by the strong performance of markets abroad and relatively easy availability of overseas investment vehicles for U.S. investors.

WHAT ARE THE ADVANTAGES OF GLOBAL INVESTING?

You, as an investor, can derive a number of important benefits from expanding the horizon of your portfolio beyond your home country: A far greater universe for stock selection, potentially greater returns, and an opportunity to reduce risk exposure. In addition, changes in currency relationships, while a double-edged sword, can enhance appreciation and offset part of the impact of price declines in foreign equity positions.

Broader Stock Selection

Global investment provides you with a much bigger pool of investment opportunities from which to choose. As Table 1 illustrates, as of June 1994, U.S. stocks accounted for only 36.2 percent of the world's total stock market capitalization. Consequently, an investor who focuses solely on domestic issues will miss nearly two-thirds of the investment opportunities in the world.

Higher Prospective Returns

Global investing offers more opportunities for achieving higher returns. Non-U.S. stocks now account for more than half the value of all global equity securities. Recent financial studies show that investors who hold a blend of foreign and U.S. stocks receive higher returns —at lower risk — than those who are fully invested in U.S. stocks.

Table 1—

World Equity Markets in Terms of Capitalization, by Country (as of June 1994)

Country	Percentage of the total
U.S.	36.2%
Japan	28.9%
Europe	26.4%
Others	8.5%
Total	100%

Source: *Morgan Stanley Capital International Perspective*, June 1994.

Figure 1 compares the performance of the major world stock markets (as measured by the *Morgan Stanley World Index)* in terms of average annual total returns over the past 10 years. As Table 2 shows, certain overseas stock markets have outpaced their U.S. counterparts over the last 10 years. In fact, foreign stocks have led in 14 of the last 23 years, and the U.S. has been the top-performing market only since 1976.

Since the impressive showing of many foreign equity markets is at least partially attributable to faster long-term economic growth in their home countries, superior returns should continue to be achieved in many cases. Further, statistics point to the more impressive showing of many foreign equity markets if we include the performances of foreign emerging markets.

Table 2—

Average Annual Total Returns by Country (for the period ended 6/30/94)

Country	Percentage Return
Hong Kong	31.42%
Belgium	25.01
Austria	24.05
Netherlands	21.33
Spain	21.13
Switzerland	20.76
France	20.13
Japan	18.81
Italy	18.02
Germany	17.84
Sweden	17.68
United Kingdom	17.39
Australia	16.02
U.S.A.	15.10
Denmark	15.05
Singapore/Malaysia	13.66
Norway	13.59

Source: Lipper Analytical Services, Inc.

Figure 1—

U.S. and Foreign Stock Returns
Compound Annual Return in U.S. Dollars
(Annualized Over 10-Year Periods)

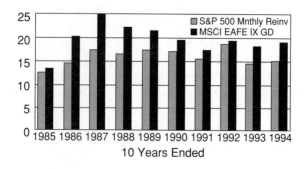

Source: Micropal, Inc.

Reduction of Risk

Adding international investments to a portfolio of
U.S. securities diversifies and reduces your risk. This
reduction of risk will be enhanced because international investments are much less influenced by the
U.S. economy and the correlation to U.S. investments is much less. Foreign markets sometimes follow different cycles than the U.S. market—and each
other.

Although foreign stocks can be riskier than
domestic issues, supplementing a domestic portfolio with a foreign component can actually reduce
your portfolio's overall volatility. The reason is that
by being diversified across many different economies which are at different points in the economic
cycle, downturns in some markets may be offset by

superior performance in others. There is considerable evidence that global diversification reduces systematic risk (*beta*) because of the relatively low cor-
relations between returns on U.S. and foreign securities.

Figure 2 illustrates this, comparing the risk reduction through diversification within the United
States to that obtainable through global diversification. A fully diversified U.S. portfolio is only 27
percent as risky as a typical individual stock, while
a globally diversified portfolio appears to be about
12 percent as risky as a typical individual stock. This
represents about 44 percent less than the U.S. figure.

Figure 2—

Risk Reduction through National and International Diversification

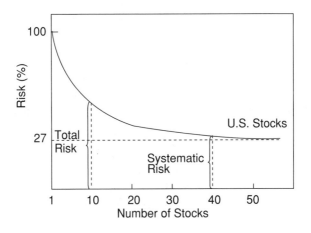

(continued)

Figure 2—*continued*

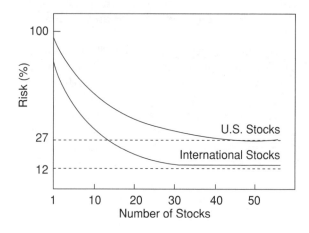

Source: B. Solnik, "Why Not Diversify Internationally Rather Than Domestically?" *Financial Analysts Journal*, July 1974, p.17.

Figure 3 demonstrates the effect over the past 10 years. Notice how adding a small percentage of foreign stocks to a domestic portfolio actually decreased its overall risk while increasing its overall return. The lowest level of volatility came from a portfolio with about 30 percent foreign stocks and 70 percent U.S. stocks. And, in fact, a portfolio with 60 percent foreign holdings and only 40 percent U.S. holdings actually approximated the risk of a 100 percent domestic portfolio, yet the average annual return was over two percentage points greater.

Figure 3—

How Foreign Stocks Have Benefitted a Domestic Portfolio

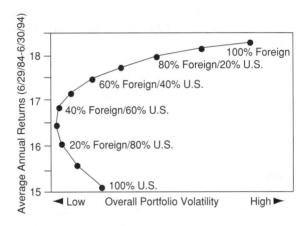

Source: Micropal, Inc.

WHAT ARE THE RISKS IN INVESTING GLOBALLY?

The advantages of lower risk must be balanced against other risks associated with foreign securities. Risks that are inherent in international investing are currency and political risks and the risks associated with emerging markets, economies and companies.

Currency (or Foreign Exchange) Risk

When you invest in a foreign market, the return on the foreign investment in terms of the U.S. dollar depends not only on the return on the foreign market in terms of local currency but also on the change in the exchange rate between the local currency and U.S. dollar. Since the exchange rates among major currencies have been volatile in recent years, exchange rate uncertainty has often been mentioned as one of the potential barriers to international investment (see Table 3).

For example, a strong dollar means that foreign currency buys less dollars; this pushes down foreign returns of the U.S. investor. The following example illustrates how a change in the dollar affects the return on a foreign investment.

Example 1—

You purchased bonds of a German firm paying 12 percent interest. You will earn that rate, assuming interest is paid and it is in Deutschemarks. What if you are paid in dollars? As Figure 4 shows, you must then convert marks to dollars before the payout has any value to you. Suppose that the dollar appreciated 10 percent against the mark during the year after purchase. (A currency appreciates when acquiring one of its units requires more units of a foreign currency). In this example, 1 mark acquired .616 dollars, and later, 1 mark acquired only .554 dollars; at the new exchange rate it would take 1.112 (.616/.554) marks to acquire .616 dollars. Thus, the dollar has appreciated while the mark has depreciated. Now, your return realized in dollars is only 10.91 percent. The adverse movement in the foreign exchange rate—the dollar's appreciation—reduced your actual yield.

Table 3—

Exchange Risk and Foreign Investment Yield

Transaction	Marks	Exchange Rate: No. of Dollars per 1 Mark	Dollars
On 1/1/19A Purchased one German bond with a 12% coupon rate	500	$.6051	$302.55
On 12/31/19A Expected interest received	60	.6051	36.31
Expected yield	12%		12%
On 12/31/19A Actual interest received	60	.5501*	33.01
Realized yield	12%		10.91%**

*$.6051/(1 + .1) = $.6051/1.1 = $.5501
**$33.01/$302.55 = .1091 = 10.91%

Currency risks can be hedged by borrowing in the local currency or selling it forward. However, this type of tool is too costly and impractical for individual investors. *Note:* Choosing countries with strong currencies and investing in international mutual funds could be an answer to minimizing currency risk.

Note, however, that currency swings work both ways. A weak dollar would boost foreign returns of U.S. investors. Table 4 is a quick reference to judge how currency swings affect your foreign returns.

Table 4—

Currency Changes vs. Foreign Returns in U.S. Dollars

Foreign Return	Change in Foreign Currency against the Dollar				
	20%	10%	0%	-10%	-20%
20%	44%	32	20	8	-4
10	32	21	10	-1	-12
0	20	10	0	-10	-20
-10	8	-1	-10	-19	-28
-20	-4	-12	-20	-28	-36

Political (or Sovereign) Risk

Political or sovereign risk is viewed by many as a major obstacle to international investment. Clearly, political factors are a major determinant of the attractiveness for investment in any country. Countries viewed as likely candidates for internal political upheaval or with a pronounced trend toward elimination of the private sector will be unattractive to all investors, foreign and domestic alike. There is no reason to believe that local investors will be systematically optimistic regarding their country's future. When political risks increase significantly, such investors will attempt to diversify from the home market as rapidly as will foreigners. As a result, prices will fall until the market deems it worthwhile to hold the securities of the risky country.

In light of political risk, how risky are investments in foreign markets? There is, of course, no easy answer. Political instability, limited track records, poor statistics —they all make gauging risk a risky business. Several companies try to evaluate the risk in some of the countries that are receiving the most attention from foreign investors. Listed at the end of this chapter are sources of country risk information.

But if domestic investors are prevented from liquidating their domestic holdings or from purchasing foreign assets by national regulations or moral suasion, the market prices may not reflect generally shared views of the political situation. Of course, if foreign investors are constrained by the same regulations, then all investors lose. A careful evaluation of the relative flexibility of domestic and foreign investment, therefore, is a key element in determining whether political risks jeopardize cross-border holdings. The risk of currency controls is one of the few political risks that is borne primarily by foreign investors.

In some cases, political risks might even favor foreign investors relative to domestic investors because risks are domestic phenomena that can be diversified away globally. As a result, they will have a greater impact on the risk of a domestic investor whose portfolio is concentrated in home assets than a globally diversified investor. Accordingly, domestic shares might well be more attractive to foreign than domestic investors in periods of perceived high political uncertainty.

Institutional Obstacles

A recurrent objection to global diversification is that the practical scope for foreign investing is limited. Many markets are perceived to be small, less liquid, and less efficient than those of the United States. Undoubtedly, there are many foreign stocks whose total capitalization and turnover are too limited for them to be of interest to most U.S. institutional investors. Further, in many markets—particularly the Japanese and West German—market capitalizations are often misleading indicators of an issue's marketability because a large proportion of the shares might be owned by banks, holding companies, or other concerns.

However, these considerations do not necessarily imply that these markets are less attractive to foreign institutional investors than to local investors. In fact, just the opposite might be the case. Domestic investors who depend primarily on their own market for liquidity and diversification are likely to be more constrained by these limitations than international investors who, through diversification, can virtually eliminate the nonmarket risk unique to individual companies even if they hold only a small number of shares in each market. International investors also do not have to rely on any single market for liquidity and, as a result, can take a longer view in regard to each market and security, even though they wish to realize profits within a reasonable period in each market and currency.

Another concern is related to the market efficiency of foreign markets. An efficient market is one where new information is quickly reflected in securities' prices and hence it is unlikely that any single investor will beat the market. Although less efficiency can be desirable from an active investment manager's perspective because it implies that superior performance is possible, it also puts the international investor at a disadvantage relative to the domestic investor, who has greater knowledge and better information. Studies of foreign markets suggest that they generally can be considered to be efficient in the sense that prices adjust rapidly to new information and that most professional managers are unable to consistently outperform the market.

There are several institutional obstacles that can make international investing costly, undesirable, or, in some cases, impossible. They include formal barriers to international transactions, such as exchange controls, double taxation of portfolio income for certain investors in particular countries, and restrictions on ownership of securities according to the nationality of the investor. These obstacles also include informal barriers, such as the difficulty of obtaining information about a market, differences in reporting practices that make international comparisons difficult, and subtle impediments to foreign investment based on traditional practice.

A major implication of the existence of such obstacles is that even if one assumes an integrated, efficient world capital market, investors with different legal domiciles or tax situations might want to hold different investments. However, it is difficult to determine by how much such portfolios should differ from the world optimal market portfolio in the absence of such obstacles. This would depend on the balancing of the effect of the obstacles against the gains from more complete diversification.

WHAT ARE THE WAYS TO INVEST GLOBALLY?

The advantages of international investing can be reaped from participation in international money and capital markets, direct or indirect.

Purchasing Foreign Stock Directly

A U.S. investor can place an order to purchase foreign securities through a U.S. brokerage firm, which will instruct its respective branch office or a local broker to buy the stock. One advantage of owning ordinary shares is a much larger selection of foreign stocks from which to choose. Also, trading is usually more active, resulting in greater liquidity.

The direct purchase of foreign securities causes the following difficulties:

1. It involves high transaction costs in terms of brokerage commissions and additional costs associated with the international clearing process.

2. It involves extensive information and research costs. Further, the information is often difficult to obtain and its reliability is questionable.

3. An investor must be familiar with the financial reporting and disclosure standards of the country in which the stock is issued.

4. When owning foreign shares, U.S. investors are subject to the rules and regulations of the foreign stock exchanges. Moreover, delays in settlement can occur. Table 5 shows stock market rules in major foreign markets.

Table 5—

Stock Market Rules in Major Markets

Country	Settlement Date	Is Inside Trading Illegal?	Percent Stake that Must Be Disclosed
Australia	Negotiable	Yes	10
Britain	Every 2 or 3 weeks	Yes (infrequent enforcement)	5
France	Monthly	Yes	5
Germany	2 business days	No (but barred by voluntary code)	25
Italy	Monthly	Yes	2
Japan	3 business days	Yes (infrequent enforcement)	5

Country	Settlement Date	Is Inside Trading Illegal?	Percent Stake that Must Be Disclosed
Netherlands	3 business days	Yes (only for directors)	10
Singapore	5 business days	Yes	n.a.
Switzerland	1 business days	Yes (no enforcement body)	5
United States	5 business days	Yes	5

How May Your Account Be Handled?

Like domestic stock purchases, the foreign stock purchased may be registered in your name or it may be registered in "Street" name—the name of the broker who initiates the transaction. In the former case, however, you must arrange to open custodian accounts at banks in the countries in which you plan to buy securities. This process can be simplified by opening a global custody account with a multinational commercial bank. This type of account enables you to utilize the foreign subsidiaries of a single institution for the safekeeping of all securities rather than having to establish accounts at separate banks around the world. Many U.S. brokers also establish their own global custody accounts overseas to act as receiving and delivery agents.

Many foreign nations impose a withholding tax on dividends, though these taxes vary from country to country. U.S. investors can file for a refund on this tax if tax treaties exist between the U.S. and the other nation involved. Most foreign shares can be held in either registered or bearer form, though in some countries foreign investors may only own stock in bearer form. If the shares are registered, the investor will receive dividends in local currency (less withholding taxes) and notices from the company in the local language. If the securities are held in bearer form, the investor can receive dividends (after deduction of withholding taxes) in U.S. dollars through the agent bank.

The following example illustrates how to determine a rough price for foreign securities in U.S. dollars. This illustration is based on "Foreign Exchange Quotation" (Table 6) and "Foreign Securities Quotations" (Table 7) from *The Wall Street Journal*, March 17, 1995.

Example 2—

The rates in Table 6 are interbank rates. As a rule of thumb, we add 2 percent to the interbank rate to determine the rate for stock transactions. To determine a rough price for foreign securities in U.S. dollars, you must multiply the price by the applicable exchange rate. For example, as of 3/17/95, in the case of Ajinomodo closing at 1,020 yen, we note that for the Japanese yen, the exchange rate is $.011204. Two percent added to this gives you an estimated exchange rate of $.011428 ($.011204 + .000224).

If you multiply the price of the stock in foreign currency by the approximate U.S. equivalent of yen, you obtain a rough per-share price of the stock in U.S. dollars.

1,020	yen (price of stock)
x $.011428	U.S.$ (rough exchange value of $1)
$ 11.6566	U.S.$ (price of stock in U.S. dollars)

Table 6—

Foreign Exhange Rates

Currency	Fgn. Currency in Dollars		Dollar in Fgn.Currency	
	3/17	3/16	3/17	3/16

Prices as of 3:00 p.m. Eastern Time.
Rates for trades of $1 million minimum.

Currency	3/17	3/16	3/17	3/16
Argentina	1.0000	1.0000	1.0000	1.0000
Australia	.7385	.7460	1.3541	1.3405
Austria	.1026	.1017	9.751	9.832
Belgium	.0348	.0350	28.71	28.54
Brazil	1.1236	1.1236	.8900	.8900
Britain	.5830	1.5870	.6317	6301
30-day fwd	1.5827	1.5868	.6318	.6302
60-day fwd	1.5821	1.5862	.6321	6304
90-day fwd	1.5815	1.5856	.6323	.6307
Canada	.7080	.7068	1.4125	1.4148
30-day fwd	.7092	.7081	1.4100	1.4122
60-day fwd	.7105	.7093	1.4075	1.4099
90-day fwd	.7114	.7103	1.4056	1.4078
Chile	.002437	.002432	410.35	411.25
China	.1189	.1189	8.4095	8.4089
Colombia	.001157	.001155	864.50	866.00
CzechRep	.0384	.0381	26.03	26.26
Denmark	.1773	.1793	5.6400	6.5781
ECU	1.30680	1.31150	.7652	.7625
Ecuador	.000417	.000417	2398.50	2398.00
Egypt	.2946	.2946	3.3940	3.3940
Finland	.2301	.2296	4.3455	4.3560
France	.2015	.2012	4.9620	4.9690
Germany	.7217	.7161	1.3857	1.3965
30-day fwd	.7224	.7168	1.3843	1.3951
60-day fwd	.7231	.7176	1.3829	1.3936
90-day fwd	.7239	.7183	1.3814	1.3922
Greece	.004405	.004376	227.00	228.50
Hong Kong	.1294	.1294	7.7308	7.7305
Hungary	.0084	.0083	119.28	119.96
India	.0319	.0322	31.350	31.040
Indonesia	.000449	.000449	2225.50	2225.65
Ireland	1.5825	1.5847	.6319	.6310
Israel	.3369	.3376	2.9686	2.9622
Italy	.000577	.000590	1734.00	1695.00

(continued)

Table 6—continued

Currency	Fgn. Currency in Dollars 3/17	3/16	Dollar in Fgn.Currency 3/17	3/16
Prices as of 3:00 p.m. Eastern Time. Rates for trades of $1 million minimum.				
Japan	.011204	.011104	89.25	90.06
30-day fwd	.011245	.011141	88.93	89.76
60-day fwd	.011280	.011181	88.65	89.44
90-day fwd	.011321	.011218	88.33	89.14
Jordan	1.4556	1.4514	.68700	.68899
Lebanon	.000611	.000611	1636.50	1637.00
Malaysia	.3920	.3928	2.5510	2.5460
Mexico	.146843	.141443	6.8100	7.0700
Netherlands	.6425	.6455	1.5565	1.5491
N. Zealand	.6470	.6507	1.5456	1.5368
Norway	.1605	.1614	6.2320	6.1945
Pakistan	.0324	.0324	30.85	30.85
Peru	.4444	.4444	2.250	2.250
Philippines	.0390	.0389	25.63	25.73
Poland	.4237	.4237	2.36	2.36
Portugal	.006807	.006768	146.90	147.75
Russia	.000211	.000211	4744.00	4744.00
Saudi Arabia	.2667	.2667	3.7500	3.7500

Table 7—

Foreign Securities Quotations

Closing Prices

JAPAN (Japanese Yen)

	Cur.	Prev.
Ajinomto	1020	1040
Alps	971	1000
Amada	855	900
Anitsu	1030	1030
Asahi Chem	600	614
Asahi Glas	1050	1050
Bank of Tokyo	1300	1340
Banyu	920	949
Bridgestone	1300	1310
Brother	472	504

In recent years, there have been an increasing trend of the shares of many firms being listed on foreign exchanges. This cross-listing is usually accomplished by depositary receipts.

AMERICAN DEPOSITARY RECEIPTS (ADRS)

American Depository Receipts (ADRs) are certificates that represent stock in foreign companies. The process of ADRs works as follows: A foreign company places shares in trust with a U.S. bank, which in turn issues depository receipts to U.S. investors. The ADRs, then, are claims to shares of stock and are essentially the same as shares. The depository bank performs all clerical functions—issuing annual reports, keeping a shareholder ledger, paying and maintaining dividend records, and what not—allowing the ADRs to trade in markets just like domestic securities trade. ADRs are traded on the NYSE, AMEX, and OTC markets as a share in stock, minus the voting rights. Examples of ADRs are Hanson, Cannon, and Smithkline Beecham.

ADRs have become an increasingly convenient and popular vehicle for investing internationally. Investors do not have to go through foreign brokers, and information on company operations is usually available in English. Therefore, ADRs are good substitutes for direct foreign investment. They are bought and sold with U.S. dollars and pay their dividends in dollars. Further, the trading and settlement costs are waived that apply in some foreign markets. The certificates are issued by depository banks (for example, the Bank of New York). To purchase ADRs, contact your stockbroker or call Bank of New York, which is the largest seller of ADRs, at (212) 815-2000.

Disadvantages of ADRs

ADRs, however, are not for everyone. The disadvantages are:

1.   ADRs carry an element of currency risk. For example, an ADR based on the stock of a British company would tend to lose in value when the dollar strengthens against the British pound, if other factors were held constant. This is because as the pound weakens, less U.S. dollars are required to buy the same shares of a U.K. company.

2.   Some thinly traded ADRs can be harder to buy and sell. This could make them more expensive to purchase than the quoted price.

3.   You may face problems obtaining reliable information on foreign companies. It may be difficult to do your own research in selecting foreign stocks. For one thing, there is a shortage of data: The annual report may be all that is available, and its reliability is questionable. Furthermore, in many instances, foreign financial reporting and accounting standards are substantially different from those accepted in the U.S.

4.   ADRs can be either sponsored or unsponsored. Many ADRs are not sponsored by the underlying companies. Nonsponsored ADRs oblige you to pay certain fees to the depository bank. The return is reduced accordingly.

5.   There are a limited number of issues available, for only a small fraction of the foreign stocks traded internationally. As of August 1993, 967 ADRs were available in the U.S. Many interesting and rewarding investment opportunities exist in shares with no ADRs.

BUYING FOREIGN BONDS

All international bonds fall within two generic classifications, Eurobonds and foreign bonds. The distinction between categories is based on whether the borrower is a domestic or a foreign resident and whether the issue is denominated in the local currency or a foreign currency.

What Is the Difference Between a Eurobond and Foreign Bond?

A *Eurobond* is underwritten by an international syndicate of banks and other securities firms, and is sold exclusively in countries other than the country in whose currency the issue is denominated. For example, a bond issued by a U.S. corporation, denominated in U.S. dollars but sold to investors in Europe and Japan (not to investors in the United States), would be a Eurobond. Eurobonds are issued by multinational corporations, large domestic corporations, sovereign governments, governmental enterprises, and international institutions. They are offered simultaneously in a number of different national capital markets, but not in the capital market of the country, nor to residents of the country, in whose currency the bond is denominated. Almost all Eurobonds are in bearer form with call provisions and sinking funds.

A *foreign bond* is underwritten by a syndicate composed of members from a single country, sold principally within that country, and denominated in the currency of that country. The issuer, however, is from another country. A bond issued by a Swedish corporation, denominated in dollars, and sold in the U.S. to U.S. investors by U.S. investment bankers would be a foreign bond. Foreign bonds have nicknames: Those sold in the U.S. are "Yankee bonds"; those sold in Japan are "Samurai bonds"; and foreign bonds sold in the United Kingdom are "Bulldogs."

Figure 4 specifically reclassifies foreign bonds from a U.S. investor's perspective.

Figure 4—

Foreign Bonds to U.S. Investors

		Sales	
		In the U.S.	In Foreign Countries
Issuer	Domestic	Domestic Bonds	Eurodollar Bonds
	Foreign	Yankee Bonds	Foreign Currency Bonds, Eurodollar Bonds

---

Foreign currency bonds are issued by foreign governments and foreign corporations, denominated in their own currency. As with domestic bonds, such bonds are priced inversely to movements in the interest rate of the country in whose currency the issue is denominated. For example, the values of German bonds fall if German interest rates rise. In addition, values of bonds denominated in foreign currencies will fall (or rise) if the dollar appreciates (or depreciates) relative to the denominated currency. Indeed, investing in foreign currency bonds is really a play on the dollar. If the dollar and foreign interest rates fall, investors in foreign currency bonds could make a nice return. It should be pointed out, however, that if both the dollar and foreign interest rates rise, investors will be hit with a double whammy.

What Are the Advantages of Foreign Convertibles?

In addition to participation in the appreciation of overseas stocks, foreign convertibles enable investors to earn greater current returns while incurring less risk compared with the underlying common stocks. Their yields are usually higher than those provided by the dividends of the underlying common stocks. Moreover, the conversion premium (the difference between the cost of acquiring the underlying stock through the conversion provisions of the bond and the current share price) on these bonds is normally quite low, allowing an investor to pick up this yield advantage at a relatively low cost. Most Japanese convertibles are issued with 5 percent premiums, for example.

Because of their hybrid nature, convertible bonds have less downside risk than the underlying common—i.e., the fixed coupon provides a price floor determined by the yields available on comparable straight debt issues. Also, convertible securities are senior to common stocks. In the event of bankruptcy, holders of convertible securities have priority over stockholders in claiming the assets of a firm. And coupon payments on Euroconvertibles are not subject to withholding taxes, while the dividend payments on the common stocks usually are.

What Does the Yield Depend On?

The yield on a foreign bond, for a U.S. investor, will depend on both the local bond market of the issuing company and how the currency in which the bond is denominated appreciates (depreciates) against the U.S. dollar. International bond funds offer an excellent alternative. They provide diversification benefits because of the low correlation between the returns of U.S. government bonds and those of most major foreign bond markets.

INVESTING IN INTERNATIONAL MONEY MARKETS

A market for short-term financial claims performs the essential service of enabling financial investment to be transformed into real investment. A well-developed money market is able to attract savings and channel them to their most efficient uses, making funds more cheaply and freely available to the business sector. Every country that has banks which accept short-term deposits (time deposits) has a money market of sorts. As the economy grows, demand would grow for a wider range of financial instruments, such as commercial paper, acceptances, and government securities, and these would be traded in a secondary market where financial claims could be freely bought and sold. As the economy expands through international transactions, the national money market becomes linked to international money markets just as the national capital market has its linkages with international capital markets.

What Are the Ways of Investing in International Money Markets?

There are three major ways of investing in international money markets. The first approach is to purchase foreign short-term money market instruments directly. By investing in foreign money market assets denominated in the foreign currency, the full impact of currency variation is reflected in returns along with the yield of the money market investments. If, for example, interest rates are higher in

England and a U.S. investor thinks sterling will strengthen or remain on the same exchange rate with the dollar, then an investment denominated in the sterling currency would make sense.

The second approach is through the Eurocurrency market, where funds are intermediated outside the country of the currency in which the funds are denominated. Thus, the Eurocurrency market comprises financial institutions that compete for dollar time deposits and make dollar loans outside the United States, for example. An example of Eurocurrency markets would be that a U.S. investor purchases Eurodollar CDs from a bank in London.

Eurocurrency banking is not subject to domestic banking regulation, such as reserve requirements and interest-rate restrictions. This enables Eurobanks to operate more efficiently, cheaply and competitively than their domestic counterparts, and to offer slightly better terms to both borrowers and lenders. Therefore, Eurodollar deposit rates are somewhat higher and effective lending rates a little lower than they are in the U.S. money market.

The third approach is to place foreign currency deposits with U.S. banks in the United States. This enables U.S. investors to conveniently take advantage of the expected weakness of the dollar relative to the currency in which the deposit is denominated.

BUYING SHARES OF U.S.-BASED MULTINATIONAL CORPORATIONS

Many investors achieve a reasonable degree of global diversification without recognizing it because many U.S. firms are multinational corporations (MNCs). Companies such as IBM, Coca-Cola, and General Motors do a considerable portion of their business outside the U.S. Further, buying shares of

MNCs not only achieves global diversification, but also avoids the high transaction costs and information problems faced by investors directly purchasing foreign securities.

A MNC owns, controls and manages income - generating assets in a variety of countries. Thus, a MNC can be viewed as representing a portfolio of globally diversified cash flows originated in different countries and currencies. Since the cash flows of a MNC are likely to be strongly influenced by foreign factors, it has been suggested that you may be able to achieve global diversification indirectly through shares in MNCs.

However, several studies have found that the share price behavior of MNCs is nearly indistinguishable from that of purely domestic firms. The share prices of MNCs show far more sensitivity to the index of their home markets than to foreign market indices. Thus, investing in domestic MNCs would not be an effective means of global diversification, though it would be one of the cheapest and the most convenient means.

INVESTING IN INTERNATIONAL MUTUAL FUNDS

You may find mutual funds attractive because they offer the services of full-time, professional managers, safekeeping of securities, the option to invest various dollar amounts (as funds offer both full and fractional shares), and the ability to reduce the amount invested without reducing diversity. Coupled with such benefits, there has been a significant increase in international mutual funds as more investors diversify globally. The next section is devoted to this subject.

GLOBAL PORTFOLIO DIVERSIFICATION VIA MUTUAL FUNDS

International mutual funds are probably the best way for you to achieve global diversification, either on a broad basis or by targeting specific countries or geographical regions. It is a relatively easy, low-cost way, and simplifies the process of investing in foreign securities.

In general, mutual funds are classified as stock funds, bond funds, and money market funds, based on the securities invested. Thus, global and international funds are made up of all three, though international money market funds are a relatively recent development.

WHAT ARE THE FEATURES OF THE VARIOUS TYPES OF INTERNATIONAL FUNDS?

Global and International Stock Funds

In terms of geographical diversity, international stock funds can be divided into four groups, ranging from highly diversified to highly focused: Global, international, regional, and single-country funds.

Global funds can invest anywhere in the world, including the United States. However, most global funds keep the majority of their assets in foreign markets. Global funds are worth considering if you are unsure about how much to allocate to foreign markets, though this is somewhat of a cop-out in that the fund's foreign allocation is not based on the specific circumstances of any single investor.

International (or foreign) funds invest only in foreign stocks. Because these funds focus only on foreign markets, they allow investors to control what portion of their personal portfolio they want to allocate to non-U.S. stocks.

International funds with a *regional focus* allow investors to narrow their sights on a particular region. There are a number of European, Asian-Pacific, and Latin American funds. Most regional funds are closed-end funds, although there are some open-end. International index funds are being introduced, such as Vanguard's.

Single-country funds are the most focused and therefore by far the most aggressive foreign stock funds. Almost all single-country funds are closed-end funds (exceptions are the Japan Fund and French Fund). This exaggerates their aggressiveness because single-country (and regional) closed-end funds have been known to sell at both large discounts and premiums to their net asset value. Thus, closed-end single-country funds are well suited for only the most sophisticated investors who are confident in their ability to assess the potential for a specific market as well as the trends in the fund's stock price versus its net asset value. *Note:* Because of their broad focus, global and international funds are less risky and therefore a better choice for the average investor than a single-country or a regional fund.

International Bond Funds

Compared with international stock funds, international bond funds are limited in the number of available funds as well as in the performance history. In selecting international bond funds, consider the following factors: open-end versus closed-end; average maturity; country focus; and currency risk. It is often suggested that you should stay short-term (typically, four years or less) and locate a fund that *hedges* some of the foreign exchange risk and invests in countries with currencies that move with the U.S. dollar.

International Money Market Funds

International money market funds are a relatively recent phenomenon. Many funds invest only in dollar-denominated foreign money market instruments, thereby eliminating the currency risk.

If you are a currency risk-averse investor, you should put your money in international money market funds.

Hedged Funds

In order to minimize exposure to currency risk, many funds try to hedge. It is a matter of degree. In general, international short-term bond funds usually hedge most of the currency risk, while longer-term funds have substantial exposure. Funds use currency options, futures, and elaborate cross-currency hedges, but the most effective hedges are expensive.

HOW DO YOU SELECT MUTUAL FUNDS?

In evaluating a mutual fund, domestic or foreign, you should look at itsobjectives, management and track record, expense ratio, and so on. It is important to note that, when considering any mutual fund, you should realize that a big part of what you are buying is management. Therefore, continuity of management is important, as evidenced by consistent track records for at least five years.

The performance of foreign mutual funds must be measured against their peers and the correct market benchmarks. For example, a broadly diversified international fund should be compared with

the EAFE index. On the other hand, the Japanese
funds should be judged against each other as well
as with the Nikkei average.

With closed-end funds, a well diversified,
multicountry fund that sells at a discount should
be sought. But if you buy at a premium, make sure
that it is at least the low-end of its range. Another
fact to consider is the fund's expense ratio relative
to other comparable funds and relative to its premium or discount level. Table 8 shows quotes of
some international closed-end funds.

Table 8—

Quotes on International Closed-End Funds

Fund Name	Stock Exch.	Market NAV	Price	Prem /Disc	52-Week Market Return
Friday, April 7, 1995					
General Equity Funds					
Adams Express	N	19.27	16 1/4	-15.7	4.2
Alliance All-Mkt	N	20.27	17 1/8	-14.3	N/A
Baker Fentress	N	18.94	15 3/8	-18.8	3.4
Bergstrom Cap	A	104.36	.92 -	-11.8	12.4
Blue Chip Value -a	N	- 7.64	6 5/8	13.3	5.4
Central Secs	A	18.43	17 1/4	3.7	22.0
Charles Allmon	N	10.39	8 3/4	-15.8	-5.6
Engex	A	9.76	7 5/8	-21.9	-18.7
Equus II	A	19.68	12 1/2	-36.5	-16.4
Gabelli Equity	N	9.76	9 3/4	-0.1	8.1
General American	N	22.66	19 1/8	15.6	0.7
Inefficient Mkt	A	12.15	9 7/8	-18.7	0.1
Jundt Growth	N	14.97	14 1/4	-4.8	6.9
Liberty All-Star	N	9.89	9 3/4	-1.4	2.7
Morgan FunShares-c	O	7.94	7 1/8	-10.3.	N/A
Morgan Gr Sm Cap	N	11.02	9 3/8	-14.9	4.7
NAIC Growth-c	C	12.60	10 1/4	18.7	6.0
Royce Value	N	13.01	11 3/8	-12.6	-2.5
Salomon SBF	N	14.01	11 5/8	-17.0	5.8

Fund Name	Stock Exch.	Market NAV	Price	Prem /Disc	52-Week Market Return

Friday, April 7, 1995
General Equity Funds

Fund Name	Stock Exch.	Market NAV	Price	Prem /Disc	52-Week Market Return
Source Capital	N	40.59	39 1/4	-3.3	3.3
Spectra	O	14.88	12 3/4	-14.3	8.4
Tri-Continental	N	25.51	21 1/8	-17.2	7.0
Z-Seven	O	17.66	17 1/2	-0.9	7.9
Zweig -a	N	10.26	10 5/8	+3.6	-9.2

Specialized Equity Funds

Fund Name	Stock Exch.	Market NAV	Price	Prem /Disc	52-Week Market Return
Alliance GI Env	N	11.53	8 3/4	-24.1	-5.4
C&S Realty	A	8.08	8 5/8	+6.7	-6.4
C&S Total Rtn -a	N	12.55	12 1/4	-2.4	-7.5
Centri Fd Canada -c	A	4.98	5	+0.4	-10.9
Counsellors Tand	N	16.26	13 7/8	-14.7	8.8
Delaware Gr Div	N	13.06	12 5/8	-3.3	-1.0
Delaware Grp GI	N	13.33	12 5/8	-5.3	-4.4
Duft&Ph Util Inc	N	7.56	8 3/8	+10.8	7.0
Emer Mkts lnfra	N	11.36	9 3/8	-17.5	-21.5

SOURCES OF INFORMATION

Country Risk

- *Euromoney* magazine's annual *Country Risk Rating* is based on a measure of different countries' access to international credit, trade finance, political risk, and a country's payment record. The rankings are generally confirmed by political risk insurers and top syndicate managers in the Euromarkets.

- Ratings by *Economist Intelligence Unit*, a New York-based subsidiary of the *Economist Group*, London, are based on such factors as external debt and trends in the current account, the consistency of the government policy, foreign-exchange reserves, and the quality of economic management.

- *International Country Risk Guide*, published by a U.S. division of International Business Communications, Ltd., London, offers a composite risk rating as well as individual ratings for political, financial, and economic risk. The political variable—which makes up half of the composite index—includes factors such as government corruption and how economic expectations diverge from reality. The financial rating looks at such things as the likelihood of losses from exchange controls and loan defaults. Finally, economic ratings consider such factors as inflation and debt-service costs.

- *Data Book* (quarterly), published by Thompson BankWatch, Inc., 61 Broadway, New York, NY 10006, provides a country rating assessing overall political and economic stability of a country in which a bank is domiciled.

Foreign Firms

The following sources provide addresses, phone numbers, areas of business, officers, directors, and financial data on foreign firms:

- *Moody's International Manual*, published annually by Moody's Investment Service, in two volumes with weekly updating.

- *International Directory of Corporate Affiliations*, published twice a year by National Register Publishing Co.

- *The International Corporate 1000*, published by Monitor Publishing Co., with annual updating.

---

*This chapter was coauthored with Dr. Yojin Jung of International Investment Advisors, Los Angeles, California.

TAX-ADVANTAGED INVESTMENTS

Many investments are designed specifically for tax benefits. Therefore, they can be excellent investment vehicles for retirement planning. They include limited partnerships, various retirement plans, such as Individual Retirement Accounts (IRAs), and annuities. You will learn the pros and cons of each in this chapter.

WHAT ARE THE RELATED TAX RULES AND APPLICATIONS?

Some important tax rules are:

1. Portfolio income is divided into investment income (and loss) and capital gain (and loss). The expenses associated with earning investment income are generally deductible only to the extent of investment income. Capital losses are generally deductible only to the extent of capital gains.

2. Dividend income is fully taxed.

3. A long-term capital gain is the excess of net proceeds on sale over the initial cost for stock owned more than one year. A capital loss is the opposite. Net long-term a capital gains (capital gains less capital losses) are taxed at the lower of your tax rate or 28 percent.

4. Net capital losses are tax deductible up to $3,000 ($1,500 for married individuals filing separately). The balance over $3,000 may be carried forward to future years.
5. A short-term capital gain is for stock owned less than one year. The tax rate for short-term capital gains is the ordinary tax rate.
6. Gains and losses from the sale of securities is reported on the trade date (date you sell the stock) not the settlement date (three business days later, when the broker pays you). The settlement date may go into the next year.
7. A way to delay the tax on the gain from the sale of stock while assuring that gain is to sell short. You may sell short close to year-end and then deliver the security to the brokerage firm and report the gain next year.
8. Passive income is defined as income received from real estate investments and limited partnership interests. Expenses associated with managing real estate or the limited partnership are deductible only against passive income.
9. Wash sale rule: The IRS disallows the loss if a position is sold at a loss and is repurchased within 30 days of the sale date. Furthermore, the IRS considers a transaction to be a wash sale if an equivalent security, such as a convertible, is purchased; if a call option, warrants, or rights are purchased; or if the customer sells a "deep in the money" put.

WHAT TAX ADVANTAGE IS THERE TO REAL ESTATE?

Tax relief comes with real estate because the investor can deduct expenses, mortgage interest, and depreciation. Two major types of real estate investments are limited partnerships and real estate investment trusts.

What Are Limited Partnerships?

Limited partnerships, now usually referred to as direct investments or private investments, are used for tax benefits. They include real estate partnerships, oil and gas partnerships, equipment leasing partnerships, cable partnerships, and the like. For example, real estate partnerships enable investors to buy into real estate projects too costly for them individually; for example, a group of investors buy a large project like a shopping mall or an apartment house. There are both general and limited partners. The *general manager* typically originates and manages the property for compensation. The *limited partners* invest money and are liable just for that investment. Limited partnerships offer the following benefits:

- Tax deductible expenses.

- Professional management.

- Exemption from the double taxation of distributions faced by a corporate structure. A limited partnership functions as a pass-through agency, so it does not have to pay taxes on the income it receives.

The disadvantages are:

- IRS rulings disallowing certain real estate losses.

- High management charges and costs (typically, 15 to 30 percent)

- High risk.

- Illiquidity from a lack of secondary market, unlike, for example, real estate investment trusts (REITs). This means you would be likely to lose money if you wish to sell your interest before it liquidates its assets. *Note:* In recent years, a new securities market has emerged—

the limited partnership secondary market. This new market offers a long-term benefit to limited partnership investors. Secondary market liquidity softens what has perhaps been the principal negative of limited partnership investing—the long-term illiquid nature of the security.

Information on the limited partnership secondary market includes:

1. *Partnership Profiles* [P.O. Box 7938, Dallas, Texas 75209, (817) 488-6115] provides quarterly research reports on actively traded partnerships. In addition, *The Perspective*, a newsletter, carries news and analysis of the partnership market, including secondary market trading prices.

2. *The Stanger Report: A Guide to Partnership Investing* [Robert A. Stanger & Company, 1129 Broad Street, Shrewsbury, NJ 07702-4790, (908) 389-3600] provides review articles on the partnership market, listings of partnerships traded in the secondary market, and listings of new issue partnerships currently being marketed.

What Are Real Estate Investment Trusts (REITs)?

REITs are another form of real estate investing. REITs are companies similar to closed-end mutual funds. REITs invest money in diversified real estate or mortgage portfolios rather than stocks or bonds. REITs are traded on the stock exchanges and over-the-counter market.

To continue their tax-exempt status, REITs must distribute 95 percent of their profit to shareholders, and in turn they are exempt from corporate taxes on income or gains.

Are REIT Yields Attractive ?

Yields might be high because there is no corporate tax on earnings, so it all flows to shareholders.

What Kinds of REITs Are There?

Three types of REITs exist: Equity REITs concentrate on income-producing properties; mortgage REITs lend to developers and builders; and hybrid REITs do both. Equity REITs are the safest, but, their total returns are lower than the others.

Are REITs for You?

You may determine the suitability of REITs for your investment objectives by considering the following factors.

How to purchase	Contact a Stockbroker
Advantages	Dividend income
	Capital appreciation potential
	Liquid investment relative to other real estate investments
	Diversification in real estate projects with smaller cash investment
Disadvantages	Risk of loss in declining real estate market
Liquidity	Because shares are traded on the stock exchange it may be sold
Taxes	Tax on capital gains and dividends

On What Basis Should You Choose a REIT?

Before investing in a REIT, review the current annual report, *The Value Line Investment Survey*, *Audit*

Investment's Newsletter, or *Realty Stock Review.* Consider:

- Profitability
- Annual cash flow
- Condition of properties
- Location of properties, good or bad areas.
- Nature of property (e.g., residential, commercial)
- Degree of leverage
- Years REIT has been in existence
- Dividend history

What Are Sources of REITs Information?

Since REITs are traded on the national exchanges, facts and financial data can be obtained through many of the same sources you would use for listed stocks, such as *S&P's Stock Guide* and *Value Line Investment Surveys. Moody's Bank and Finance Manual,* published annually with twice weekly supplements by Moody's Investment Service (also available on CD-ROM), covers 109 REITs, giving detailed financial information. For a list of current REITs, contact *National Association of Real Estate Investment Trusts,* (202)785-8717.

HOW ABOUT OIL AND GAS PROGRAMS?

Limited partnerships exist for oil and gas. They include:

1. Drilling programs, exploratory drilling (wildcatting) in an unproven area, and development drilling in or near proven fields.

2.   Income programs that acquire producing prop-
     erties.

Oil and gas programs may deduct "intangible
drilling costs and a "depletion allowance" reflecting the depletion of estimated reserves.

• Recapture rules: The tax breaks are "recaptured" by the IRS when the asset is sold. For
  example, if tangible property is sold, all depreciation is recaptured and taxed upon sale.

• Alternative minimum tax (AMT): If an investor relies on "tax preference" items to reduce
  his regular tax liability excessively, the alternative computation adds back the preference
  items to the investor's taxable income, and a
  flat 24 percent tax rate is applied to the "alternative income."

WHAT ARE THE TAX IMPLICATIONS OF RETIREMENT PLANS?

Retirement plans are either "tax qualified" or
"non-tax qualified." Tax qualified plan contributions are deductible against the contributor's taxable income. Earnings in the plan build up tax deferred. When distributions are taken from the plan,
the entire distribution is taxable at that time.

Non-tax qualified plan contributions are not deductible against the contributor's taxable income.
Earnings in the plan build up tax-deferred. When
distributions are taken from the plan, the portion
of the distribution that represents that build up is
taxable.

Tax-deferred investments are important parts
of any retirement planning effort. A key to this is
that earnings, including dividends and capital
gains, will compound tax-deferred until they are
distributed. To see how tax-deferred growth can

make a significant difference over the years, consider the following example.

Example 1—

Assume that you earn 8 percent return on
your investment annually and that your
current income tax rate is 15 percent. Assume also that you will be taxed at a 31 percent rate 30 years from now when you retire. If you make annual tax-deferred contributions of $2,000 for 30 years (such as to
an IRA account), you could build a nest egg
of $226,566, while the same investment in
a taxable account may produce $145,376.

There are two types of pension funds: Company
and individual.

1. Company-sponsored pension plans:
   — Qualified company retirement plans
   — Profit-sharing plans
   — 401(k) salary reduction plans
   — Tax-sheltered annuities (TSA)
   — Employee stock ownership plans (ESOP)
   — Simplified employee pension plan (SEP)
2. Individual retirement plans:
   — Individual retirement accounts (IRAs)
   — Keoghs
   — Annuities

Each of these types of pension plans are now
discussed.

Qualified company retirement plans. The IRS allows a company to contribute to a pension plan that is qualified; that is, the plan satisfies certain criteria so that contributions are tax deductible. Investment income accumulates tax-free.

Profit-sharing plans. A category defined contribution plan. Different from other qualified plans, you need not retire to obtain payments. *Note*: Because contributions are made only if there is profit, there is uncertainty as to the amount of retirement benefit.

401(k) salary reduction plans. A 401(k) plan postpones part of your salary until you retire. Each salary payment is lower. Employers often match a percentage of employee's contributions (50 percent matches are common at many companies). With a 401(k), you can put away up to $9,240 tax-deferred each year. Interest accumulates tax-free until you retire. The untaxed compounding effect enhances your retirement savings.

Example 2—

You save 15 percent of your $60,000 annual salary in a 401(k) plan.

	Take-home Pay With 401(k) Plan	Take-home Pay Without 401(k) Plan
Base pay	$60,000	$60,000
Salary reduction	9,000	None
Taxable income	$51,000	$60,000
Federal and FICA taxes	10,000	12,000
Savings after taxes	None	9,000
Take-home pay	$41,000	$39,000

Incremental take-home pay under plan = $2,000.

Tax-sheltered annuities (TSA). This applies if you work for a nonprofit entity. It is like a 401(k), but you may take out money at any age and not incur a tax penalty. The withdrawals are subject to ordinary tax rates.

Employee stock ownership plans (ESOP). A stock-bonus plan in which employer contributions are tax deductible.

Simplified employee pension (SEP). SEP, sometimes referred to as "super IRA," is a plan whereby an employer who could not afford or did not want the administrative burden of establishing a Keogh plan makes annual payments for the employee to an IRA established by the employee.

Once a contribution is made to a SEP, it is nonforfeitable. The money contributed belongs to the employee and cannot be returned to the employer. If employment is terminated, the entire balance in the SEP account belongs to the former employee. As in the case with most qualified plans, employers receive a deduction for contributions made to a SEP plan. SEPs have higher contribution limits: You may contribute up to 15 percent of each employee's annual compensation or $30,000, whichever is less, to their SEP accounts.

KEEPING YOUR EYE ON RETIREMENT

When you retire, how much you will have depends on such factors as interest rates and managing funds for the best return. The following example illustrates the power of tax-deferred compounding.

Example 3—

Assume a $2,000 annual investment at the beginning of each year, an 8 percent fixed return, and a 39.6 percent tax bracket. The after-tax dollar amount of the tax-deferred investment upon withdrawal at retirement (assuming that contributions were not deductible) would be $226,566 while taxable investment would grow only to $129,107, as shown in Figure 1.

Figure 1—

The Power of Tax-Deferred Growth

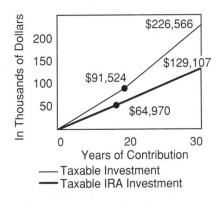

A couple of percentage points mean a lot. A $50,000 tax-free pension fund earning 6 percent will be $287,150 after 30 years. The same amount invested at 9 percent will give you $663,400 after 30 years.

Example 4—

$10,000 invested at 10%, 12%, or 15% after
30 years:

	10%	12%	15%
Amount invested	$ 10,000	$10,000	$10,000
Future value of $1 (Table 1, Chapter 7)	17.449	29.960	66.212
Compound amount after 30 years	$174,490	$299,600	$662,120

Even if your pension plan is professionally
managed, you may select different investments
based on return rate and risk. With the privilege of
periodic switching, you may apportion your savings, say from stocks to bonds.

What interest rate are you earning? The interest rate should exceed the inflation rate. Compound
tax-free interest will make your pension grow.

Do You Qualify for an IRA?

If you are not covered through a company pension
plan, or want to save privately, you may set up your
own IRA, Keogh, or annuity plan.

The IRA is a retirement savings plan that individuals set up themselves. If you do not have a company retirement plan, you can take an IRA tax deduction from adjusted gross income (AGI) up to
$2,000. If you are self-employed, you can establish
a Keogh plan. A married couple may contribute
up to $4,000 provided each earns $2,000 (maximum
of $2,250 if there is a nonworking spouse). IRA con-
tributions accumulate tax-free and are also either
tax deductible or exempt from your income. Several things to remember:

1. An individual covered by an employer's pension plan, or whose spouse is covered by such a plan (assuming a joint tax return is filed), may only qualify for a partial deduction—or no deduction—based on the adjusted gross income (AGI). The deduction phases out (that is, the allowable deductions are reduced $1 for each $5 increase in income) when the taxpayer's income increases over a specified amount, and is eliminated when it exceeds a higher amount. The following IRS guideline is used for this purpose.

Filing status:	Deduction is reduced if AGI is within range of:	Deduction is eliminated if AGI is:
Single, or head of household	$25,000 - $35,000	$35,000 or more
Married-joint return, or qualifying widow(er)	$40,000 - $50,000	$50,000 or more
Married-separate return	$0 - $10,000	$10,000 or more

Example 5—

You are single and have an adjusted gross income of $28,000. You can deduct an IRA contribution of:

$2,000 - [($28,000 - $25,000)/$5 x $1] = $1,400

2. Withdrawals before age 59 1/2 will incur a 10 percent penalty except under special circumstances. Premature withdrawals are taxed as ordinary income.

3. It is not mandatory that distributions begin until the age of 70 1/2. If you do not need the income, allow the account to further accumulate

past age 59 1/2 so as to add a considerable amount to the corpus of your IRA.

4. Nonwithdrawals after 70 1/2 will incur a 50 percent penalty on the minimum amount that should have been withdrawn.

5. If you are over 70 1/2 years of age, you are not allowed to contribute to an IRA.

Are You Eligible for a Keogh Plan?

A Keogh pension plan, also called an HR 10 plan, is tax-deferred for self-employed people satisfying specified criteria. It can take three forms: a profit-sharing plan, a money purchase pension plan, or a combination of both. The maximum contribution rate is 25 percent of "after Keogh deduction" earnings or $30,000, whichever is less. Thus, the effective contribution rate is 20 percent.

Example 6—

Net earnings	$100,000
Keogh contribution	20,000 (effective 20%)
After Keogh earnings	80,000

The Keogh contribution of $20,000 is 25 percent of the "after Keogh deduction" earnings of $80,000.

How Do Annuities Work?

Annuities are insurance contracts. You can pay a single, large premium, annual premiums, or flexible premiums to the company, and at retirement you can obtain periodic payments for a specified time (the maximum being lifetime) or take periodic withdrawals. The periodic withdrawals have limits set by the insurance company. The payments accumulate tax-free and are subject to tax only when withdrawn when you retire. Hopefully, your tax-rate will be lower at that time. Annuity payments begin at retirement. The two types of annuities are fixed and variable.

Fixed (guaranteed) annuities. You are guaranteed for a year or more your principal plus a minimum interest. There is *no* capital gains (or appreciation) potential with fixed annuities. There is low risk with this policy. You get both a "minimum" interest rate plus an "extra" interest rate based on prevailing rates in the market. The following is a summary of fixed annuities.

Tax-deferred income	Yes
Price stability	Yes
Capital gain (or loss) potential	No
Different payout options	Yes
Different payment options	Yes
Contribution limits	No (except due to age)
Source of funds	Not restricted to earned income
Choice of underlying investments	No
Federal deposit insurance	No
Surrender charge	Yes
IRS early withdrawal penalty	Yes
Mandatory withdrawals	Typically, by age 85
Rate-guaranteed periods	For 1, 3, 5, 7, or 10 years

Like a bond or a bond fund, a fixed annuity may fail to provide a satisfactory inflation hedge, thereby subjecting the investor to purchasing-power risk.

Variable annuities. A variable annuity has none of the guarantees of fixed annuities. The policy value changes with the performance of an underlying investment fund, much like a mutual fund within a family of funds. Investment risk lies with the investor. Many insurance companies permit you to change to a different fund of a variable type and to change the percentage mix of the funds as frequently as the annuity contract allows. You pay taxes on the amount distributed from the capital appreciation of the annuity value.

Here is a summary of variable annuities.

Tax-deferred income	Yes
Price stability	No
Capital-gain (or loss) potential	Yes
Different payout options	Yes
Different payment options	Yes
Contribution limits	No (except due to age)
Source of funds	Not restricted to earned income
Choice of underlying investments	Yes
Federal deposit insurance	No
Grace period	Yes
Surrender charge	Yes
IRS early withdrawal penalty	Yes
Mandatory withdrawals	Typically, by age 85
Rate-guaranteed periods	No

What Are Advantages of Annuities?

Annuities offer these advantages:

- Tax-deferred compounding of interest.
- Unlike retirement plans, annual contributions are not restricted.
- Another form of savings plan.

What Are the Disadvantages of Annuities?

Disadvantages of annuities are:

- Commission (usually 7 or 8 percent) is often high.

- You cannot withdraw funds before age 59 1/2. Otherwise, a tax penalty will be assessed (10 percent charge). Also, there are penalties called *surrender charges* imposed by the insurance carrier if you cash in the policy early. However, no penalty would apply if you become disabled or die. (One way to avoid the early withdrawal penalty is to annuitize, taking regular payments for the remainder of your life). Such charges may start around 7 percent for withdrawals in the first year and phase down by one percentage point each year after that.

- The interest earned may not keep up with and/or be less than the return on alternative investment opportunities.

- Annuity income is taxed as income, not as capital gains, which can be stiff if you are in a high tax bracket.

- They are *nonqualified* annuities, meaning annuities having a tax-deferral benefit but paid in after-tax dollars.

What Are Qualified Annuities?

Qualified annuities, on the other hand, fund pension plans. The contributions accumulate tax-free and are either tax deductible or exempt from your income. If you qualify, always take advantage of IRAs and Keoghs, because contributions are in pre-tax dollars.

What Are Some Types of Annuities?

Annuities may include:

Life annuity. The annuity continues for the life of the annuitant. This usually results in the highest periodic payment.

Life annuity with period certain. The annuity covers the life of the annuitant, but if that person dies early, the annuity continues for a specified minimum period.

Joint and last survivor annuity. If the annuitant dies, the annuity continues for the life of another person (usually the spouse).

What Sales Charges Exist?

You can invest in variable annuity contracts by making lump-sum investments or by signing a long-term investment contract (contractual plans). The plan custodian is required to send investors a statement of total charges within 60 days after the plan certificate is issued, and inform you of the right to withdraw within 45 days from the date the notice is mailed. Sales charges vary.

Front-end load. Up to 50 percent of the sales charges may be deducted from the first 12 monthly payments (in equal amounts). If the plan is liquidated within 18 months, you receive a refund of sales charges paid in excess of 15 percent of the total invested.

Spread-load plan. Up to 64 percent of all sales charges over the first four years can be deducted, but no more than 20 percent in any one year.

How Do You Purchase Annuities?

Advice in purchasing annuities follows.

- Be wary of unusually high "teaser" rates, which are a sign of a financially weak company. Deal with a firm that is financially sound and strong. There was an instance where Baldwin-United, a leading annuity seller, filed for bankruptcy.
- Purchase annuities only from highly rated insurance companies. Refer to A.M. Best's publication, *Best's Insurance Reports.* Also refer to Standard & Poor's, Moody's, and Duff & Phelps rating publications.
- Diversify among insurance companies to get a blending of rates and maturities. In fact, dozens of mutual fund families manage variable annuity portfolios.
- Evaluate the insurance companies' investment performance.
- Diversify the variable annuities.
- Consider all service charges as well as contract features and terms.
- Closely review the prospectus.
- Compare insurance companies.

Note: For comparison shopping, refer to the monthly *Morningstar Variable Annuity/Life Performance Report,* (800) 876-5005, and *Lipper Mutual Fund Quarterly on Variable Annuities and Life Accounts* appearing in *Barron's.*

When Is an Annuity Right for You?

Consider an annuity if you:

- Do not have other tax-free pension plans, such as Keoghs
- Want to receive fixed payments over a stated time period (e.g., retirees)

- Want the assurance of a guaranteed check when you retire.
- Aren't comfortable with selecting your own investments, such as stocks.

    You shouldn't consider annuities if you:

- Have alternative tax-deferred savings plans.
- Anticipate adequate income and savings from other sources.

MUTUAL FUNDS

If you are an investor with limited resources who wants funds managed by experts, you can get diversification by investing in a mutual fund. A mutual fund is an investment company that is in the business of investing and managing other people's money. It invests in a variety of securities. When you buy shares in a mutual fund, you become a part owner of such a portfolio of securities.

WHAT IS MUTUAL FUND INVESTING?

A mutual fund is managed by professionals. It uses investors' money to buy diversified securities portfolios. Ownership is in the form of proportionate shares.

Example 1—

Mutual Fund X has the securities below:

Stock	Number of Shares
GE	200
AT&T	300
ITT	500

If you have a 3 percent ownership in the fund, it equals:

6 shares of GE, 9 shares of AT&T, and 15 shares of ITT.

WHAT ARE THE ATTRIBUTES OF MUTUAL FUNDS?

Mutual fund investing is characterized by:

1. *Diversification.* Your investment money may be used to buy a broad range of equity, debt, and other securities. Diversification reduces your risk.
2. *Automatic reinvestment.* Dividends, interest, and capital gains may be reinvested into the fund, usually at no charge
3. *Automatic withdrawals.* Funds may be withdrawn, usually at no charge.
4. *Liquidity.* You can redeem your shares at any time.
5. *Switching.* You can go from one fund type to another in a family of funds.
6. *Small minimum investment.* Some mutual funds can be bought into initially for less than $1,000.

WHAT ARE COMMON SERVICES OFFERED BY MUTUAL FUNDS?

A major reason for the attractiveness of mutual funds is the many convenient services offered to their shareholders. Some can be useful in your investment strategy. Common services are summarized in Table 1.

Table 1—
Major Services of Mutual Funds

1. Accounting and reporting for tax purposes
2. Safekeeping and custodian services

3. Automatic reinvestment
4. Exchange privileges
5. Periodic withdrawals
6. Checking privileges
7. Acceptance of small investments
8. Tax-sheltered plan (e.g., IRA and Keogh)
9. Guardianship under the Uniform Gift to Minor Act
10. Pre-authorized check plan

HOW IS NET ASSET VALUE (NAV) DETERMINED?

The price of a mutual fund share is stated as net asset value (NAV). It is computed as follows:

$$\frac{\text{Fund's total assets - debt}}{\text{Number of shares outstanding in the fund}}$$

Example 2—

Assume that on a given date the following market values apply. The fund has liabilities of $4,500. The NAV of the fund is calculated below:

(a) GE—$100 per share x 200 shares	=	$20,000
(b) Westinghouse—$50 per share x 300 shares	=	15,000
(c) CBS—$75 per share x 100 shares	=	7,500
Total assets		$42,500
(d) Liabilities		4,500
(e) Net asset value of the fund's portfolio		$38,000
(f) Number of shares outstanding in the fund		1,000
(g) Net asset value (NAV) per share = (E)/(F)		$38

Assume you own 3 percent of the fund.
Your investment is worth:

3% x 1,000 shares = 30 shares; 30 shares x $38 = $1,140

HOW DO YOU MAKE MONEY IN A MUTUAL FUND?

You make money from the change in net asset value, dividends, and capital gains.

Dividends

Mutual funds typically pay out a large percentage of their income. You are fully taxed on dividends.

Capital Gains Distribution

Capital gains are distributed each year to fund holders. You are taxed at the maximum capital gains rate of 28 percent. Do not just consider NAV. It only shows the current market value of your portfolio. Look at the number of shares you own and total value. Your shares will increase over time from dividends and capital gains reinvestment into more shares.

Multiply the number of shares you own by the net asset value per share to determine value.

WHAT IS THE TOTAL RETURN ON THE MUTUAL FUND?

Total return equals:

(dividends + capital gains distributed
+ price appreciation in fund)

The percentage return equals:

(Dividends + capital gain distributions
+ (ending NAV - beginning NAV))

Beginning NAV

where (ending NAV - beginning NAV) is price appreciation.

Example 3—

Your mutual fund paid dividends of $1.00 per share and capital gain distributions of $.40 per share this year. NAV at the beginning of the year was $10.00 per share, and $12 at year-end. Percentage return equals:

$$\frac{\$1.00 + \$.40 + (\$12 - \$10)}{\$10} = \frac{\$3.40}{\$10} = 34\%$$

HOW MUCH WILL MUTUAL FUNDS CHARGE YOU?

If you invest in a mutual fund, there will be some kind of fee. When shopping for funds, you should take a close look at these charges. The charges may be classified as follows: load, management fee, 12b-1 fees, back-end loads, deferred loads, and reinvestment loads.

Load

A load is the fee to buy shares as a form of sales charge.

Such charges may range from 1 to 8.5 percent (maximum legal limit) of the amount invested. That means if you invested $1,000 in a fund with an 8.5 percent load, only $915 would go into the fund. Mutual fund prices are stated in "bid" and "ask" form. The bid is the price the fund will buy back its shares (at the NAV). The ask or "offer" is the price the investor must pay to buy shares. The difference between the offer and bid is the load. "No-load" mutual funds have no sales fees so there is the same bid and ask prices. *Note:* A sales fee does not mean better performance of the fund. The fee will reduce your net return rate. Load funds do not perform better than no-load funds.

Management and Expense Fees

All funds ("no load" or "load") charge a fee to pay a portfolio manager. It typically ranges from 0.5 percent to 1 percent of the fund's assets.

12b-1 Fees

These charges are for advertising and promotion. They typically range from 0.25 percent to 0.30 percent, but some run as high as 1.25 percent.

Back-end Loads, or Redemption Fees

These are charged when you sell your shares. They are based on a percentage of the shares' net asset value, so steep back-end loads can reduce your profits or increase your loss.

Deferred Load, or Contingent Deferred Sales Fees

These are deducted from your original investment if you sell shares before a specified period.

Reinvestment Loads

These fees are taken out of reinvested interest, dividends, and capital gains. For example, if you receive a capital gains distribution of $150 and the reinvestment fee is 7 percent, the fund will keep $10.50 and reinvest $139.50.

WHAT KINDS OF MUTUAL FUNDS EXIST?

Mutual funds are categorized by type depending on purpose, structure, fees, switching privileges, return potential, and risk. You can virtually invest in any type of fund based on your investment goals.

There are two basic types of funds: open-end funds, commonly called mutual funds, which can sell an unlimited number of ownership shares, and closed-end funds, which can issue only a limited (fixed) number.

What Is the Difference between Open-End and Closed-End Funds?

In *open-end funds*, you purchase from and sell shares back to the fund. You can redeem shares when you so desire. Shares are bought at NAV plus service fee and redeemed at NAV less a commission. In *closed-end funds* there is a fixed number of shares traded on the stock exchange or over-the-counter market. Share price is determined independently of NAV by factors of supply and demand. Management fees are assessed by all funds.

Table 2 summarizes the differences between open-end funds, known simply as mutual funds, and closed-end investment companies.

Table 2—

Differences Between Open-End and Closed-End Funds

	Mutual Funds	Closed-end Funds
Number of shares	Fluctuates	Fixed
Traded at net asset value (NAV)	Yes	No—a discount or premium from NAV
Liquidity	Almost immediate	3 business days
Dividends and capital gain	Can be reinvested	Some offer automatic reinvestment
Accessibility	Yes; via a toll-free phone; check-writing privileges	Limited
Method of purchase	Direct from fund or fund salesperson	Stock exchange or OTC
Flexibility	Yes, exchange privileges	No
Commission	Load or no-load	Yes

What Are the Types of Mutual Funds?

Mutual funds may be categorized as follows:

Money market funds. Money market funds invest solely in short-term debt securities. The price of the fund is constant, so it is very conservative. You can buy and sell shares at $1.00. Money market funds provide high interest income with safe principal.

Growth funds. Growth funds want high return via capital gains. They usually invest in companies with growth exceeding the inflation rate. The stocks have constant, long-term, current income. Like other growth investments, the aim of these funds is to increase share value, not pay dividends.

Aggressive growth (capital appreciation) funds. Funds taking greater risk for high capital appreciation. Dividend income is secondary. They concentrate on new, high-tech businesses. They offer the greatest potential for growth, but also the greater risk. *Note*: These funds are appropriate if you are not especially worried about near-term variability in return but want long-term appreciation. Aggressive strategies taken may consist of leverage purchases, short selling, call options, put options, and buying stock.

Income funds. Income funds generate current income through investments in securities that pay interest or a cash dividend. These securities include dividend-paying stocks, corporate bonds, and a variety of government securities. Generally, the higher the income sought, the riskier the underlying investments. They offer current income with low to high risk.

Growth and income funds. Growth and income funds emphasize current dividend or interest and capital appreciation. They offer moderate growth potential and moderate risk. The objective is long-term growth. Share value should be stable.

Balanced funds. Balanced funds seek preservation of capital while seeking growth and income. The aim of these funds is to "balance" the portfolio with

the best ratio of stocks and bonds within the funds'
investment objective guidelines. This is done to
adjust to prevailing market conditions. Balanced
funds tend to underperform all-stock funds in
strong bull markets.

Index funds. Index funds invest in a broad group
of stocks based on an index such as the Standard &
Poor's 500. Vanguard Index Trust Fund matches
the stock index.

Sector (specialized) funds. Sector funds invest by
industry (ies). High risk exists because the fortunes
of the fund depend of the performance of the specific industry. If an industry, such as pharmaceuti-
cals, takes a "hit" huge losses will ensue.

International funds. International funds invest in
securities of overseas (foreign) companies. Some
international funds invest in one geographic area,
such as Fidelity Canada Fund and Vanguard Trust-
ees Commingled International Portfolio. Fund
value increases if the dollar decreases due to exchange rates.

Municipal tax-exempt funds. Tax-free funds seek
current, tax-free income by investing for the most
part in tax-exempt bonds issued by municipalities
to build schools, highways and public projects.
They offer current tax-exempt income, with low to
high risk depending on the yield sought and individual investments.

WHAT INVESTMENT PROGRAMS ARE
TIED WITH MUTUAL FUNDS?

There many different kinds of mutual funds as well
as diverse ways to buy them. You should consider

your financial status and investment objectives. Some available investment programs follow:

Accumulation Plan. You invest periodically (e.g, monthly). Minimum investments may be required (e.g., $100 per month). This approach is advisable for long-term investors.

Withdrawal Plan. You obtain periodic payments (e.g., quarterly) of a given sum.

Life Insurance-Mutual Fund Plans. A combination of life insurance and shares of a mutual fund. If the fund performs well, it pays your insurance premiums. If not, you must pay the premium.

Automatic Dividend Reinvestment. Fund proceeds (dividends and capital gains) are automatically reinvested.

Individual Retirement Accounts (IRA). You contribute $2,000 before-tax-income each year. When you take out money at retirement, you do so at a lower tax rate.

Payroll Deduction Plans. Amounts are withheld from your salary and used to buy fund shares. Typically, there is no load.

403 (B) Plan. This is for employees working for non-profit entities.

HOW DOES A BOND (INCOME) FUND WORK?

In selecting a bond fund, consider:

- *Quality*. How is the fund rated by Standard & Poor's and Moody's?

- *Maturity*. What is the life? What effect will changing interest rates have? A longer maturity means wider price fluctuations. For example, a 10-year bond varies more in price than a 5-year bond. *Note:* Check out the *duration* of your bond fund. Some bond funds manage to produce top returns without undue volatility. For example, Harbor Bond Fund has returned a respectable return—an annualized 11.5 percent over the past five years. Yet its duration is a middle-of-road 5.3 years.

- *Premium or discount*. Funds selling at a premium are above face value. Such funds are less susceptible to losses if interest rates increase. Funds selling at a discount are below face value. Bonds trading at a discount to face value can lose most.

- *Total return*. Bonds generate more than interest payouts. There is also the question of capital gains or losses, which can make a huge difference in performance. Total return reflects both interest and price changes.

- *Commissions, loads, or fees*. Check fees. The difference between yields on the best and worst bond funds is often slight, and such fees can be more important to total return than the money manager. Check out the expense ratio.

- *Prepayment risk* and *currency risk*. Prepayment risk exists with funds that invest in mortgage-backed securities, such as Ginnie Maes. Mortgage prepayments accelerate when interest rates decline, and can appreciably shorten your expected long-term string of high payments. Currency risk exists with international bond funds. For example, some international funds frequently generate handsome returns, not because of higher interest abroad, but because of a fall in the U.S. dollar value.

What Are Some Guidelines to Follow When Investing in a Bond Fund?

You must remember the following guidelines:

- Increasing interest rates means lower NAV of bond funds. Therefore, instead of concentrating just on current yield, consider the total return (yield plus capital gains from declining interest rates or less capital losses if interest rates increase).

- All bond funds do not react the same way when interest rates decline. If you believe interest rates will drop, purchase funds that invest in U.S. Treasuries or high-quality corporate bonds. Consider high-yield junk bonds if you think interest rates will be stable or up. Consider the *duration* of the fund in measuring interest rate risk.

- Bond funds vary greatly. Some are aggressively managed and contain high risks; others buy only government issues and are best suited for conservative investors. Read the prospectus.

- Consider the taxability of interest payments. Interest payments on municipal bonds are generally free from federal income tax and from some state taxes if issued within that state, which is particularly important for investors living in states with high tax rates.

  Note: Bond funds are rated on the basis of *standardized (SEC) yield.*

ARE TAX-EXEMPT MUNICIPAL BOND FUNDS FOR YOU?

Increases in tax rates have brought tax-free income more attention lately. But you don't need to be in the top brackets to benefit from municipal bonds.

As long as your federal rate is 28 percent, you should give serious consideration to municipal bond funds. When trying to decide how much better (or worse) off you would be with a tax-exempt bond fund than with a taxable bond fund, it's useful to examine your taxable equivalent yield, which was discussed earlier.

If similar but taxable bond funds yield less than your taxable equivalent yield, then you are better off in the muni fund; if taxable funds yield more, you are better off in the taxable fund. What is meant by "similar"? It is important to compare bond funds with a similar average maturity and credit quality. Comparing, for example, the taxable equivalent yield of a short-term muni portfolio with a long-term, high-yield corporate fund is not meaningful. *Note*: Muni-bond funds have call risk, which refers to the danger that a bond carrying a relatively high coupon will be called in for early redemption by its issuer. Nearly all municipal bonds have some sort of call provision.

In picking a muni-bond fund, what factors should you consider?

1. *Portfolio composition*. What sectors does the fund invest in? Is this diversified enough?

2. *Credit quality*. Look at the breakdown of the fund in terms of credit rating. The larger the proportion of investment-grade bonds, the lower the credit risk.

3. *Duration*. The longer the duration, the greater the interest rate risk.

4. *Standard deviation*. The most common statistical indicator of an asset's risk.

5. *Yield*. Based on the standardized SEC 30-day yield and total return.

6. *Expense ratio*.

ARE UNIT INVESTMENT TRUSTS FOR YOU?

Similar to a mutual fund, a unit investment trust (UIT) gives investors the benefits of a professionally managed, diversified portfolio. But, unlike a mutual fund, the portfolio is constant—after the initial selections are made, active management ceases. Unit investment trusts include tax-free municipals, corporate bonds, preferred stock, and common stock. Unit trusts are good for those on fixed income and who are guaranteed a return on capital. Investors' shares are redeemed when the fund terminates.

WHAT HAS BEEN THE PERFORMANCE OF THEIR MUTUAL FUND?

Mutual funds, like any other investments, are evaluated on the basis of return and risk.

What Is the Return on the Mutual Fund?

The return on a mutual fund equals (1) dividend (interest) income, (2) capital gains, and (3) change in NAV of the fund. Using the statement you get from the mutual fund, complete the form in Figure 1.

The following example uses the data provided in Figure 2.

Figure 1—

Figuring Your Personal Rate of Return

	Example	*Your Fund*
1. The number of months for which your fund's performance is being measured.	5	_____
2. Your investment at the beginning of the period. (Multiply the total number of shares owned by the NAV.) [(0 + 246.063) x $10.16]	$2,500.00	_____
3. The ending value of your investment. (Multiply the number of shares you currently own by the current NAV.) (578.537 x $11.91)	$6,890.38	_____
4. Total dividends and capital gains received in cash—not reinvested ($0)	0.00	_____
5. All additional investments (any redemptions subtracted) ($2,500+1,000)	$3,500.00	_____

6. Computation of your gain or loss

Step (a):	Add line 2 to 1/2 of the total on line 5 [$2500 + 1/2($3500)]	$4,250.00	_____
Step (b):	Add line 3 and line 4, then subtract 1/2 of the total on line 5 [($6890.38 + $0) - 1/2($3500)]	$5,140.38	_____
Step (c):	Divide the Step (b) sum by the Step (a) sum ($5140.38/$4250)	1.2095	_____

Step (d): Subtract the
numeral 1 from the
result of Step (c),
then multiply by 100
[(1.2095 - 1) x 100]   20.95   _____

7. Compute your
annualized return.
(Divide the number of
months on line 1 into
12; multiply the result by
the Step (d) %.)   50.28   _____
[(12/5) x 20.95]

Figure 2—

Your Mutual Fund, Inc.

Date (19X1)	Transaction	Dollar Amount	Share Price	Shares	Shares Owned
	Beginning balance				0.000
07/19	Purchase	$2,500.00	$10.16	246.063	246.063
08/17	Purchase	2,500.00	10.87	229.991	476.054
11/30	Purchase	1,000.00	11.27	88.731	564.785
12/22	Dividend reinvest .09	50.83	11.91	4.268	569.053
12/22	Short-term Cg rein .07	39.53	11.91	3.319	572.372
12/22	Reinvest cap gain .13	73.42	11.91	6.165	578.537
12/22	Ending balance	$6,890.38	11.91		578.537

WHAT ARE THE MEASURES OF RISK (OR VOLATILITY) OF A MUTUAL FUND?

In evaluating fund performance, consider the published measures of risk or volatility of the funds to ascertain the amount of risk. There are three popular measures of risk: Beta, R-squared, and standard deviation.

What Is Beta?

Beta shows how volatile a mutual fund is compared with the market as a whole, as measured by the Standard & Poor's 500 index on the equity side and the Lehman Brothers Aggregate Index on the bond side.

Beta	Meaning
1.0	A fund goes up in price the same as the market.
>1.0	The fund goes higher in bull markets and lower in bear markets than the market.
<1.0	The fund is risky relative to the market.

Example 4—

A fund with a 1.10 beta is expected to perform 10 percent better than the market in up markets, and 10 percent worse in down markets. By the same token, a fund with a beta of 0.75 should capture 75 percent of the market gains in a rally and lose only 75 percent as much in a decline.

What Are R-Squared and Standard Deviation?

Some analysts prefer to use R-squared or standard deviation, shown as "R^2" or "Std. Dev." in mutual fund tables such as those in Morningstar's Mutual Fund Values. R-squared, ranging from 0 to 100, gives you an idea about what percentage of a fund's performance is explained by that of the benchmark (such as S&P). The higher the R-squared, the higher the relationship between the funds and the benchmark and thus the more relevant is the beta figure.

Standard deviation says that in 95 cases out of 100, the fund's period-ending price will be plus or minus a certain percentage of its price at the beginning of the period, usually a month. In general, the higher the standard deviation, the greater the volatility or risk.

Note: If beta, R^2, and/or standard deviation are used to help pick a fund, these measures should cover at least *three years* to give the most accurate picture about the risk and instability of the fund. All these numbers, of course, should be weighed against other indicators, including total return over at least five years, performance in up and down markets, and the experience of the fund manager.

Risk measures such as beta, R^2, and standard deviation for mutual funds are published in many investment publications, including *Value Line Mutual Fund Survey* and *Morningstar's Mutual Fund Values.* See Figure 3 for a sample "Mutual Fund Values Report" by Morningstar.

Figure 3—

	Alpha	Beta	R^2	Std.Dev
	-1.7	0.83	96	4.85
Pct. Rank — All Funds	49	59	8	50
Objective	22	22	9	23

Percentile Ranks: 1=Highest   100=Lowest
Except MFV RISK: 1=Lowest   100=Highest

WHAT IS ALPHA VALUE?

Alpha value of a security, also called *average differential return*, is the difference between the actual return and the return predicted by the overall mutual fund *beta*. It has been used to evaluate performance of mutual funds. Generally, a positive alpha (excess return) indicates superior performance, while a negative value leads to the opposite conclusion.

Example 5—

Assume that the market return (r_m) is 8 percent and the risk-free rate (r_f) is 5 percent. XYZ fund, with a beta of 1.5, returned 7.5 percent. The expected return is then 9.5 percent (5% + 1.5(8% - 5%)]. That means the fund has a negative alpha of 1.5 percent (9.5% - 8%).

Note: (1)"Keep your alpha high and your beta low" is a basic strategy for those who wish to generate good investment performance.

(2) A key question for investors is: Can a fund consistently perform at positive alpha levels?

Note: Morningstar's Mutual Fund Values (Figure 3) shows the alpha value as well as beta, R^2, and standard deviation.

HOW DO YOU CHOOSE A MUTUAL FUND?

Selecting the "right" mutual fund for you involves the following steps:

1. Prepare a fund listing to check what type of fund is appropriate for your risk tolerance and investment needs and objectives.

2. Read the prospectus to choose a fund satisfying your requirements and risk level. The prospectus includes the fund's purpose, selection criteria, performance statistics, fees, and financial condition. Read the statement of objectives as well as risk considerations and investment constraints. Look at the "Statement of Additional Information," containing charges and investment portfolio. Review for annual and quarterly financial information.

3. Does the fund match your requirements?

4. How has the fund performed in both good and bad times over the past 10 years? Compare this fund to comparable funds and market averages of the same type. Examine standard deviation in financial publications. What is the trend in per-share and dollar values?

     Note: Many magazines, such as *Business Week, Kiplinger's Personal Finance, Worth, Consumer Reports, Financial World, Forbes,* and *U.S. News and World Report* publish mutual fund performance statistics. Investment newsletters, such as *Morningstar* and *Lipper Analytical,* publish the fund ranking (to be discussed later), which may be a place to start.

5. How good is fund management? *Note:* The
    Value Line Mutual Fund Survey has recently
    added a "Manager Ratings" box to its one-page
    fund reviews to give investors an idea of how
    that fund manager's performance ranks against
    those of his or her peers. Keep in mind that your
    fund is only going to do as well as its
    manager(s).

6. What is the quality of the stock portfolio? How
    diversified is it? *Note: Morningstar Mutual Funds*
    has recently added a special securities section
    to its fund-data page to show what percentage
    of a fund's assets were invested in derivatives,
    which are regarded risky securities.

7. Check out a fund's expense ratio, which is the
    percentage of a fund's net assets going annu-
    ally to cover management fees, transaction
    costs, administrative overhead, legal and audit-
    ing fees, and marketing costs (12b-1 fees). You
    find this information in the prospectus under
    the heading "Annual Fund Operating Ex-
    penses." Compare expense ratios in similar
    funds (see the table below) since they can af-
    fect a fund's overall performance. For example,
    one recent study of fund performance found
    that a $10,000 investment in two no-load funds,
    each earning 9 percent over 20 years, would
    grow to $30,475 in a fund with a 3 percent ex-
    pense ratio and $45,840 in a fund with a 1 per-
    cent expense ratio.

Fund	Average Expense Ratio
Stock funds	1.5%
Taxable bond funds	1.0
Municipal bond funds	0.75

8. Compare sales and redemption fees and share-
    holder services.

9. Check out fund rankings provided by various ranking services, such as *Lipper Analytical Services, Inc.* and *Morningstar.* The so-called performance benchmarking can be used as a way to objectively measure a fund's performance.

WHAT IS PERFORMANCE BENCHMARKING?

One way to objectively measure your fund's performance is to compare it to similar groups of investments —mutual fund peer groups and market indexes. Mutual fund peer group rankings report performance for funds with similar asset classes, strategies, objectives, and risk level.

More about Mutual Fund Peer Group Rankings

Peer group is one objective source of information that can assist you in picking the right fund. Typically, funds are first sliced into various categories based on their investment goals. Then each fund is ranked according to a chosen criteria (such as a five-year total return, risk, or risk-adjusted return) by where it falls among all funds in its category. For example, funds in the top 20 percent get a "1" ranking and the bottom 20 percent get a "5." The following is a partial list of ranking sources.

Morningstar Rankings

This is a risk measurement system for comparing more than 2,000 mutual funds' long-term performance, available from Chicago-based Morningstar. The system rates stock and bond funds from five stars (the best) to no stars (the worst, or unrated). Morningstar uses a proprietary system that measures a mutual fund's price and dividend performance as well as the risks taken by the fund management to get those results. The rankings are then made from comparing a fund both in its own category and against the industry as a whole. Thus, the best-performing fund in a category that has been a weak market sector might get only two or three stars.

When choosing among mutual funds, investors can use Morningstar rankings to find potentially better-performing investments. Many brokerages and financial planning firms limit their clients' investments to 5-star and 4-star funds. But choosing a 5-star fund over a 3-star fund is not always the correct choice. For one, Morningstar's rankings reflect past performance and that often slants the reviews toward funds with recently successful investment styles.

In addition, within each category—notably a poorly performing sector—the highest rated fund may have succeeded by limiting its exposure to certain risks. If an investor believed that an out-of-favor market sector was ready to return, he might want to buy a fund with a lower rating that was more fully invested in that sector. *Lipper Mutual Fund Rankings* and *Value Line Mutual Fund Survey* are two other important sources.

Magazine Rankings

Before buying or selling a fund, you should consult other fund-watching sources. *Business Week, Fortune, Forbes*, and *Money* magazines all print periodic analyses of individual funds and their rankings, as do many newsletters and newspapers.

WHAT MARKET INDEXES ARE USED AS BENCHMARKS?

Each fund describes its strategy and objective and also lists relevant market indexes (see Figure 4). These market indexes are also found in *The Wall Street Journal*, *Barron's*, and *Investor's Business Daily*. First, find the total average annual return for the 1-, 5-, and 10-year periods for the benchmark and compare those figures with the fund's returns for the exact same periods. Compare bid positive and negative differences between the two before making a decision about getting into the fund or staying in it.

Figure 4—

Typical Market Indexes Used as Performance Benchmarks

Funds	*Index*
Domestic	
Growth	S&P 500
Aggressive Growth	Value Line
Small Company	Russell 2000
Government Bond	Various Lehman Bros. Government/Corporate Bond Indexes
Municipal Bond	Lehman Bros. Municipal Bond Index
International	
Global	Morgan Stanley International World Index, Morgan Stanley Europe, Australia, and the Far East (EAFE) Indexes
Foreign Bond	Salomon Bros. Non-U.S. Dollar World Bond Index
Global Bond	Shearson World Bond Index

WHAT RISK-REDUCING STRATEGIES FOR INVESTING IN MUTUAL FUNDS ARE AVAILABLE?

In a bearish market, minimizing or spreading risks is particularly important. Below are five proven risk-reducing strategies for making money in mutual funds.

1. Shoot for low-cost funds.

    Especially in difficult times, fees and expenses will loom larger, deepening losses and prolonging subsequent recoveries.

2. Build a well-balanced, diversified portfolio.

    Sensible diversification will spread (or minimize) risks.

3. Use the dollar-cost average method.

    Investing a fixed amount of money at regular intervals keeps you from committing your whole savings at a market peak. This is how the technique works. If your fund's NAV drops, your next payment automatically picks up more of the low-priced shares, cuts your average cost per share, and raises your ultimate gain. This is discussed later.

4. Divide your money among fund managers with different styles and philosophies.

    Funds with differing styles will take turns outperforming, and being outperformed by, those with other styles. In a nutshell, you should diversify across mutual funds or a family of funds.

5. Concentrate on short- or intermediate-term bond funds.

    Typically, the longer the maturity of the bonds in a fund's portfolio, the greater the fund's return—but also the deeper its losses as interest rates rise.

HOW DOES DOLLAR-COST AVERAGING WORK?

Dollar-cost averaging is an investment strategy designed to take advantage of the market's long-term upward bias while reducing risk over time. It simply means that you invest the same amount of money on a regular schedule, whatever the market price. It eliminates the need to predict share-price movements and to figure out the right time to buy, and it protects you from putting too much money into the market at just the wrong time. Under this strategy, you buy more shares when the share price of your fund is down and fewer shares when the price of the fund is high, which can potentially lower your average cost per share and allow you to buy more shares. And lowering your cost can reduce your downside risk. It also ensures that the entire portfolio will not be purchased at temporarily inflated prices.

Dollar-cost averaging has proven most effective for mutual fund investing, whose typically small investment minimums allow you to implement this strategy easily in a cost-effective way. Many funds and brokerages make this process easy by allowing purchases through direct deductions from investors' checking accounts or paychecks.

You may unknowingly be using this strategy as part of employer-sponsored savings plans such as 401(k) retirement programs. Many of these benefit plans routinely make equal purchases of assets at set periods, quietly accomplishing dollar-cost averaging.

Dollar-cost averaging will work as long as prices of the fund targeted by the strategy rise over the long haul. Figure 5 shows how dollar-cost averaging works for a no-load mutual fund and compares in a hypothetical situation with two other investment strategies: lump-sum, up-front investment

and lump-sum investment after saving (see Figure
6).

Figure 5—

Dollar-Costing Based Mutual Fund Purchase Plan

Period	Amount Invested	Share Price	Shares Purchased
1	$100	$12.50	8
2	100	8.00	12.5
3	100	10.00	10
4	100	8.00	12.5
5	100	10.00	10
6	100	12.50	8
7	100	14.28	7
8	100	12.50	8
9	100	16.67	6
10	100	20.00	5
	$1,000	$124.45	87.0

Average share price = $124.45/10 = $12.45.
Total shares owned = 87.
Average share cost = $1,000/87.0 shares = $11.49.
Total market value now = 87 shares x $20 = $1,740.

Figure 6—

Lump-Sum, Up-Front Investment

Period	Amount Invested	Share Price	Shares Purchased
1	$1,000	$12.50	80
2	0	10.00	0
10	0	20.00	0

Average share price = $12.45.
Total shares owned = 80.
Average share cost = $1,000/80 shares = $12.50.
Total market value now = 80 shares x $20 = $1,600.

Lump-Sum, Up-Front Investment after $1,000 is Saved

Period	Amount Invested	Share Price	Shares Purchased
10	$1,000	$20.00	50

Average share price = $20.00.
Total shares owned = 50.
Average share cost = $1,000/50 shares = $20.00.
Total market value now = 50 shares x $20 = $1,000.

Note that by the process of dollar-cost averaging, you have purchased 87 shares, now worth $20 apiece, for a total market value of $1,740 ($20 x 87 shares). You have invested only $1,000 over the period. In other words, your average share cost of $11.49 is lower than the average ($12.45) of the market price of the fund's shares during the periods in which they are accumulated. So you've actually made money through this process. It works because you bought more shares when they are cheap and fewer shares when they were dear.

Note: Dollar-cost averaging can result in high transaction costs that can lower returns over time. That is why mutual funds, which often charge either no sales fee or a flat commission, are a popular way to implement this strategy.

INVESTING IN INDEX FUNDS: NO-BRAINER INVESTMENT METHOD

If you want the returns of the stock or bond market, but not the risk that your fund manager makes the wrong bet, some experts suggest that you should consider an index fund. It is a sensible method for investors who are not interested in the ongoing process of evaluating funds and wish to obtain the market's return with absolutely no effort and a minimal expense. There are several mutual funds based on the S&P 500 index, which represents approximately 70 percent of the market value of all outstanding U.S. common stocks. (Very recently some index funds, emulating the broader Wilshire 5,000-Stock Index have appeared.) According to a study by Lipper Analytical Services of New York, 83 percent of the basic stock mutual funds did *not* beat the S&P 500 index for the year 1994. Furthermore, stock fund managers have been beaten by the S&P 500 in 10 of the past 15 years. What are the advantages of index funds?

1. You simply send one check, need make no further decisions, and are guaranteed the same annual return as the market as a whole.

2. Lower management costs typically are passed to the fund owner. Index funds are cheap to run since there is no need for any research staff. The average index-fund charges about 0.3 percent, or $3 for every $1,000 invested.

3. Index funds usually have all their money in stocks or bonds, with no cash cushion needed. The typical actively managed fund keeps a cash cushion of 3 to 10 percent of the portfolio, which is used to handle investor withdrawals and to seek new opportunities. Cash, being the worst-performing asset, has been a drag on long-term performance.

4. There is a tax savings advantage. Index funds rarely trade the securities they hold, meaning significantly less capital gains and thus less taxes.

Note: 1. There are also index funds available that track foreign securities markets. They typically emulate the EAFE (Europe and Far East) index. These are excellent vehicles for obtaining risk reduction and profit opportunities from international diversification.

2. *Vanguard* has the widest selections of stock, bond, and EAFE index funds. Others include *DFA* and *Wells Fargo Bank's Stagecoach* funds.

WHERE CAN YOU OBTAIN MUTUAL FUND INFORMATION AND RATINGS?

With 6,000-plus mutual funds in existence today, there is not one source that will satisfy your information needs completely. You may refer to the following important sources of mutual fund information:

1. *Mutual Fund Fact Book* and *A Guide to Mutual Funds.* The Investment Company Institute, 1775 K Street NW, Suite 600, Washington, D.C. 20006, and *Wiesenberger Investment Companies Service,* Warren, Gorham & Lamont, 210 South St., Boston, MA 02111.

   These list most mutual funds, broken down by investment objective, statistics on specific funds, background on trends in the mutual fund industry, and brief mutual fund term definitions.

2. *The Individual Investor's Guide to No-Load Mutual Funds.* The American Association of Individual Investors, 625 North Michigan Avenue, Department NLG, Chicago, IL 60611, (312) 280-0170.

   This classic guide provides investment objectives, operating statistics, and various performance measures covering 436 mutual funds.

3. *Investor's Directory* and *No-Load Mutual Fund Resource List.* No-Load Mutual Fund Association, P.O. Box 2004, JAF Station, New York, NY 10116.
4. *The Investor's Guide to Closed-End Funds,* Thomas J. Herzfeld Advisors, Inc., P. O. Box 161465 Miami, FL 33116, and *The Complete Guide to Closed-End Funds,* International Publishing Corporation, 625 North Michigan, Chicago, IL 60611. They are excellent publications providing a description of various fund characteristics, covering the over 160 traded closed-end funds on the NYSE, AMEX, and OTC markets.

These publications offer a bibliography of newsletters, magazines, books, other publications and organizations, including advisory services. For more sources of mutual fund information, refer to Chapter 13 (Investment Advisory and Newsletters).

You can get help in selecting mutual funds from a number of sources, including investment advisory services that charge fees. More readily available sources, however, are various magazines that include *Money, Forbes, Barron's,* and *The Kiplinger Personal Finance. Money* has a "Fund Watch" column appearing in each monthly issue. In addition, it ranks about 450 funds twice a year reporting each fund's 1-, 5-, and 10-year performances along with a risk rating. The Kiplinger Magazine publishes its review in October.

Forbes has an annual report covering each fund's performance in both up and down markets. In terms of grading, the top 12.5 percent get an A+; the next 12.5 percent, an A; the next 25 percent, a B; and so on. *Value Line Investment Survey* shows the make-up of the fund's portfolio beta values. *Note*: You should not choose a fund only on the basis of its performance rating. You should consider both performance and risk.

You can read up on mutual funds in various newspapers, including *The Wall Street Journal.* College and public libraries are stocked with these publications, as well as books on the subject.

Most funds have toll-free telephone services through which you can get detailed information on each family of funds. Toll-free numbers can easily be obtained by calling the toll-free directory service (800) 555-1212.

HOW DO YOU PICK THE RIGHT FUND BY USING THE PC?

One way to select a mutual fund is with the help of the PC. For example, *CompuServe* has seized upon the mutual fund boom by developing an array of in-depth databases for small investors. Its *FundWatch On-line* by *Money* magazine allows you to quickly screen over 1,700 mutual funds using criteria which mirror your investment philosophy, to find only the ones which are consistent with your goals, and directly obtain a detailed report on a fund by entering its name or ticker symbol. GO MONEYMAG is the command at any CompuServe ! prompt. Screening criteria include:

1. Investment objective (for example, aggressive growth, growth, international, municipal, etc.).
2. Fees (no-load or load) and expense ratios.
3. Performance ratings and rankings.
4. Total asset size.
5. Management company.
6. Dividend yield.
7. Risk ratings (for example, beta and alpha).

A menu of funds found by *CompuServe* can then be summarized and displayed on your screen ranked by return over one of seven different time periods, including the latest bull and bear markets.

From this menu, you simply select which funds you would like to investigate, and detailed reports for each will be provided. These detailed reports include comprehensive descriptive and performance information, along with sector and portfolio holdings for many funds.

Note: More and more easy-to-use software products for mutual fund selection are being introduced to individual investors, including *Mutual Fund Selector* by Intuit (619) 550-5002, the maker of *Quicken* and *TurboTax*.

WHAT ABOUT INVESTING IN MONEY MARKET FUNDS?

Money market funds are a special form of mutual funds. for a small investment, the investor can own a portfolio of high-yielding CDs, T-bills, and other similar securities of short-term nature. There is a great deal of liquidity and flexibility in withdrawing funds through check-writing privileges. They are therefore called "cash equivalents." Money market funds are considered very conservative, because most of the securities purchased by the funds are quite safe.

The yield, however, fluctuates daily. Despite the myth that all money funds perform about the same, some regularly offer significantly higher yields than others, chiefly because they keep their expenses low.

What are the advantages of money market mutual funds?

• No-load.

• Interest earned.

• Possible small initial investment.

• Possible check-writing priveleges.

The disadvantage is that these funds are not federally insured.

What questions should be asked in picking a
money market fund?

1. What is the average maturity? *Note:* The shorter
    the average maturity, the safer the fund is likely
    to be and the faster it will begin offering com-
    petitive yields if interest rates rise.

2. Can you write checks against your fund with-
    out charge?

3. What is the minimum check amount, $200, $250,
    or $500? *Note:* The smaller the amount, the more
    often you can use your fund to park funds for
    future investment or for an emergency.

4. How much do you need to open an account?

5. What is the expense ratio? The expense ratios
    of money-market funds range from about 0.3
    to 2 percent annually.

What Sources of Information Exist, Including On-Line Services?

Most mutual fund families offer a money market
fund. Current yield quotes and average maturity
can be found weekly in *The Wall Street Journal*,
Barron's, and daily newspapers. For more in-depth
information, see *IBC/Donoghue*'s weekly and annual
reports, which track the performance and portfolio
holdings of 750 money market mutual funds. Current and historical quotes are also available from
on-line services such as Prodigy, Compuserve, Dow
Jones News/Retrieval, and Telescan Analyzer. For
example, CompuServe's *Rategram* (!GO
RATEGRAM is the command) ranks the highest
yielding taxable and tax-exempt money market
funds available. In addition, each report identifies
the fund and provides its telephone number, the
minimum required deposit, a safety index rating,
average maturity, and yields.

HOW DO CLOSED-END FUNDS WORK?

Closed-end funds have features similar to both mutual funds and common stocks. They do differ from open-end funds in two ways: First, they operate with a fixed number of shares outstanding, which trade among individuals in secondary markets like common stocks. That is, if you wish to invest in a closed-end fund, you must purchase shares from someone willing to sell them. In the same manner, in order to sell shares you must locate a buyer. Transactions involving closed-end mutual funds are easy to arrange, however, since most of these funds are traded on the New York Stock Exchange, the American Stock Exchange, or the over-the-counter market. Second, the price of a closed-end fund is based on a demand/supply relationship because the shares are traded on the stock exchange. New shares are not issued. Therefore, the net asset value of the fund may be more or less than its current market price of stock. A major point of closed-end funds is the size of *discount* or *premium*. Many funds of this type sell at discounts, which enhances their investment appeal.

When the market price is above its NAV, it is said to be selling at a premium; when market price is below the NAV, it is selling at a discount. A number of publications, such as *The Wall Street Journal* and *Barron's*, report the share premiums or discounts of closed-end funds.

What Are the Advantages and Disadvantages of Closed-End Funds?

Advantages are:

1. Professional management.
2. Diversification.

3.   The opportunity to buy at a discount.
      Note: Closed-end funds are well suited for income investors and those seeking international diversification.

Disadvantages are:

1.   High management fees, ranging from 1/2 to 1 1/2 percent.

2.   Brokerage commissions vary widely. *Note:* Negotiate or use a discount broker if you can.
      Note: You may examine trends in *Herzfeld Closed-End Average,* which tracks 20 closed-end mutual funds accounting for about 50 percent of the value of all the funds traded on the exchanges. It is published in *Barron's.* An upward trend is a positive sign in a bullish market.

Sources of Information and On-Line Services for Closed-End Funds

In addition to *The Wall Street Journal* and *Barron's,* current and historical data are provided in the following publications:

1.   *Morningstar Closed-End Funds,* Morningstar Inc., (800) 876-5005.

2.   *S&P Stock Reports* and *S&P Stock Guide,* Standard & Poor's Corp., (212) 208-8800.

3.   *The Complete Guide to Closed-End Funds,* International Publishing Corp., (800) 488-4149.

Current and historical quotes are also available in on-line services such as Prodigy, Compuserve, Dow Jones News/Retrieval, and Telescan Analyzer.

TAX TIPS FOR MUTUAL FUNDS

Unless you are investing in a tax-deferred IRA or a tax-free bond fund, the capital gains from mutual fund investing are taxable. Capital gains distributions usually come once during the year, typically in December. If you purchase shares right before a distribution, you can be caught in a tax bind. A portion of the price you paid will be returned to you as a taxable gain. In general, a fund that turns over securities frequently in pursuit of a high return may generate more taxable gains than one that holds onto securities that are climbing in value. For this reason, *Consumer Reports* has recently added to their ratings a new column, "Tax Efficiency."

Here are some tax tips in connection with mutual fund investing.

1. Never buy shares of a mutual fund late in the year without going over its distribution, or "ex-dividend," date.

2. Try to sell the shares with the highest original cost.

3. Check out tax consequences when you have to move your money from one fund to another. Such switches are viewed as a taxable event by the IRS.

4. Use tax efficiency as an added screening device—try to pick the fund showing the best tax benefit.

DIVERSIFICATION, PORTFOLIO CONSTRUCTION, AND ASSET ALLOCATION

The key question for an individual investor is: How do I structure an investment portfolio to achieve my financial goals? That depends on many factors, as was discussed in Chapter 1: What your investment goals are; the level of risk you are willing to assume without losing sleep; your tax bracket; and so on.

DIVERSIFICATION IS THE KEY

No matter what your goal, proper diversification—allocating investment assets among different types of investments in order to balance risk and return—is a major element of structuring a successful portfolio, as illustrated in Figure 1.

Figure 1—

A Systematic Approach to Portfolio Construction

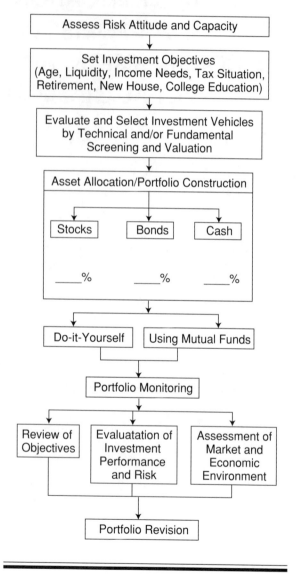

CAN YOU ALLOCATE ASSETS THROUGH MUTUAL FUNDS?

Asset allocation measures the weighting of various types of investments in a portfolio. Undoubtedly, one of the best ways to allocate assets is through mutual funds. Further, allocating assets among several types of mutual funds may be even more profitable. Different segments of the market react differently to the same economic conditions. For example, a cut in interest rates may lower yields on your bond funds, but that news could spark a rally in stocks that would benefit your stock funds. A poor economy that tends to depress the domestic markets may be offset by diversifying in international funds. Spreading your investment money among a family of funds is strongly recommended. More specifically:

1. Diversify among different classes of investments—for example, cash and cash equivalents (such as money market funds), stock funds, bond funds, and so on.
2. Diversify within each class of funds—for example, small company stock funds, large company stock funds, sector funds, international funds, and so on.
3. Go on even further—for example, diversifying among tax-exempt funds and taxable funds.

Investing in an Asset Allocation Fund

As an alternative to constructing your own portfolio, many mutual fund companies offer a variety of *asset allocation funds*. An asset allocation fund is a mutual fund seeking to reduce risk by investing in the right securities at the right time. These funds stress consistent performance at the expense of spectacular gains.

Some funds, such as Vanguard's Star Fund, use fixed weightings; others, such as Fidelity's Asset Manager, have flexible weights that are altered within predefined limits. In fact, Fidelity offers several asset allocation funds designed for various investment objectives (i.e., Fidelity Asset Manager, Asset Manager-Growth, and Asset Manager-Income.).

WHAT IS DO-IT-YOURSELF PORTFOLIO CONSTRUCTION?

Do-it-yourself portfolio construction is a difficult task. Asset allocation, a time-tested approach to portfolio management, distributes funds within your portfolio among several asset categories or classes, typically cash and cash-equivalents (investments with maturities of less than one year, such as CDs or money market funds), equities (stocks and stock funds), and fixed income securities (bonds and bond funds). Stock market diversification is also critical, such as spreading your money across broad sectors, large-company stocks, small-company stocks, and foreign stocks.

This mix of instruments is based on your financial goals, resources, total return (yield plus price change), and the level of tolerance of risk. The highly personalized process of asset allocation first takes into account each of your unique investment needs and objectives, earnings ability, and the financial resources you have available to meet them. Also, your age may be a big factor. For example,

- Do you need to build funds for retirement or a child's college education?

- Is reducing your tax liability a priority?

- Do you need to generate current income (or yield) or need funds soon or at some point in the future? Which one is more important to you, current income or capital appreciation?

Answers to these questions will determine whether your portfolio should be split among the following three classes of investment vehicles:

1. *Liquidity investments.* These investments are liquid enough to be turned into cash as needed with minimum risk or penalty (for example, short-term CDs, money market funds, money market deposit accounts).

2. *Income investments.* These have the ability to provide present and/or future income. For example, various corporate bonds and tax-free municipal bonds, fixed annuities providing tax-deferred future income, and U.S. savings bonds fall in this category.

3. *Growth investments.* These are intended to appreciate in value over a given period of time (for example, growth stocks, stock funds, and variable annuities).

Asset allocation must take into account your risk comfort level. You should ask yourself: Am I conservative, moderate, or aggressive? Where is your sleeping point? (In other words, would you want to eat well or sleep well?)

One approach is based on the investor's time frame. Longer-term portfolios permit investors to assume additional risk. The investor can increase the amount invested in stocks, precious metals, and such. Changes in asset mix would have to be made as the investor's time horizon decreases or as gains or losses alter the portfolio's composition.

Another approach is to time changes in asset allocation to market changes, preferably in step with market cycles. In bull markets, investors desire to be heavily into stocks, for instance. In bear markets, cash, bond, or precious metal allocations would be high. There is controversy whether investors can profitability time market waves.

HOW DO YOU CALCULATE YOUR ALLOCATION MIX?

To determine asset allocation mix, you can add holdings of stocks, bonds, and cash, and divide each sum by the total value of the portfolio. However, in today's complex investment world, determining what asset class certain investments belong to can be confusing. You will have to give some thought to how you allocate mixed investments, such as balanced mutual funds that own both stocks and bonds, or how to treat convertible securities, which are half-bond and half-stock.

The calculation can be done by hand or by using spreadsheet software. Personal finance software, such as *Meca's Managing Your Money,* can also help. The Dreyfus Group mutual funds and the Shearson Lehman Brothers brokerage will do the calculation for no charge. Also, Fidelity has developed *Fidelity PortfolioMatch,* a guidebook that provides a defined process for evaluating your existing investment, as well as action steps tailored to your individual needs.

A grid serves as an easy way to calculate asset allocation. Figure 2 provides a completed grid as an example and a blank grid for your own use.

Figure 2—
Asset Allocation Grids

INVESTMENT	(A) AMOUNT	(B) %STOCK	(C) % BOND	(D) % CASH	$$ IN STOCK (A*B)	$$ IN BONDS (A*C)	$$ IN CASH (A*D)
BLT common	$10,000	100%	0	0	$10,000	0	0
Jaytown Balanced Fund	$15,000	60%	30%	10%	$9,000	$4,500	$1,500
Certificate of deposit	$,8,000	0	0	100%	0	0	$8,000
Burgh Water District bond	$5,000	0	100%	0	0	$5,000	0
TOTAL	(E) $38,000				(F) $19,000	(G) $9,500	(H) $9,500
ASSET ALLOCATION					(F÷E) 50%	(G÷E) 25%	(H÷E) 25%

(continued)

Figure 2—*continued*

For you to do your own:

INVESTMENT	(A) AMOUNT	(B) %STOCK	(C) % BOND	(D) % CASH	$$ IN STOCK (A*B)	$$ IN BONDS (A*C)	$$ IN CASH (A*D)
TOTAL	(E)				(F)	(G)	(H)
ASSET ALLOCATION					(F÷E) %	(G÷E) %	(H÷E) %

HOW DO YOU FINE-TUNE YOUR ASSET MIX?

The beauty of asset allocation is that as such factors as your financial circumstances, goals, and age change, your allocations can change as well. Four reasons for fine-tuning or rebalancing your asset mix are:

1. When there occur external events, such as stock market corrections or low yields, that have thrown off your original target allocation.

2. When you experience a major life event (such as having a child, losing a spouse, getting married, or retiring) that alters your investment goals.

3. When the weight of one investment class in your portfolio surges or shrinks significantly.

4. When you are within a year or so of achieving your particular goal.

    Note: If you intend to rebalance your asset mix too often, consider sticking with mutual funds that have no front- and back-end loads.

CAN YOU OBTAIN HELP FOR CONSTRUCTING AN ASSET ALLOCATION PORTFOLIO?

There are a number of sources that can be referred to when trying to construct a portfolio, including the following:

1. Most major brokerages maintain a recommended asset allocation (or model portfolio) that is updated to keep pace with the investment climate (see Figures 3 and 4). It will tell you how much you should have in each sector of the economy.

2. Each quarter, *The Wall Street Journal* tracks Wall Street firms' recommendations of asset allocation.

3. In addition, many market newsletters and money management firms also tell investors what they believe are good allocations for the times.

4. Every issue of *Worth* magazine provides you with a breakdown of what sectors and companies you should own.

Figure 3—

T. Rowe Price Portfolio Suggestions

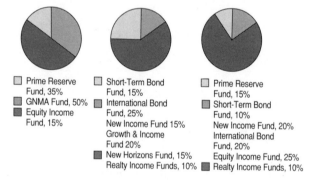

☐ Prime Reserve
   Fund, 35%
■ GNMA Fund, 50%
■ Equity Income
   Fund, 15%

☐ Short-Term Bond
   Fund, 15%
■ International Bond
   Fund, 25%
   New Income Fund 15%
   Growth & Income
   Fund 20%
■ New Horizons Fund, 15%
   Realty Income Funds, 10%

☐ Prime Reserve
   Fund, 15%
■ Short-Term Bond
   Fund, 10%
   New Income Fund, 20%
   International Bond
   Fund, 20%
   Equity Income Fund, 25%
■ Realty Income Funds, 10%

Source: T. Rowe Price.

Figure 4—

Merrill Lynch Asset Allocation Recommendations

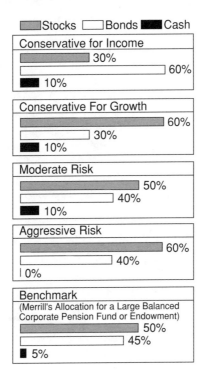

Source: Merrill Lynch.

5. Surveys by organizations such as *Money* magazine and American Association of Individual Investors (AAII) give you some idea on what other investors are doing. These surveys are briefly described below.

MONEY'S SMALL INVESTOR INDEX

Small Investor Index, developed by *Money* magazine, measures gains and losses of the average investor relative to a base of 100 set on 12/27/1991. It is based on a portfolio including types of investments held by average small investors.

This index can be used to measure the average investor's gains and losses. It is based on a portfolio that includes 10 types of investments held in proportions consistent with Federal Reserve data on what the average household owns. The index is reported weekly each Monday in daily papers like *USA Today* and the *Orange County Register* and monthly as part of *Money*'s "Investor's Scorecard." The investments included and their proportions in the small investor's portfolio are shown in Figure 5.

From Figure 5, the value of the index on March 17, 1995 was 104.32, which reflected a 1.15 percent gain for the week and an 4.15 percent gain over a year earlier.

Although this index is not widely used on Wall Street, its importance lies in the fact that it provides the individual investor with a standard against which he or she can assess both the composition and performance of his or her portfolio. *Note:* This index is by no means an optimal allocation for every investor.

AAII surveys periodically where individuals commit their assets, as shown in Figure 6.

Figure 5—

Investments Included in Money's Small Investor Index (The Second Week of March, 1995)

Category	Current	Year Ago
Big Stocks	23.34%	24.51%
Small Stocks	7.37	7.74
Equity Funds	10.29	9.31
Taxable Bonds	12.54	10.80
Municipals	4.34	4.55
Bond Funds	6.23	6.91
CDs	13.58	12.45
Money Funds	20.80	22.20
Real Estate	0.99	0.88
Gold	0.52	0.66

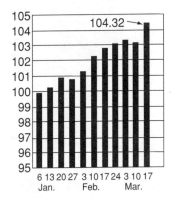

Source: Orange County Register.

Figure 6—

AAII Allocation Survey

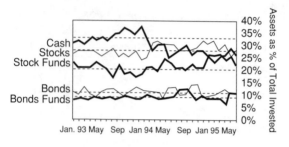

Source: *AAII Journal*, August 1992.

HOW CAN YOU USE BETA FOR ASSET ALLOCATION?

You can construct and/or adjust your own portfolio based on beta coefficients. If you desire higher returns and high risk, you would select securities with higher betas (or at least mix high and low beta securities such that the overall beta is higher than 1.0). The beta of a portfolio can be estimated by weighting the individual securities that comprise the portfolio. Table 1 illustrates the calculation of a portfolio's beta.

Table 1—
Calculation of a Portfolio's Beta

Stock	Beta	Percent of Portfolio (%)	Portfolio Beta
Coca-Cola	1.10	30%	.33
Calif. Water	.50	20	.10
Liz Clairborne	1.50	50	.75
		100%	1.18

The beta of this portfolio is 1.18.

Adding a security with a high beta will increase the portfolio's beta, while adding a low beta stock will reduce the portfolio's risk. The higher the beta or risk, the higher the return expected from the portfolio. Thus, to get a higher long-run rate of return, you should just increase the beta of your portfolio.

LIFECYCLE GUIDE: RECOMMENDED ASSET ALLOCATION

Investment strategy must be tailored to a lifecycle. It depends to a large extent on the following factors:

1. How capable an individual is of bearing risk and his/her attitude toward risk. Do you have a stomach for risk? How much loss can you take? Some people just can't sleep at night knowing their assets might take a dip, no matter how small.

2. Income needs and desire for growth. A retiree or someone close to retirement might look for a steady income, while younger people might be able to afford the luxury of long-term growth.

There is also a trade-off between income and growth.

3. Time horizon. By and large, a longer time horizon allows you to take on greater risks—with a greater return potential—because it increases the capacity to take risk. As retirement approaches, a large percentage of assets needs to be shifted into more conservative, less risky investments. *One rule of thumb:* Subtract your age from 100; that is the percentage that stocks should account for in your portfolio.

4. Tax exposure. The bottom line to every investor is not how much you earn, but how much you keep—what's left after taxes. Investors who are in higher income tax brackets need to be concerned with the tax implications of their investments. Table 2 provides a capsule summary of the four elements of the individual investment profile, while Table 3 shows how an investor's profile may change with age, given these assumptions: (1) everybody is essentially risk-averse and (2) the younger have more capacity for risk than the older. Of course, your own profile may be very different than this one. Table 4 is a suggested allocation mix.

Table 2—

Individual Investment Profile

Elements	*Degree/ Level*	*Investment Vehicles Identified with Each Category*
Risk tolerance		
	Low (0 - 5% loss)	Cash, CDs, money market funds
	Moderate (6 - 15%)	Conservative high-dividend stocks, bonds
	High (16 - 25%)	Growth stocks

Elements	Degree/ Level	Investment Vehicles Identified with Each Category
Income needs	Income	Bonds, preferred stocks
	Growth/ Income	Growth/income funds, high-dividend stocks
	Growth	Growth stocks
Time/age factor	Short (1 - 2 years)	Cash, CDs, money market funds, short-term bonds
	Medium (3 - 5 years)	Intermediate-term bonds, growth stocks
	Long (over 5 years)	Aggressive growth stocks
Tax exposure	Low	Bonds and other fixed income securities
	Moderate	High-dividend stocks, preferred stocks
	High	Municipal bonds, nondividend-paying growth stocks

Table 3—

Lifecycle Investing: An Example of a Changing Profile

	20s	30s	40s-50s	60s
Risk Tolerance	High	High	Moderate	Low
Return Needs	Growth	Growth	Growth/ Income	Income
Time Horizon	Long	Long	Short/ Long	Short/ Long
Tax Exposure	Lower	Higher	Lower	Lower

Table 4—

Suggested Asset Mix

	20s	30s	Midlife	60s
Money market funds	5%	5%	5%	10%
Bond funds	25%	35%	45%	60%
Zero-coupon				
T-bonds				
High grade				
Stocks funds	70%	60%	50%	30%
Growth				
Income				
Income & growth				

HOW YOUR FAMILY SITUATION AFFECT YOUR FINANCIAL GOALS AND INVESTMENT CONDITIONS?

In addition to your age, your family situation would dictate investment goals and strategies. Table 5 provides some general conditions of typical goals at various family situations.

Table 5—

Family Situation	Typical Financial Goals	Conditions
1. Young, single working	To start a business; to buy an auto	• Stress on capital growth • No great need for liquidity • Time-horizon, 3-5 years • Capacity for substantial risk

Family Situation	Typical Financial Goals	Conditions
2. Young couple, with no children	To buy a house	• Similar to Situation 1
3. Young couple, with two children	For a college education fund	• Similar to Situation 1 • Time-horizon, 10-15 yrs. • Moderate risk preferred
4. Middle-aged married couple with no children	For retirement fund	• Balance between growth and income • Moderate risk preferred • Time-horizon, 5-10 yrs.
5. Divorced mother, working, with children	To supplement income	• Similar to Situation 4 • Low risk preferred
6. Married couple in retirement	To supplement retirement	• Stress on preservation of capital • Need for liquidity and current income • Low risk

ASSET ALLOCATION BY PC

Asset allocation software programs are designed to perform asset allocation functions. They try to show how to allocate funds among assets in a portfolio to minimize risk and maximize return by means of the well known Markowitz procedure. They also evaluate the potential risks and returns on different types of investments, such as cash, stocks, and bonds, which allows you to allocate your funds among them for maximum returns at acceptable levels of risk. Below is a list of popular asset allocation software.

Asset Allocator and Stock Portfolio Allocator (DOS)
Portfolio Software, (617) 328-8248

Asset Allocation Expert (DOS)
Sponsor-Software Systems, Inc., (212) 724-7535

AAT (Asset Allocation Tools) (DOS)
Scientific Press, (415) 366-2577

Asset Mix Optimizer (DOS)
CDA Investment Technologies, Inc., (301) 590-1330

PORTFOLIO MANAGEMENT BY PC

Portfolio management can be done on-line, using
such services as *CompuServe*, *Prodigy*, and *America
Online*. They offer the built-in ability to access
on-line services and update the prices on the securities in your portfolio. On-line or not, portfolio
management programs are designed to help you
monitor your investment portfolios and provide detailed reports on your portfolio, covering security
and portfolio betas and dividend yields; a calendar
listing maturity dates of bonds, options, and futures,
along with expected dividend amounts and payment dates; and a breakdown of the industries and
asset classes of your securities; and your asset allocation. Below is a list of popular portfolio management software.

Managing Your Money (DOS, Windows, Mac)
MECA Software, Inc., (203) 255-1441

Financial Navigator (DOS, Windows)
Financial Navigator International, (800) 468-3636 or
(415) 962-0300

Quicken (DOS, Windows, Mac)
Intuit, (800) 624-8742 or (415) 322-0573

WealthBuilder by *Money* Magazine (DOS, Mac)
Reality Technologies, Inc., (800) 346-2024 or (215) 277-7600

CAPTOOL and Global Investor (DOS)
Techserve, Inc., (800) 826-8082 or (206) 865-0249

Centerpiece and Performance Monitor (DOS)
Performance Technologies, Inc., (800) 528-9595 or (919) 876-355

Equalizer (DOS) and Streetsmart (Windows)
Charles Schwab & Co., Inc., (800) 334-4455 or (415) 627-7000

Fidelity On-line Xpress (DOS)
Fidelity Investments, (800) 544-0246

Market Manager Plus (DOS, Mac)
Dow Jones & Co., Inc., (800) 815-5100 or (609) 520-4641

Mutual Fund Investor (DOS)
American River Software, (916) 483-1600

Personal Portfolio Analyzer (DOS)
Charles L. Pack, (415) 949-0887

Pulse Portfolio Management System (DOS)
EQUIS International, (800) 882-3040 or (801) 265-8886

Money Fund Vision (DOS, Windows)
IBC/Donoghue, Inc., (800) 343-5413 or (508) 881-2800

CHAPTER 13

INVESTMENT ADVISORY AND NEWSLETTERS

Investors often find that newsletters help them choose a right investment vehicle or decide when to get in and out of an investment. There were more than 200 market-oriented newsletters published in the U.S. in 1994, reaching about 2 million subscribers. They range in price from about $30 a year to more than $600, and their strategies are as varied as their numbers.

HOW DO YOU PICK A NEWSLETTER?

Here are four areas to consider before you take the plunge on a newsletter.

1. *Performance.* Performance is the most important criterion, focusing on long-term (such as 5- and 10-year) performance. Be sure to compare the newsletter's track record with that of the market. The market may be the Wilshire 5000, a broad index of small- and large-company stocks, or the S&P 500 index.

2. *Risk.* Pick a newsletter whose willingness to risk matches your own. Letters that chalk up the biggest gains typically take on more risks than

those with more modest results. The strategies are diverse, ranging from stocks, bonds, and gold to mutual funds. There are chartists, timers, shorters, speculators, option traders, and sector chasers.

3. *Time.* How much time do you have, or want to devote, to follow the letter's advice? Is this letter long-term oriented or relying on frequent changes?

4. *Transaction costs.* In case you follow the letter's advice and have to execute your orders frequently, shop around for lower commissions. Commissions can erode respectable gains. In the case of mutual fund investing, stick to no-load funds.

For comprehensive coverage of newsletters, refer to: (1) McGowan, Spencer, *The Investor's Investment Source Book,* NYIF, 1995, and Shim, Jae K. and Joel Siegel, *The Source: The Complete Guide to Investment Information,* International Publishing Corporation, 1992. A major source about newsletters is *The Hulbert Financial Digest* (316 Commerce St., Alexandria, VA 22314, (703)683-5905), which tracks some 130 newsletters. This digest judges the quality and value of advice in investment letters. For example, it provides a list of newsletters that beat the market over the past five years. The following are ten of the top-performing newsletters (those that are ahead of the market on a risk-adjusted basis from the August 1987 precrash high through the end of 1994's first quarter), tracked by *The Hulbert Financial Digest.*

Systems and Forecasts
Signalert Corp., (516) 829-11021
    Technical analysis. Covers stock, mutual funds, and market timing.

InvesTech Mutual Fund Advisor
InvesTech, Inc., (800) 955-8500
   Technical analysis. Covers mutual funds and market timing.

BI Research
BI Research Inc., (203) 270-9244
   Detailed research profiles of high-growth or overlooked stocks and mutual funds, with continuing advice on whether to buy, hold, or sell.

Zweig Forecast
Zweig, (800) 633-2252, ext. 9000
   Technical analysis. There are comments on sentiment and other indicators that make for superior stock market performance.

Fund Exchange
Paul A. Merriman & Associates, Inc., (800) 423-4893
   Fundamental analysis. Covers mutual funds and market timing.

Investment Quality Trends
Geraldine Weiss, (619) 459-3818
   Technical and fundamental analysis. Covers stocks, mutual funds, and charts.

Fidelity Monitor
Jack Bowers, (800) 397-3094
   Covers Fidelity mutual funds.

The Chartist
The Chartist, (310) 596-2385
   It charts various stocks and recommends buys and sells based on technical signals. It also publishes the monthly *Chartist Mutual Fund Timer*, the fifth-ranked fund letter over the past five years.

Peter Dag Investment Letter
Peter Dag & Associates, Inc., (216) 644-2782
Fundamental analysis. Covers stocks, bonds, and precious metals.

Fundline
David H. Menashe & Co., (818) 346-5637
Technical analysis. Covers mutual funds and market timing.

The following is a list of newsletters that have performed well over the years.

The Insiders
The Institute for Econometric Research
3471 N. Federal Hwy.
Fort Lauderdale, FL 33306
(monthly)
A publication based on the notion that company officials and directors who trade in their own stock know something. It collects and translates SEC data on buying and selling by insiders and makes recommendations.

Individual Investor Special Situations Report
New York
(212) 689-2777
(monthly)
It focuses on OTC stocks.

Medical Technology Stock Letter
P.O. Box 40460
Berkeley, CA 94704
(biweekly)
A solid source of information on biotechnology and other emerging health fields. It provides aggressive investors with timely insights into the leading companies in the field.

MTP Review
Lake Tahoe, NV 89504
(702) 831-1396
(monthly)
   It focuses on OTC stocks.

The Oberweis Report
Aurora, IL 60507
(708) 801-4766
(monthly)
   It focuses on no-load mutual funds.

OTC Insight
P.O. Box 1329
El Cerrito, CA 94530
(800) 955-9566
(monthly)
   A computerized stock-selector for investors in OTC stocks. There are model portfolios and risk ratings.

The Prudent Speculator
P.O. Box 1767
Santa Monica, CA 90406
(monthly)
   It finds undervalued issues and gives sell signals. It is classic stock research.

Value Line Investment Survey
Value Line, Inc.
711 Third Avenue
New York, NY 10017
(weekly)
   This loose-leaf booklet covers the business activities of major corporations in a variety of industries. There are many charts and graphs. The *Survey* ranks and updates about 1,700 stocks and speculates on the course of the market.

Value Line OTC Special Situations Report
Value Line, Inc.
711 Third Avenue
New York, NY 10017
(biweekly)
    This loose-leaf newsletter contains detailed rec-
ommendations and reports on OTC stocks and all
issues Value Line believes have unusual potential
for reasons unrelated to the broad market's direction.

    The following sections list popular newsletters
by investment categories. This is not intended as
an exhaustive list, but as a reference.

WARRANTS, OPTIONS, AND CONVERTIBLES

The Ney Option Report
P.O. Box 90215
Pasadena, CA 91109
(semimonthly; every six months)
    A letter for option traders, with recommenda-
tions and analysis.

RHM Survey of Warrants, Options & Low-Price Stocks
RHM Associates, Inc.
172 Forest Avenue
Glen Cove, NY 11542
(weekly)
    There is investment advice on warrants, call and
put options, and low-priced stocks. Tables and
charts are presented.

The Stock Option Trading Form
P.O. Drawer 24242
Fort Lauderdale, FL 33307
(monthly)
    It looks like a racing form, with puts and calls
to buy and sell. There is little explanatory text.

Value Line Options & Convertibles
Value Line, Inc.
711 Third Avenue
New York, NY 10017
(weekly)
An evaluation and analysis of hundreds of convertible bonds, warrants, and options. It is most probably the pre-eminent source of this information for active investors.

COMMODITIES

The Addison Report
P.O. Box 402
Franklin, MA 02038
(every three weeks; six months)
It offers quick comments and recommendations on stocks, bonds, and commodities.

The COINfidential Report
P.O. Box 2727
New Orleans, LA 70176
(monthly)
A coin and stock market newsletter and advisory.

Commodity Closeup
P.O. Box 6
Cedar Falls, IA 50613
(weekly)
It tracks futures prices and trading in financials, metals, grains, and meats.

Commodity Service
Dunn & Hargitt, Inc.
22 N. 2nd Street, Box 1100
Lafayette, IN 47902
(weekly)

The service charts 34 of the most actively traded commodities, including buy and sell recommendations.

Commodity Traders Consumer Report
1731 Howe Ave., Suite 149
Sacramento, CA 95825
(bimonthly)
A wide-ranging look at future markets, with specific recommendations, plus commentaries and interviews concerning trading strategies.

Dines Letter
James Dine & Company
Box 22
Belvedere, CA 94920
(monthly)
It is a respected advisory on stocks, gold and metals, and economics. It combines important technical, psychological, and business indicators concerning the markets.

Dunn & Hargitt Commodity Service
22 N. Second St.
Lafayette, IN 47902
(weekly; six months)
There are charts and action comments for investors and traders in commodities from British pounds to gold, heating oil, and pork bellies.

Gann Angles
245-A Washington St., Suite 2
Monterey, CA 93940
(monthly)
A technical market-timing advisory, heavy on commodities. It's based on the system of W.D. Gann, a turn-of-the-century trader who ascribed price movements to regular mathematical patterns.

Hard Money Digest
3608 Grand Ave.
Oakland, CA 94610
(monthly)
  A summary and comparison of opinions from various other newsletters on gold, silver, interest rates, stocks, and economics.

The Hume Moneyletter
835 Franklin Court
Marietta, GA 30067
(monthly)
  It keeps track of commodity prices.

International Asset Investor
HMR Publishing Co.
P.O. Box 471
Barrington, IL 60010
(monthly)
  There are comments and statistics on commodities and currencies for investors who send money abroad.

The Kondratieff Wave Analyst
P.O. Box 977
Crystal Lake, IL 60014
(monthly)
  An economic commentary and interpretation of trading actions, with much attention on long cycles and a section on precious metals.

Managed Account Reports
5513 Twin Knolls Rd., Suite 213
Columbia, MD 21045
(bimonthly)
  There are alternating reports on the futures industry and on the performance of commodity pools. An authoritative source for commodities traders who use managed funds. It monitors commodities trading advisors (CTAs), private pools, and public funds.

The McKeever Strategy Letter
P.O. Box 4130
Medford, OR 97501
(monthly)
    Mr. McKeever leads off his longer-than-aver-
age letters with essays on economic or market topics, before giving advice on stocks, bonds, metals,
and currencies.

Silver and Gold Report
P.O. Box 510
Bethel, CT 06801
(annual)
    It keeps an eye on dealers around the country
and publishes an annual survey with comparative
prices.

Trendway Advisory Service
P.O. Box 7184
Louisville, KY 40207
(bimonthly)
    A current analysis of stocks, money markets
and gold, with an eye for waves and other chart
patterns.

Value Forecaster
P.O. Box 50
Pilot Hill, CA 95664
(monthly)
    An analysis of COMEX warehouse bullion
stocks of silver and other precious metals.

The Wellington Letter
1800 Grosvenor Center
733 Bishop St.
Honolulu, HA 96813
(monthly)
    A thorough and respected advisory, Wellington
covers stocks, bonds, currencies and metals.

WHERE CAN YOU OBTAIN MUTUAL FUND INFORMATION?

Mutual fund investors often find that a newsletter or two helps them choose among hundreds of funds or decide when to get in and out of an investment. Letters also identify good funds that you haven't heard about elsewhere in print and explain long-term fund performance rankings.

However, before you begin looking for a letter to suit your needs, you should understand that fund publications serve differing objectives. Some, such as *Telephone Switch Newsletter* and *Weber's Fund Advisor*, tell you which funds to buy and sell, and when, according to a rigid trading formula. Unless you're going to follow the system, the letters are useless.

Another group, which includes *Growth Fund Guide*, *Mutual Fund Letter*, and *United Mutual Fund Selector*, represent educational and journalistic enterprises. They run articles (often based on original research) about assorted topics of interest to shareholders, such as how the funds have done through the years or why funds are increasing certain fees and charges.

The third group of letters is largely databases, in which you can look up scores of funds and their rankings by objectives, time periods, and size. These include *Morningstar's Mutual Fund Values*, *CDA Mutual Fund Report*, *Schabacker's Mutual Fund Analysis Guide*, and *Wiesenberger Investment Companies Service*.

Because of intense competition between publishers, most discount their subscription rates for new subscribers. But even better are the short-term trial offers, which may include one free issue. Write or call their toll-free numbers for details or watch for letters' advertisements in financial magazines and newspapers.

Examples of advisory services and newsletters follow.

CDA Mutual Fund Report
CDA Investment Technologies
11501 Georgia Ave.
Silver Spring, MD 20902
(monthly)

A comprehensive directory and data service that rates 850 funds many ways, ranks them by short-term and long-term performance, and assigns an overall rating based on a combination of factors.

Donoghue's Moneyletter
The Donoghue Organization
P.O. Box 411
Holliston, MA 01746
(508) 429-5930
(bimonthly)

This report includes a pullout called "Fundletter," which follows a portfolio of money market funds for "safety, liquidity, yield and catastrophe-proofing." This letter also tackles bread-and-butter investments like municipal bonds, mutual funds, and bank accounts. There is wise counsel on current strategies.

Income & Safety
The Institute for Econometric Research
3471 N. Federal Hwy.
Fort Lauderdale, FL 33306
(305) 563-9000 (FL only)
(800) 327-6720
(monthly)

This is a directory of over 200 mutual funds that indicates each fund's primary portfolio holding, yield, minimum investment, services available, and load, if any. It recommends "best buys."

International Fund Monitor
P.O. Box 5754
Washington, DC 20016
(monthly)

It covers closed-end international funds.

Jay Schabacker's Mutual Fund Investing
Phillips Publishing Inc.
7811 Montrose Rd.
Potomac, MD 20854
(800) 722-9000
(monthly)

For less experienced fund investors than the audience for Schabacker's other letters, this newsletter contains a smorgasbord of features, model portfolios, question-and-answer sections, and a brief market commentary.

Mannie Webb's Sector Fund Connection
8949 LaRiviera Dr.
Sacramento, CA 95826
(monthly)

Another switching advisory, covering several families of no-load funds that specialize in certain industries.

Mutual Fund Forecaster
The Institute for Econometric Research
3471 N. Federal Hwy.
Fort Lauderdale, FL 33306
(800) 327-6720
(305) 563-9000
(monthly)

The institute takes more than 300 mutual funds and projects performance based on a reading of the market and the funds' characteristics. A directory is included in which performance measures, 1-year income projections, and risk ratings are given.

Mutual Fund Values
Morningstar
53 West Jackson Blvd.
Chicago, IL 60604
(monthly)

This brings you value added information such as yields, alpha, beta, R-squared (R^2), and standard deviation. It rates each fund on its risk-adjusted performance and provides straightforward buy and sell recommendations.

Retirement Fund Advisory
Schabacker Investment Management Inc.
8943 Shady Grove Ct.
Gaithersburg, MD 20877
(monthly)

An abridged version of the same company's *Switch Fund Advisory*, with emphasis on funds suitable for IRA and Keogh investors.

Schabacker's Mutual Fund Analysis Guide
Schabacker Investment Management Inc.
8943 Shady Grove Ct.
Gaithersburg, MD 20877
(monthly)

Another comprehensive, statistical report and advisory service that, in addition, grades funds on a scale from A+ to D.

Sector Funds Newsletter
P.O. Box 1210
Escondido, CA 92025
(monthly)

It provides model portfolios and signals to switch funds. It emphasizes the Fidelity mutual funds.

United Mutual Fund Selector
United Business Service
101 Prescott St.
Wellesley Hills, MA 02181
(617) 267-8855
(semi-monthly)

This report rates mutual funds, including bond and municipal bond funds. It is very well organized and full of performance charts and descriptions of funds, plus industry developments.

REAL ESTATE—REAL ESTATE INVESTMENT TRUSTS (REITS), LIMITED PARTNERSHIPS, AND TAX SHELTERS

Brennan Reports
Valley Forge Office Colony
P.O. Box 882, Suite 200
Valley Forge, PA 19482
(monthly)

It examines tax-advantaged investments, such as real estate, single-premium life insurance, oil and gas deals, and other tax shelters. This excellent letter also coaches you on tax planning.

Brennan's IRA Advisor
Valley Forge Office Colony
P.O. Box 882, Suite 200
Valley Forge, PA 19482
(monthly)

An offshoot of *Brennan Reports* that discusses the ins and outs of unusual IRA investments, such as income real estate limited partnerships.

Income Investor Perspectives
Uniplan, Inc.
3907 N. Green Bay Ave.
Milwaukee, WI 53206
(every three weeks)

It updates tax-advantaged and income-oriented investments, such as utility stocks and REITs. It is useful for safety-and-yield investors.

Oil and Gas Quarterly
1275 Broadway
Albany, NY 12204
(quarterly)

As the title suggests, this focuses on oil and gas.

The Real Estate Digest
P.O. Box 26444
Birmingham, AL 35226
(monthly)

This monthly newsletter covers real estate investments, including tax strategies, title insurance, real estate financing, and management.

ON-LINE DATA SERVICE AND INVESTMENT SOFTWARE

An investor with a modem-equipped personal computer (PC) can now dial a database, such as *Prodigy*, that are oriented to investors and include financial data, current and historical information on stock quotes, commodity quotes, access to *Disclosure*'s SEC reports, and much more.

There has been a geometric explosion of information available to investors, both at libraries and on-line. The investment information available on-line falls into two basic categories. One is raw data, such as stock quotes, market reports, corporate filings, and news releases. Some of the raw data can be obtained through the *Internet*. The other is analytical tools, which include research reports, portfolio services, and investment forums.

The raw data can either be quickly "downloaded" onto a floppy disk or into your computer memory to be analyzed later, or it can be read directly into a software program designed to perform calculations on the raw data.

A recent survey conducted by the American Association of Individual Investors found that 80 percent of its members used a PC, 57 percent used their computer for stock analysis, and a smaller portion, 21 percent, made stock transactions on-line.

This chapter covers topics such as automated news/retrieval, on-line computer databases, and investment software.

ON-LINE DATABASES AND NEWS/ RETRIEVAL

Just as hardware is useless without software, PCs are not as useful without news/retrieval capabilities and databases. Databases are organized collections of information, both historical and current. Investment analyses require considerable amounts of economic and financial information, and the more current it is, the better.

Investors are in constant contact with many news sources, and they buy/or sell securities almost automatically when important events take place. In addition to having access to current news, the PC owner can use this same news to update his or her database.

WHAT DO ON-LINE DATABASES OFFER?

All databases don't have the same information. The following discusses the similarities and differences between various on-line databases.

Numbers

Throughout the day, you can get current prices on securities. Generally, securities quotes are 15 to 20 minutes behind the market. If you pay a little more though, you can get up-to-the-minute quotes.

Databases give you information on trading volume, low and closing stock prices, and other technical data going back many years. You can obtain financial data, including historical, current, and projected information.

Some databases can provide current and historical data on mutual funds, corporate and municipal bonds, commodities and options, indexes, and the state of the economy.

Information and News

Textual information can be obtained on an industry, on any company you're interested in, or on the economy as a whole. This information could include a company's profile, its product lines, or important industry developments.

You may get this kind of information by reading *The Wall Street Journal* or the *Value Line Investment Survey*. Databases make it available more quickly, and they can cover more companies than, say, Value Line's 1600. A database lets you zero in on a particular company or a particular item that you might otherwise miss.

Shortly after the market's close, you can get information on closing prices and also the kind of report and commentary on the day's activity that you will find in tomorrow's paper. Getting a jump on the market this way can help you act quickly.

Analysis and Advice

Some databases will analyze their data for you or will dispense its own advice or that of "experts."

Databases provide on-line fundamental or technical analysis. These databases produce the charts or do the screening on-line instead of supplying data to be used by your fundamental or technical analysis software.

Some examples of databases include:

1. *CompuServe* can select securities that meet your criteria among 46,000 securities. A somewhat limited list of criteria can be selected from the database, or you can use its new service, *Coscreen*, to more thoroughly screen 9,500 stocks using the Disclosure II database and 24 screening categories.

2. *Telescan Analyzer* provides graphs of a wide range of fundamental and technical indicators, with up to 13 years of data on 2,000 mutual funds, more than 8,000 stocks, and 150 market indices. You can compare the performance of stocks with the performance of the industry group, or the performance of the industry group with any of several overall market averages. This saves you time, but may add some loss in control over the output.

A large number of databases can relay the advice and analysis of others. Examples of this include:

1. *Dow Jones News-Retrieval (DJN/R)* provides recommendations from Standard & Poor's and access to market analysis and the financial press' research reports.

2. *Equalizer* provides access to recommendations and analysis from *Standard & Poor's MarketScope* (a source used by pros).

Investment Organizer

An example that organizes your investment accounts includes:

Investment Record (Claude E. Cleeton, 122 109th Avenue S.E., Bellevue, WA 98004, (206) 451-0293) tracks up to 10 accounts, each having up to 150 investments in 10 categories. Two reports are generated: (a) a personal income statement giving a detailed description of the investor's actual and estimated financial performance for the year, including yield and tax status and (b) a capital asset statement providing detailed information on all owned investment assets.

On-line Trading

The database can help you place buy and sell orders directly to a broker from your computer. You do this electronically by sending the same information you would have given your broker by phone. Fewer people are involved and the danger of a delay or error is decreased. An example of this includes *Fidelity Investor's Express*, available on DJN/R. Your order goes directly to the appropriate stock exchange from your computer and is reviewed only by Fidelity's computer. You can also place your order on weekends or at night and have it ordered when the market opens.

Many discount brokers think databases make their services more attractive because of the research and investment data they would miss out on by not using a full-service broker. Other programs offered include the *Equalizer* program of Schwab and Co., which offers a full range of investment services, as well as on-line trading through Max Ule & Co. and *Quickway* through Quick & Reilly.

Only the Equalizer charges no on-line fee for checking up on your account or entering orders. There is an $8 per month account fee by Fidelity and time charges of 30 cents per minute in prime time and 10 cents in non-primetime for all baud rates.

WHAT DO POPULAR ON-LINE SERVICES OFFER?

There are presently other major sources of data that are available for use on-line and are on an interactive, time-sharing basis. Almost all on-line services provide stock quotes, investor bulletin boards where members can exchange information, and general market updates, such as the Dow Jones Industrial Average. The following includes a list of popular on-line services and what they cover.

America OnLine, *(800) 827-6364*

- AAII—a library of articles on investment basics and computerized investing from back issues
- Morningstar—performance data and reports on 3,300 mutual funds
- "Nightly Business Report" Online—information about the TV program, including upcoming interviews with investment experts.
- Reuters—Financial news service
- Tax Forum—Subscribers can ask tax questions on message boards and download files from the software library

CompuServe, *(800) 848-8199*

- CoScreen—provides financial information on publicly traded companies
- FundWatch Online—*Money* magazine monitors performance of 1,900 funds
- Citibank Global Report—provides foreign exchange and commodity quotes

- E Trade Securities—on-line discount brokerage conducted through Quick & Reilly
- MMS International—financial forecasts including interest-rate trends and major economic indicators
- Executive News Service—enables investors to track and clip news coverage of specific companies

Delphi Internet Services Corp., (800) 695-4005

- Trendvest Portfolio Analysis—a stock rating system
- MarketPulse—provides snapshot of the market
- RateGram—provides reports on certificates of deposit
- News services including Business Wire, Dow Jones Averages, UPI Business News, and Reuters
- Donoghue Money Fund Reports

Prodigy, (800) 776-3449

- *Kiplinger's Personal Finance Magazine*—a library of articles from back issues
- PCFN or the PC Financial Network—discount brokerage service and investment reports
- Wall Street Edge—summaries of information collected from security analysts' newsletters
- Strategic Investor—provides investors with information (such as important ratios and research) on more than 5,000 companies and over 3,400 mutual funds

- Money Talk—electronic bulletin board where members can exchange information and ideas
- Online banking—Members can pay bills and manage their bank and investment accounts.

World Wide Web

This is a portion of the *Internet* that uses menus and graphics to display information. The two best sites to visit are *Edgar (Electronic Data Gathering, Analysis, and Retrieval)* and *NETworth.*

Edgar is a database of documents that publicly traded companies file with the SEC. NETworth is an investor service that is supported by companies that want exposure for their products. It has a variety of information, including reports from market experts, stock quotes and fundamentals, and a weekly market update. One of the latest additions is from Disclosure Inc., which provides SEC document and database services.

WHAT DATABASES ARE OF PARTICULAR INTEREST TO INVESTORS?

Some databases offering fundamental and technical screening devices are easily accessible through PCs. Not all databases offer the same information. They are useful for analyzing large numbers of companies in a short time period. Ratios can be created, analyzed, and compared. Trends and regression analysis can be performed. Searches can be implemented for specific kinds of companies. For example, one could read through the screen for companies meeting certain parameters, such as:

1. Dividend yield greater than 7 percent.
2. Earnings growth greater than 20 percent per year.

3. Price/earnings ratio less than 10 times.
4. Market price less than book value.

Some databases provide useful economic and monetary data for the U.S. economy, while others contain international economic and company data.

Value LineDatabase II

It provides financial and statistical information for over 1,600 companies, representing 95 percent of the dollar value of stocks traded on major U.S. companies. This database can be accessed by *CompuServe*.

Stock Investor

From the American Association of Individual Investors (625 North Michigan Avenue, Department NLG, Chicago, IL 60611, (312) 280-0170), provides an easy, convenient way to screen stocks, enabling you to screen through data on over 7,000 stocks using a menu-driven program. You can research stocks by using over 100 predetermined financial variables or by creating your own variables. The program data is updated quarterly and covers all stocks on the NYSE, Amex, OTC, and OTC Small-Cap. It also provides *IBES* earnings estimates.

CompuServe's FundWatch Online

FundWatch Online by *Money* magazine allows you to quickly screen over 1,700 mutual funds using criteria which mirror your investment philosophy, to find only the ones which are consistent with your goals, and directly obtain a detailed report on a fund by entering its name or ticker symbol. It also allows you to conduct in-depth research on a particular stock with such services as *Disclosure II*, *S&P On-line*, and *Value Line Database II*.

Prodigy's Strategic Investor

It enables you to screen, select, and evaluate over 5,200 stocks and 4,000 mutual funds. Prodigy also has the following on-line services:

1. TradeLine—provides price and volume charts and data on virtually any security or mutual fund.
2. Company Reports—has comprehensive data on over 6,000 public companies.
3. Mutual Fund Center—provides detailed information on funds.

CompuServe's RATEGRAM

This service ranks the highest yielding taxable and tax-exempt money market funds available. It also identifies the institution and provides its telephone number, the minimum required deposit, and a safety index rating.

IBES—Institutional Brokers Estimate System Summary

Further investigation of a company can be performed through *CompuServe*. It contains consensus earnings forecasts compiled from estimates made by over 3,400 analysts at 130 brokerage and research firms. It also compares the estimates with the stock's current price to predict forward price/earnings (P/E) ratios.

Compustat

From Standard & Poor's, it contains financial data
from more than 9,000 publicly held companies' annual and quarterly reports and SEC filings. The database is updated annually. You can choose from
various reports that summarize background, outlook, performance, business earnings and yield,
market performance, balance sheet, and company
history. This database can be accessed by
CompuServe.

CRSP (Center for Research in Security Prices)

Published by the University of Chicago, it consists
of three stock market history files: The daily AMEX/
NYSE returns since 1967, the monthly returns since
1926, and the daily NASDAQ returns since 1972.

Disclosure

From Disclosure Incorporated (5161 River Road,
Bethesda, MD 20816; (301)951-1300), database containing financial and textual data from SEC documents on about 11,000 public companies. Also included are over 250 variables such as company
name, address, phone number, financial statements,
financial ratios, and weekly prices for each company.

GLOBAL Vantage

From Standard & Poor's, it provides financial data
for approximately 7,600 companies from 33 countries around the world.The distribution includes
companies in Europe (16 countries), North America

(2), Pacific Basin (8), and other regions of the world (7).

COINTEL (Company Information for Telebase)

Within the *CompuServe* network, it provides information on European companies.

FRB (Federal Reserve Board)

Published by the Board of Governors of the Federal Reserve System, it contains financial statements and supporting schedules for more than 15,000 banks. This database is updated annually and has five years' data on-line.

CITIBASE

From Citicorp, a database of time-series data summarizing economic and other conditions in the U.S. The database is updated quarterly.

HOW TO CHOOSE A RIGHT DATABASE?

While investment databases have much to offer, they are expensive. When choosing a database, answer these questions:

- Is any database worth the cost?
- Do I want more than just investment information?
- Is there a database that offers what I want at an affordable price?

Here are further points to consider in choosing between the databases.

Coverage

The number of securities and companies covered, the depth of financial information, and the availability of historical data vary for different databases and on-line services; so does the availability of analysis and advice.

Data Organization

Even when several on-line services get information from the same database, each has its own way of organizing the information for the user. This organization will determine how difficult it is to get around the database, especially if you don't do it everyday, and it may also determine how much it costs you to use the database.

Format

The databases also differ in the way they organize data. As a result, the time it takes to get the data will be different for each service. For example, getting graphs from Telescan, using Telescan software, takes about one-tenth the time it takes on other databases.

The on-line time required to get specific data also depends on the software you use to get to the database. Because most investment software get data from only one or two databases, comparison of the time required from each database is difficult.

Cost

More of the on-line services are offering a flat-rate option in which users pay a standard monthly charge for unlimited access. Prodigy offers *Strategic Investor* for $15 per month, which allows unlimited access to stock and mutual fund databases with wide security coverage. Limited custom screening, however, is a weakness with this service. *Telescan ProSearch* offers a good balance of wide company coverage, a variety of screening variables, flexible screening options, and integrated software. Telescan also offers a variety of pricing options ranging from a pay-as-you-use option to unlimited screening with different prices for primetime or nonprime-time access.

Number of Screening Variables

Obtain a listing of available screening variables to determine if the program will support those variables you find important.

For example, *Value/Screen III* allows you to screen companies based upon Value Line's rankings and projected growth rates, which may be more important for some investors than a complete database. Telescan's ProSearch program is the only service that combines both fundamental and technical factors for screening.

Support Services

The availability and quality of a database's support services are important, just as for other products or services. For example, communicating is difficult and, when something goes wrong, it is hard to know whether the fault lies with the software, the com-

munications system, or the database. It is important to have someone who is knowledgeable and
helpful to walk you through the problem.

(1) On-line services all have customer support
services with an 800 number.

(2) Before you choose a database service, try to
get hands-on experience with at least a few. Some
offer a demonstration diskette with a sample of the
kind of material you will get on-line; others offer
free sample time. Or find or a users' group with a
service that you can try out at a predetermined cost.

(3) Dow Jones News/Retrieval and Equalizer
have the most services for the individual investor.
Their hourly charges are also the highest. Do get
many of Dow Jones' features, it is worth the cost. If
not, you may be able to find what you want on
CompuServe or Prodigy. For price quotations, technical analysis, or other specific data, look at other
databases that may fill your needs at less cost.

WHAT INVESTMENT SOFTWARE ARE AVAILABLE?

A good investment software package makes your
PC a valuable tool for identifying securities to buy
and sell, placing orders on-line, and monitoring securities after you buy them.

Databases that contain thousands of stocks can
be sorted for those that meet your own investment
criteria. You can perform complex technical analysis on individual securities, and generate scores of
market indicators.

Various programs create and analyze charts of
the technical behavior of price movements, and others evaluate the financial data from balance sheets
and income statements. You can access the Dow
Jones News Retrieval System by using the Dow
Jones Investment Evaluator and obtain information

for stocks, bonds, warrants, options, mutual funds, or Treasury issues. Information related to earnings growth rates, 10-K statements, ratios, earnings per share forecasts, and so forth are available on 2,400 companies. The correct data is entered into these software programs, which then it creates standardized analysis from preprogrammed instructions.

New programs are currently able to transfer data from a news retrieval service into a spreadsheet program such as Lotus 1-2-3. An example of this includes the *Dow Jones Spreadsheet Link,* which enables corporate planners, investors, researchers, and competitive analysts to extract data from News/Retrieval for extensive analysis with *Lotus 1-2-3, Quattro Pro,* or *Microsoft's Excel.* It increases the value of spreadsheets by linking them with key financial data. Automatically, the program logs on, collects specified data, and enters it into the spreadsheet for further analysis. Time and money are saved, and it allows individuals flexibility to create their own financial analysis.

What Are Types of Investment Software?

Three main categories of investment software are: fundamental screening and analysis, portfolio management, , and technical analysis. Also, there are two more types of investment software dealing specifically with investments other than stocks; that is, (a) options and futures and (b) fixed income securities.

1. *Fundamental Screening and Analysis.* Most fundamental analysis software is a stock-screening package, which allows you to search through many stocks and identify only those meeting certain, specified criteria. For example,

you may want to identify all stocks on the NYSE that have a market price per share less than $35, a price/earnings ratio less than the S&P 500 Index, a dividend yield greater than 6 percent, and beta less than 1.5. Stock screening packages can narrow your choices in a few minutes.

Normally, you receive a monthly database disk containing up-to-date financial information on a group of stocks.

The type and amount of information available for screening varies with the software package. There are a lot of DOS, Macintosh, and on-line screening software, including:

DOS Programs

1. *Stock Investor,* by AAII
2. *WealthBuilder/Smart Investor,* by Reality Technologies
3. *Value/Screen I,I* by Value Line

Macintosh Programs

1. *WealthBuilder/Smart Investor,* by Reality Technologies
2. *Value/Screen II,* by Value Line

On-Line Services

1. *Telescan Analyzer (Telescan Edge),* by Telescan, Inc.
2. *Strategic Investor,* by Prodigy
3. *Dow Jones News/Retrieval,* by Dow Jones
4. *CompuServe,* by H&R Block

Note: When selecting a stock-screening package:

(1) Compare the number of industries and companies that can be screened, the exchanges on which the stocks are listed, and the frequency with which data are updated.

(2) Check each package for the following types of information: earnings, dividends, assets, market price, sales, liabilities, financial ratios, and proprietary items.

2. *Portfolio Management.* With this software, you can enter the names of the securities you own or want to follow into one or more portfolios, manually enter current prices or get automatic updates from an on-line service, and generate a variety of portfolio status reports.

   These reports show the portfolio's current status. They list each security you own along with information about its type, method of purchase (for cash or on margin), purchase price, number of shares or units owned, current price, and unrealized gain or loss.

   Other types of reports convey vital income tax information. For each security you sell during the tax year, you get the name, number of shares, sale date, total cost, total proceeds, purchase date and gain or loss. The information you need to complete your federal income tax return is included in this report.

   Alternative reports reflect dividend and interest income. Also, reports often provide advance notice of dividends coming due and options expiring.

3. *Technical Analysis.* Technical analysis software is usually for charting. It gives you the ability to plot standard high-low-close-volume bar charts, along with various technical indicators and studies.

As such software requires the input of extensive information, it is wise to compare the kinds of data required to use each package you consider and the sources for such data. An example of this is that if you want to see a basic high-low-close-volume bar chart for General Electric for a 120-day period, the program will require 600 pieces of data. You could always enter the information into the computer little by little, although you might prefer a program that can get it from an on-line service such as the Dow Jones New/Retrieval and Telescan Analyzer, thus greatly reducing the time it takes to create a chart.

A good program will offer a variety of charting abilities.

Note: In selecting a good program, ask:

(1) Can you plot sophisticated indicators to analyze individual securities and the overall stock market?

(2) Are you limited to simple moving-average lines and a few basic charting tools?

(3) Can any data the software collects be easily transferred for use for further analysis in other software programs?

(4) Are the rates charged reasonable?

(5) Can the program show multiple charts on the same screen to permit you to compare the activity in two different stocks or to examine a number of technical indicators at the same time?

(6) Is there an "auto-run" feature? Although programs with this capability are frequently more expensive, they can save a lot of time by allowing you to automatically prepare and print a series of charts you want on a regular basis. You simply enter the auto-run mode, leave the com-

puter, and return later to pick up your printed charts.

(7) Which technical indicators and studies can be plotted?

How Do You Do Comparison Shopping?

There are more than 550 investment software packages on the market, and your neighborhood computer store won't be much help in sorting through the choices. Because of its specialized nature, most investment software is sold only through the mail, meaning you'll have to pay several hundred dollars in advance for software that, in many cases, is not returnable for a refund. Charge it with a credit card. Get all the facts you can before you decide what to buy. Below is a checklist.

* Do market research—look at who's selling what.

    (1) Refer to an excellent user guide, AAII's *Computerized Investing*, published by the *American Association of Individual Investors (AAII)*. Updated annually, the guide contains a description of most investment software packages on the market, and PC and Mac magazines and financial magazines for their independent ratings and reviews.

    (2) Look at the support policies of the company: Do they offer telephone support and, if so, when is it available? Some vendors charge for providing help. Some may operate a bulletin board system (BBS) or forum that you can connect to—not only to solve problems, but also to get operating tips.

    (3) Communicate with other investors at a local investment club or through BBS or Internet.

    (4) Request information from each vendor. Match the features offered with those on your checklist and eliminate packages that don't meet your needs. *Note:* For a nominal amount, many software vendors offer a demonstration package containing a disk and written material that illustrate the features of their software packages.

- List the features you believe absolutely necessary, and be specific. For example, if you want to break down your stocks by industry group to analyze portfolio diversification, write that down. When you're finished, you'll have a checklist of features to look for as you review actual software.

GLOSSARY

All-or-Nothing Order: A type of order for the purchase of stock or options which specifies that the full quantity of your order be filled, or else none of it.

Advisory Letters: Specialized newsletters on investment media usually costing a lot.

Aggressive Growth Fund: Or *maximum capital gain*, *capital appreciation*, or *small-company growth fund*. Type of mutual fund assuming greater risk so as to obtain maximum appreciation (rather than dividend income). It essentially invests in the stocks of beginning, and high-tech firms. Return can be great but so can risk.

Alpha: A measure of risk-adjusted return of a mutual fund. It is the difference between the fund's actual performance and its anticipated performance in light of market risk (beta) and the market's behavior.

American Depository Receipts (ADRs): Foreign company securities traded in the U.S. markets. They are similar to common stock, as each one constitutes a specific number of shares in a given foreign firm.

American Stock Exchange (AMEX) Market Value Index: An unweighted index of the *American Stock*

Exchange (AMEX) stocks. It is calculated by adding all of the plus net changes and minus net changes above or below previous closing prices. The sum is divided by the number of issues listed and the result is added to or subtracted from the prior close. It is more like an average than an index because there is no base period.

Analytical Information: Information used with forecasts and recommendations concerning potential investments.

Annual Report: A glossy, magazine-style report prepared each year by a company for its stockholders. The annual report contains the president's letter, management's discussion of operations, balance sheet, income statement, statement of cash flows, footnotes, and the audit report.

Ask Price: Or *offer price.* The lowest price at which a dealer will sell a security to an investor.

Asset: Financial resources expected to generate benefits to a person, company, or an institution. Examples of assets are land, securities, equipment, and inventory.

Asset Allocation: Percent of the fund in cash, fixed income securities, and common stocks.

At-the-Money: Term used when the striking price of an option is equal to the price of the underlying stock.

Automated Clearing House (ACH): A bank network that allows participating banks to send and receive funds electronically.

Averages: Numbers used to measure the general behavior of security prices by considering the arithmetic average price behavior of a typical group of securities for a specified time period.

Back-End Load: Or *deferred sales charges*. A fee assessed for redeeming mutual fund shares. These charges discourage constant trading in the fund.

Baby Bond: Bond with less than $1,000 par (face) value.

Balance Sheet: A statement showing the nature and amount of a company's assets, debt, and stockholders' equity at a specified date. The balance sheet indicates what the firm owns and owes and its net worth.

Balanced (Mutual) Fund: A mutual fund combining investments in common stock, preferred stock, and bonds. It attempts to generate income and capital appreciation. Balanced funds underperform all-stock funds in markets of increasing prices.

Bargain Hunters: Investors looking to buy shares at reduced prices in a period of market decline.

Barron's: A weekly publication by Dow Jones containing stories on specific companies and industries as well as data on the financial markets.

Basis Point: A unit of measure for the change in interest rates for bonds and notes. One basis point is equal to 1/100th of a percent, that is, 0.01 percent. Thus, 100 basis points is equal to 1 percent. For example, an increase in a bond's yield from 6.0 percent to 6.5 percent is a rise of 50 basis points.

Bear: Someone who thinks the market will decline.

Bear Market: When security prices decline (a bear's claws point down).

Bearer Bond: A bond which does not have the owner's name recorded; its coupons can be clipped and cashed by any holder.

Bearish: The anticipation of a decline in the price of a stock or the overall market.

Benchmark: An index or fund average used in fund reports to compare performance. Benchmarks include the S&P 500 Stock Index, Europe, Austria, and Far East (EAFE) Index, and Lipper Averages or Indexes.

Beta: A measure of systematic (nondiversifiable) risk. It reveals how the price of a security or a mutual fund reacts to market forces. The market has a beta of 1. The higher the beta, the riskier the security or fund.

Bid and Asked: Also called a quotation or quote. The bid is the highest price anyone has declared that he wants to pay for a security at a particular time; the asked is the lowest price anyone will take at the same time.

Big Board: New York Stock Exchange.

Black Monday: Refers to the October 19, 1987 plunge that saw the Dow Jones Industrial Average fall a record 22.6 percent. (See also Great Crash).

Blue Chip: A stock of a high-quality, financially sound company (blue chips in poker are worth more than red or white chips).

Bond: A debt obligation of a company, municipality, or government, stated at a specified interest rate and a maturity date.

Bond Funds: Mutual funds investing mostly in bonds, so as to generate current income.

Bond Ratings: Letter grades of the quality of a bond.

Bond Yield: Effective rate of interest earned on a bond taking into account the nominal interest and any discount or premium.

Book: A record kept by a specialist in a security of buy and sell orders at stated prices, in sequence of receipt, which are left with him by other brokers.

Book-Entry Bond: No certificate is issued, but a computerized record of ownership is kept.

Book Value: The net assets (assets minus liabilities) divided by the number of common shares outstanding. Book value may be substantially different from market value.

Broker: An agent who executes buy and sell orders of stocks, bonds, and so forth. For this service a commission is charged.

Bull: A person expecting increasing security prices.

Bull Market: A period of increasing prices (a bull's horns thrust upward).

Bullish: The anticipation of increasing prices of a specific stock or the overall market.

Business Cycle: An indication of the present economic state. It is the fluctuation in economic activity.

Call: The right to purchase 100 shares of a particular stock at a set price per share (the exercise price) for a specified time period (until expiration).

Callable: A bond or preferred stock redeemable by the issuing company.

Capital Gain or Capital Loss: Profit or loss from selling a capital asset. It may be either short-term (one year or less) or long-term (more than one year).

Capital Gains Distribution: Income for investors arising from net long-term profits of a mutual fund realized when portfolio securities are sold at a gain. The gains are distributed by fund managers to shareholders at least yearly.

Capital Stock: Ownership shares in a company, including common and preferred stock.

Capital Market: The long-term financial market in which long-term securities (e.g., stocks and bonds) are bought and sold.

Capitalization: Total amount of the different types of securities, such as common stock and bonds, issued by a company. Bonds are typically stated on the books of the issuing company at face value. Common and preferred shares are stated at par value.

Cash Flow: (1) Net income plus noncash expenses (e.g., depreciation) less noncash revenue (e.g., amortization of deferred revenue) equals cash flow from operations. (2) Cash receipts less cash payments.

Certificate of Deposit (CD): A term account offering higher interest than passbook or other savings accounts. There is a penalty for early withdrawal.

Chicago Board Options Exchange (CBOE): Organized national market where foreign currency, index, and interest rate options are traded by members for their own and customers' accounts.

Chicago Board of Trade (CBOT): Exchange that trades commodity futures and futures options.

Circuit Breakers: A post-1987 crash system of rules to temporarily halt trading of stocks and futures contracts when prices plummet. (See also Black Monday).

Commodity Futures Trading Commission (CFTC): Federal agency regulating commodities traded in organized contract markets.

Closed-End Mutual Fund: A mutual fund operating with a fixed number of outstanding shares.

Chicago Mercantile Exchange (CME): Trades futures contracts in commodities and options.

Churning: Practice by a broker to make frequent buy and sell trades in an account without benefiting the investor. It is unethical and illegal.

Collateral: Securities or other assets pledged by a borrower to obtain a loan.

Closing Tick: The difference between the number of companies whose last trade of the day was on a downtick from those closing trades which were on an uptick. (See also Tick).

Commission: The broker's fee to purchase and sell securities for an investor.

Commodity Exchange, Inc. (COMEX): Trades futures and futures options and is located in the Commodity Exchange Center of New York City.

Common Stock: Securities representing an equity interest in a company. If the firm has also issued preferred shares, both common and preferred have ownership rights, but the preferred usually has prior claim on dividends and, in bankruptcy, assets. Stockholders come after bondholders or other creditors of the business.

Compounding: The process of earning interest on the interest already accumulated.

Computerized Program Trading: A computer-run strategy enabling big institutional investors to make lightening-quick trades of huge amounts of stocks, stock index futures, and options on index futures in attempts to profit from price disparities.

Consolidated Balance Sheet: A balance sheet presenting the financial position of a parent and one or more subsidiaries.

Consolidated Income Statement: An income statement detailing a company's revenue, expenses, and profit or loss for a given period. It includes all of the company's operations and subsidiaries.

Contingencies: In an annual report, a section that discusses claims and litigations against the company and assesses whether they would have a significant impact on finances or operations.

Convertible: A bond or preferred share which may be converted by the owner for common stock or another security, typically of the same company, in conformity with the terms of the issue.

Correction: A reverse movement, usually downward, in the overall stock market, or in the price of an individual stock, bond, commodity, or index.

Cost Basis: The price paid for an investment. This is used to compute capital gains or losses when shares are sold.

Coupon Bond: A bearer bond on which interest payments are made when the attached coupons are presented to the paying agent.

Covered Options: Options written against stock owned. For example, a call can be written on stock you hold.

Credit Rating: An assessment of a bond's quality as determined by a rating agency such as Moody's or Standard & Poor's.

Credit Risk: The risk of a bond that its issuer will default on interest or principal payments.

Cumulative Preferred: A stock with a provision that if dividends are omitted, the omitted dividends must be paid before dividends may be paid to common stockholders.

Curb Exchange: Former name of the American Stock Exchange, the second largest U.S. exchange. The term comes from the market's origin on the streets of downtown New York.

Currency Futures: Futures contracts on foreign currencies stated in dollars per unit of the underlying foreign currency.

Current Exchange Risk: The risk that the return on an international security would be negatively affected by a change in the value of a currency relative to the foreign currency. For example, a weak dollar would boost the security's return to U.S. investors, while a strong dollar would lower its return.

Currency Options: Call and put options written on foreign currencies.

Current Yield: Current income an investment provides compared to the prevailing market price.

Custodian: The bank or trust company that maintains a mutual fund's assets, including its portfolio of securities or some record of them. It provides safe-keeping of securities but has no role in portfolio management.

Cyclical Stock: A stock that varies in market price with changes in the economy. It increases in price during an upturn in business conditions and decreases in price during downturns.

Dealer: A buyer and seller of securities who keeps an inventory of the issues traded in; different from the broker, who serves as the buyer's or seller's representative for a fee.

Debenture: A promissory note secured by the general credit and assets of a company and typically not backed by collateral or a lien on specific assets.

Default Risk: See Credit Risk.

Defensive Stock: A stock fairly constant in price during business downturns and upturns.

Delivery: Transfer of securities from buyer to seller. The certificate shows shares purchased "regular way" on the New York Stock Exchange. Usually delivered to the buyer's broker on the third business day after the transaction.

Descriptive Information: Factual information on the prior behavior of the economy, stock market, industry, or some investment instrument.

Discount: A security selling for below its face or par value.

Discount Broker: A stockbroker charging a low fee and not furnishing investment advice.

Discount Rate: The interest rate charged to banks for loans by the Federal Reserve Bank.

Discretionary Account: A customer giving his broker the right to use his judgement in buying and selling securities.

Distribution: (1) A payment of dividends or capital gains to shareholders. (2) A redemption from a retirement account. (3) Selling over a period of time of a large block of securities without unduly lowering the market price.

Dividend Reinvestment: Dividends that an investor reinvests in the company or mutual fund by buying additional shares. A mutual fund does not assess a sales commission on reinvested dividends.

Dollar-Cost Averaging: The technique of investing a fixed sum at regular intervals regardless of stock market movements. This reduces average share costs to the investor, who acquires more shares in periods of lower prices and fewer shares in periods of higher prices. In this way, investment risk is spread over time.

Dow Jones Bond Averages: Mathematical averages of ending prices for categories of utility, industrial, and corporate bonds.

Dow Jones Industrial Average (DJIA): A stock average of 30 blue-chip industrial stocks chosen for total market value and overall public ownership. Considered to depict broad market activity.

Diversification: Spreading investments among different companies in different industries. Diversification exists by owning securities of many companies having negative or no correlation.

Dividend: The payment approved by the board of directors to be distributed proportionally based on the shares outstanding.

Dividend Yield: Dividends per share divided by either market price per share or initial cost per share. It is used by an investor as a return measure.

Dow Theory: A way of evaluating market trends by identifying the movement of the Dow-Jones industrial and transportation averages. A bull market is presumed to continue as long as one average makes new highs which are "confirmed" by the other. A reversal is indicated when one average refuses to confirm the other; a bear market is presumed to continue as long as one average makes new lows which are confirmed by the other.

Downtick: Or *minus tick*. A transaction of securities executed at a price below that in the preceding transaction. For example, if a stock has been selling at $23 per share, the next transaction is a downtick if it is at $22 1/8.

Duration: The number of years a bond takes to recover its investment. It is widely regarded as a more accurate measure of maturity of a bond since it considers the effect of rate changes on the security's price. It is used as a gauge of a bond or bond portfolio's interest rate risk.

EAFE Index: More exactly, Morgan Stanley Capital International Europe, Austria, and Far East Index. It is a market-weighted index composed of 1,041 companies representing the stock markets of Europe, New Zealand, and the Far East.

Earnings per Share (EPS): Net income divided by outstanding common shares.

Equipment Trust Certificate: A type of security to pay for equipment. Title to the asset is held by a trustee until the notes are paid. It is a lien on the property.

Equity: (1) The ownership interest of stockholders. (2) Excess value of securities over the debit balance in a margin account.

Equity REIT: A type of REIT buying a portfolio of specific properties to generate both current income and capital gains.

Exchange Privilege: Or *switching privilege.* The right to transfer from one mutual fund to another, generally within the same fund family, at little or no cost.

Ex-dividend: A synonym for "without dividend." Stocks have record dates for the payment of dividends and interest. The New York Stock Exchange establishes dates a few days before the transfer of the stock. Investors who purchase stocks to this date receive this dividend; investors who purchase after it do not.

Exercise: Meeting the provisions of the option contract. The number of shares of the underlying stock are purchased or sold at the price stated in the option contract.

Exit Fees: Or *redemption fees.* Charges to redeem mutual fund shares irrespective of the time period the investor owned the shares.

Expense Ratio: The ratio of total expenses (such as management fees and other administrative expenses) to net assets of the mutual fund. The ratio is listed in the fund's prospectus.

Expiration: The day the option contract expires unless previously exercised. All option contracts expire on the Saturday after the third Friday of the expiration month.

Ex-Rights: Without the rights.

Extra: "Extra dividend" beyond the regular dividend, which may be in cash or stock.

Face Value: The amount of the promise to pay shown on the face of a bond.

Family of Funds: A group of mutual funds, each having different investment objectives, that are under the same management company. A shareholder can transfer between the funds, sometimes at no charge, as investment objectives change.

Federal National Mortgage Association (FNMA): Also known as Fannie Mae. A government-sponsored corporation that buys and sells FHA, FHDA, or VA mortgages.

Federal Reserve Bulletin: Summarizes economic and business conditions, employment statistics, retail prices, and industrial production.

Financial Highlight: Usually the third page of an annual report. It is a table containing the sales, net income or loss, and earnings per share (EPS). Many of these tables contain percentage changes from previous years.

Financial Information Services: Services providing historical, financial, market and economic data, and current stock market prices and financial news. Information is obtained by accessing an on-line database.

Financial Futures: Futures contracts in which the underlying commodities are financial assets. Examples are debt securities, foreign currencies, or market baskets of common stocks.

Financial Planner: A person having expertise in providing personal financial planning services to individuals. He may be an independent professional (e.g., CFP) or associated with a large investment, insurance, or other institution.

Fiscal Year: A company's accounting year other than Jan. 1 through Dec. 31. An example is July 1 to June 30.

Fixed Charges: Constant expenses, such as bond interest, taxes, and royalties, that a business must incur regardless of profitability.

Fixed Income Securities: Investments providing a fixed, periodic return, such as bonds paying semi-annual interest.

Form 10-K: A report filed with the Securities and Exchange Commission (SEC) once a year by every company that has more than 500 shareholders, has stock traded on a public exchange, or has issued a registered security, such as a stock or bond. The 10-K discloses sales, profits, and losses for the past five years and other significant information. All data must be audited by an independent accounting firm.

Front-End Load: Initial sales charge at the date of the purchase of mutual funds. Administration and management fees are charged annually regardless of a fund being a front-end load, back-end load (12b-1), or no-load.

Full-Service Brokerage House: A brokerage house that provides research reports, investment advice, and a broker to act as a sounding board for ideas.

Fundamental Analysis: The evaluation of a company's financial statements, including footnotes.

Futures Contract: A contract to deliver a specified amount of an item by some given future date.

Futures Market: Or *futures exchange*. The commodity market that trades futures contracts. It is a self-regulating body whose aim is to decide the terms for acceptance of members, their trading restrictions, and their behavior in trading. Examples are Amex Commodity Exchange, The Commodity Exchange, Inc. (COMEX), the New York Mercantile Exchange, the Chicago Board of Trade, and the Chicago Mercantile Exchange.

General Mortgage Bond: A bond collateralized by a blanket mortgage on a company's property, usually subordinated to specific pledges against specified properties.

Global Fund: A mutual fund that invests in both U.S. and foreign securities.

Good-Till-Canceled (G.T.C. Order): This is an order for the purchase or sale of a security remaining in effect until filled or canceled.

Government Bonds: Obligations of the U.S. Government, considered as the highest grade because they have the least risk.

Government National Mortgage Association (GNMA): Government-owned corporation, nick-named *Ginnie Mae*. GNMA issues pass-through securities. These pass through all payments of interest and principal received on a pool of federally insured mortgage loans. GNMA guarantees all payments of principal and interest on the mortgages on a timely basis.

Great Crash: The stock market collapse that occurred on the original Black Monday October 28, 1929, when the Dow Jones Average dropped 12.8 percent. The historic event helped trigger the Depression of the 1930s.

Growth and Income Fund: A mutual fund with the objective of periodic dividends and capital gains by investing in quality securities.

Growth Fund: A mutual fund having the objective of maximizing its return through capital gains. It usually invests in the stocks of potential companies which are anticipated to increase in value faster than inflation.

Growth Stock: A company having good prospects for future growth in earnings and activities.

Hedging: Protecting oneself from wide market changes by taking both buy and sell positions in a security or commodity.

Holding Company: A business that owns the voting shares of other companies.

Horizontal Analysis: The percentage change in an account or category over the years to reveal trends.

Income Bonds: Bonds promising to repay principal at the maturity date, but will pay interest only as it is earned. The issuer typically promises to add any unpaid interest to the face amount of the income bond when it is paid off.

Income Fund: A mutual fund that primarily seeks current income rather than growth of capital. It will tend to invest in stocks and bonds that normally pay high dividends and interest.

Indenture: A written contract under which bonds are issued, stipulating the maturity date, interest rate, collateral, and so on.

Index: An index differs from an average in that it weights changes in prices by size for the companies affected. The Standard & Poor's Index of 500 stocks computes changes in prices as if all the shares of each company were sold every day, thus giving a big company like General Motors its greater weight.

Index Arbitrage: The purchase of a stock-index future in one market and sale of the stocks that constitute that index in another market, or vice versa, in order to profit from temporary price differences in the two markets. Index arbitrage is the most widely used form of *computerized program trading.*

Index Fund: A mutual fund that has as its major objective the matching of the performance of a specific stock index, such as the *Standard & Poor's 500 Composite Stock Price Index.* An example is Vanguard's Index 500 Fund.

Index Options: Option contracts on stock indexes. Since there is no single underlying asset, covered writing is not possible with stock indexes.

Individual Investor: An individual whose major concerns in the purchase of a security are regular dividend income, safety of the original investment, and, if possible, capital appreciation.

Insider Trading: Buying and selling of stock by insiders, such as corporate executives, who have inside information concerning a company that is not known to others.

Institutional Investor: An institution such as a mutual fund, bank, insurance company, or pension fund, operating on behalf of a broad client base that trades large blocks of securities.

Interest Rate Futures: Futures contracts on fixed income securities. As interest rates decrease, the value of the contract increases. A basis point equals 1/100 of 1 percent.

Interest Rate Options: Put and call options written on fixed income securities.

International Fund: A mutual fund that invests in securities of foreign companies. It makes substantial gains when the dollar is falling and foreign stock prices are increasing. Some funds invest in many overseas markets, while others only concentrate on particular foreign areas. Examples are T.Rowe Price International Stock Fund, T. Rowe Price Europe Fund, Fidelity Pacific Basin Fund, and Fidelity Canada Fund.

In-the-Money: A call option with a striking price less than the market price of the underlying security; a put option with a striking price greater than the market price of the underlying security.

Intrinsic Value: The intrinsic value of an option is what its premium would be if the price of the underlying stock would remain at its current level until expiration.

Investment: The use of money to make more money, to earn income or capital appreciation, or both.

Investment Banker: Also referred to as an underwriter. The middleman between the corporation raising money and the public. When an investment banker or syndicate underwrites a new issue, it stands ready to buy the new securities if they cannot be sold to the public.

Investment Club: A group who combine their funds to buy and sell stocks, bonds, and so on.

Investment Company: See Investment Trust.

Investment Counselor: A professional engaged in performing investment advisory services.

Investment-Grade Bond: Any bond rated in the top four categories; i.e., triple-B or higher. (See also Junk Bond).

Investment Letters: Newsletters providing, on a subscription basis, the evaluations and recommendations of experts in different aspects of investment instruments.

Investment Software: Computer programs that track investments in shares, cost, and income. The programs update the market value of securities, show unrealized gains or losses, present accumulated dividends, and the like. Examples of investment software are Dow Jones Market Manager PLUS and Value/Screen II.

Investment Trust: A company that invests in other companies after which it sells its own shares to the public. If it is a closed-end company, it sells its shares only. If it is an open-end company or a mutual fund, it repeatedly buys and sells its shares.

Issue: Any of a company's securities, or the act of distributing such securities.

Junk Bonds: Bonds with a speculative credit rating of BB or less by financial rating services. They are generally more volatile, but pay higher yields than investment-grade bonds. They are issued by companies without long track records of sales or earnings, or by those with questionable credit strength. They have been key to financing takeovers in recent years.

Leverage: A broad term to describe using a smaller amount of an investment to control the total amount of the investment. Buying a stock on "margin," for example, permits an investor to borrow up to half the price of the stock. The ratio of dollars controlled to dollars invested in that case would be 2:1.

Limit Order: A customer's order to a broker to buy or sell at a given price or better.

Limited Partnership (Syndicate): Partnership in which the limited partner is obligated for the initial investment. The general partner (typically the organizer) who operates the syndicate has unlimited financial liability.

Lipper Average and Lipper Index: Calculated by Lipper Analytical Services, the average total return of funds in the same investment category and a hypothetical return which measures the performance of a specific market sector. These returns are often used to compare a fund's return to the performance of similar funds or the market sector.

Liquidation: The process of converting securities or property into cash. Or the dissolution of a company, with cash remaining after sale of its assets and payment of all indebtedness being distributed to the shareholders.

Liquidity: The degree of ease with which a security can be sold for cash.

Listed Stock: The stock of a company traded on a national securities exchange, and for which a listing application and a registration statement, providing detailed data about the company and its activities, have been filed with the SEC and the exchange involved.

Load (Sales Charge): A sales fee charged to buy shares in many mutual funds sold by brokers or other members of a salesforce. Typically, the charge ranges from 2 to 8.5 percent of the initial investment. The charge is added to the net asset value (NAV) per share when determining the offer price. Not all mutual funds have a load.

Load (Mutual) Fund: A mutual fund sold to the public that charges sales commissions, typically called a *front-end load* when purchased.

Long: Signifies ownership of securities. "I am long 200 Merck" means the speaker owns 200 shares in that company. This term is used as the opposite of being "short" on an investment.

Low-Load Fund: A mutual fund that charges a minimal commission.

M: Abbreviation for 1,000. It is used to specify the face value of a bond.

Management: The board of directors, elected by the stockholders, and the officers of the corporation, appointed by the board of directors.

Management Fee: The fee paid for fund or portfolio management, expressed as a percentage of the fund's assets.

Management Letter: In an annual report, a letter from the chairman or chief executive officer (CEO) informing shareholders about the company's operations for the past year. It is designed to address significant events at the company and give some analysis of its financial state.

Margin: The amount paid by the customer when he uses credit to purchase a security, the balance being advanced by the broker. According to Federal Reserve regulations, the initial margin required in the past 20 years has ranged from 40 percent of the purchase price all the way to 100 percent.

Margin Call: A demand upon a customer to send additional money or securities to the broker. The call is made when a purchase is made; also if a customer's equity in a margin account drops below a minimum standard established by an exchange or by the firm.

Margin Purchases (Buying): The buying of securities using some borrowed funds. The percentage of borrowed funds is limited by both law and brokerage firms.

Margin Requirement: Provision stating what percentage of each dollar used to buy a security must be provided by the investor.

Market Maker: Firm specializing in making markets for given securities. The market maker buys

and sells the security receiving the difference between the purchase price and selling price as compensation.

Market Order: An order by a customer to a broker
to purchase or sell at the best price available when
the order reaches the trading floor.

Market Price: For a security, market price is typically considered the last reported price at which it
sold.

Market Return: The average return on all stocks,
such as those in the S&P 500 Stock Composite Index.

Market Risk: For bond investors, the risk that interest rates will be moving higher, pushing bond
prices down. For equity investors, the risk that equity prices will decline.

Maturity: The number of years until a bond's principal is repaid. Generally, long-term bond prices are
more volatile to changes in interest rates than short-
term counterparts.

Money Market: Market in which short-term debt
securities, such as T-bills and certificates of deposit
(CDs), are purchased and sold.

Money Market (Mutual) Fund: A mutual fund investing high-yielding, short-term money market
instruments such as U.S. T-bills and commercial
paper.

Moody's Investors Services: A company that publishes a variety of investment reference manuals,
such as *Moody's Manuals.*

Mortgage REITs: REITs investing in long-term
mortgage bonds. (See also Real Estate Investment
Trust.)

Municipal Bonds: Debt securities of state or local governments or other public agencies. Their interest is exempt from federal income tax and from state income tax for residents of that state.

Mutual Fund: A company that uses its capital to invest in other companies. There are two major types: closed-end and open-end. Shares in closed-end investment trusts are readily transferable in the open market and are bought and sold like other shares. Capitalization of these companies is fixed. Open-end funds sell their own new shares to investors, stand ready to buy back their old shares, and are not listed. Open-end funds are so called because their capitalization is not fixed and they issue more shares as investors want them.

Naked: An uncovered option strategy. It is an investment in which the written options are *not* matched with a long stock position or a long option position that expires no earlier than the written options. The loss potential with such a strategy is unlimited.

National Association of Securities Dealers (NASD): A self-regulatory organization that has jurisdiction over certain broker-dealers who trade over-the-counter (OTC) securities. The NASD requires member broker-dealers to register, and conducts examinations for compliance with net capital requirements and other regulations.

NASDAQ Indexes: Measures of current price behavior of securities sold in the over-the counter (OTC) market.

Negotiable: Refers to a security, title to which, when properly endorsed by the owner, is transferable by delivery.

Net Asset Value (NAV): The current market worth of a mutual fund share. Mutual funds compute their assets daily by summing the market value of all securities owned. All liabilities are subtracted, and the balance divided by the number of shares outstanding. The ensuing figure is the net asset value per share.

Net Change: Change in the price of a security from the closing price on one day to the closing price on the next trading day. If a stock is entitled to a dividend one day, but is traded "ex-dividend" the next, the dividend is considered in computing the change. For example, if the ending market price of a stock on Tuesday—the last day it was entitled to receive a $1 dividend—was $65 a share, and $66 at the close of the next day, when it was "ex-dividend," the price would be considered unchanged. With a stock split, a stock selling at $70 the day before a 2-for-1 split and trading the next day at $35 would also be considered unchanged. If it sold at $37, it would be considered up $2. The net change is typically the last figure in a stock price list.

New Issue: A stock or bond sold by a company for the first time. Proceeds may be used to retire outstanding securities of the company, for new plant or equipment, or for additional working capital.

New York Stock Exchange Indexes: Measure of the current price behavior of the stocks traded on the NYSE.

No-Load Fund: A commission-free mutual fund that sells its shares at net asset value (NAV), either directly to the public or through an affiliated distributor, without the addition of a sales charge.

Nominal Yield: (1) The stated rate of interest (or coupon rate) on a debt security or loan. It may not be the true rate earned. In the case of bonds, the terms *nominal interest rate* and *coupon rate* are synonymous. The interest received on a bond investment equals the nominal interest rate times the face value of the bond. For example, on an 8%, $10,000 bond, the investor would receive annual interest income of $800 ($10,000 x 8%). (2) The interest rate without adjusting it for inflation.

Noncumulative: A preferred stock on which unpaid dividends are lost.

Options Clearing Corporation (OCC): A company issuing calls listed on the options exchanges. Orders are placed with this corporation, which then issues the calls or closes the position.

Odd Lot: An amount of stock less that the established 100-share unit or 10-share unit of trading: From 1 to 99 shares for the great majority of issues; 1 to 9 for so-called inactive stocks.

Offer: The price at which a person will sell, Opposed to bid, the price at which one will buy.

On-Line Database: A service, such as Dow Jones News/Retrieval or CompuServe, furnishing historical, financial, market, and economic data or current stock market prices and financial news obtained via telecommunications.

Open-End (Mutual) Funds: A mutual fund that offers to sell and redeem shares on a continual basis for an indefinite time period. Shares are bought at net asset value (NAV) plus commission (if any) and redeemed at NAV less a service charge (if any).

Open Order: Buy or sell order for a security at a stated price. An open order continues until executed or canceled by the customer.

Option: A contract allowing an investor to reserve the right to buy or sell a stipulated number of shares of stock at a fixed price per share for a limited time period. There are two types of option contracts: calls and puts.

Out-of-the-Money: Term used when the striking price of an option is below the price of the underlying stock for a call option, or greater than the price of the underlying stock for a put option.

Overnight Orders: Orders placed to buy and sell securities after the market is closed.

Over-the-Counter (OTC): Trading of securities through a broker-dealer, typically through a computer or over the telephone, without using the facilities of an exchange. The securities may or may not be listed on an exchange.

Pacific Stock Exchange (PSE): Exchange that handles trading of West Coast companies.

Paper Profit: An unrealized gain on a security still held. Paper profits become realized when the security is sold.

Par Value: For a stock, the dollar amount assigned each share of stock in the company's charter. For preferred issues and bonds, the value on which the issuer promises to pay dividends.

Participating Preferred: A stock entitled to receive a proportionate share of excess dividends after common stockholders have received their regular dividend.

Passed Dividend: Omission of a scheduled dividend.

Penny Stocks: Low-priced, usually risky stocks, which typically sell for $5.00 or less per share. Penny stocks are traded in the over-the counter (OTC) market.

Performance (Go-Go) Fund: A mutual fund portfolio of speculative securities designed to achieve very high returns. However, they carry considerable risk.

Point: (1) In the case of shares of stock, a point is $1. For example, if GM shares increase 3 points, each share has risen $3. (2) In the case of bonds, a point means $10, because a bond is quoted as a percentage of $1,000. A bond which rises 4 points gains 4 per cent of $1,000, or $40 in value. (3) In the case of market averages, point means merely that; it is not equivalent to any fixed sum of money.

Portfolio: Holdings of securities by an individual or institution. A portfolio may include bonds, preferred stocks, and common stocks of different types of companies.

Position: (1) An investor's holding of particular securities. (2) A chosen "strategy." For example, an option position is an investment comprised of one or more options.

Precious Metals: Tangible assets including gold, silver, and platinum.

Preferred Stock: A category of stock having a claim on the company's profits before payment may be made on the common stock and typically entitled to priority over common stock if the company fails. Preferred stockholders are usually entitled to dividends at a certain rate and before payment of a dividend on the common stock, depending upon the terms of the issue.

Premium: (1) A market term meaning an excess over an expected norm. A preferred stock or bond selling at a premium brings more than its par value. A new issue that rises quickly from its issuing price sells at a premium. When the redemption price of a bond or preferred issue is higher than par, redemption is at a premium. (2) The purchasing or selling price of an option contract.

Price/Earnings (P/E) Ratio: Also called earnings multiple or market multiple, current market price of a stock divided by the last year's earnings per share (EPS), i.e., the total EPS of the last four reported quarters.

Price-to-Book Ratio: Market price per share divided by book value (tangible assets less all liabilities) per share. A measure of stock valuation relative to net assets.

Primary Distribution: Or *primary offering*. The initial sale of a company's securities.

Primary Market: A market of new securities issues.

Prime Rate: The interest rate charged by banks to their most financially strong customers for short-term loans.

Principal: The individual for whom a broker executes an order, or a dealer buying or selling for his own account. The term "principal" may also refer to a person's capital or to the face amount of a bond.

Profit Diagram: A chart showing the relationship between the price of a security and the corresponding gain or loss to an investor.

Profit Margin: Net income divided by sales.

Profit Taking: Realizing a gain through sale of a security or commodity.

Profit Table: A table showing the relationship between the price of a security and corresponding gain or loss to an investor.

Program Trading: The term used to describe the use of computer software to formulate security trading decisions. The software has built-in guidelines that instantaneously trigger buy and sell orders when differences in the prices of the securities are great enough to generate profit. Program trading is used by institutional investors, who place buy and sell orders in large blocks of 10,000 or more units. This type of large trade tends to substantially impact the prices of securities in the market. Sometimes, the program trading orders reach the trading floors from a number of firms. This impact can be seen most readily during what is called *triple witching hours* (or *days*). The triple witching hour occurs four times annually in the hour prior to the moment (4:00 P.M. EST, on the third Friday of March, June, September, and December) when listed stock options, listed stock index options, and commodity index futures all expire at once. During this hour, the Dow Jones Industrial Average and other indices may change drastically.

Prospectus: A circular, required by the Securities Act of 1933, that describes securities being offered for sale. Its objective is full disclosure, particularly of any negative prospects for the issuer. It discloses facts regarding the issuer's activities, including the experience of its management, its financial position, any expected legal issues that could impact the company, and potential risks of investing in the business.

Proxy: Written permission given by a stockholder to someone else to represent him and vote his shares at a shareholders' meeting.

Proxy Statement: Information required by the SEC to be given to stockholders as a prerequisite to solicitation of proxies.

Prudent Man Rule: A rule stating that a fiduciary, such as a trustee, may invest only in a list of securities allowed by the state. In other states, the trustee may invest in a security in a prudent, conservative manner.

Put: An option contract giving the right to sell 100 shares of a particular stock at a set price per share (the striking price) for a limited time (until expiration).

Puts and Calls: Options giving the right to buy or sell a fixed amount of a certain stock at a specified price within a particular time. A put gives the holder the right to sell the stock; a call the right to buy it. Puts are bought by those who believe a stock may go down. A put obligates the seller to take delivery of the stock and pay the specified price to the owner of the option within the contract's time limit. Calls are purchased by those who believe a stock may rise. A call gives the holder the right to buy the stock at the specified price within a fixed period of time. Put and call contracts are written for 30, 60, or 90 days, or longer. If the purchaser of a put or call does not want to exercise the option, the price he paid for the option becomes a loss.

Quotation: Or *quote*. The highest bid to buy and the lowest offer to sell a security in a particular market at a given time. If you ask your broker for a quotation on a stock, he/she may say, for example, "30 1/4 to 30 3/4." This means that $30.25 was the highest price any buyer wished to pay (bid) at the time the quotation was given on the exchange and that $30.75 was the lowest price at which any holder of the stock offered to sell.

Rally: A significant increase following a decline in the general price level of the market or of a specific stock.

Real Estate Investment Trust (REIT): A type of closed-end investment company that invests money, obtained through the issuance of shares to investors, in different kinds of real estate and/or mortgages.

Realized Yield: The rate of return earned over a period of time that is less than the life of the issue.

Record Date: The date on which you must be registered on the company's books as a shareholder to receive a dividend or to vote.

Redemption Price: The price at which a bond may be repurchased before maturity, or a preferred stock retired, at the issuer's option.

Regional Stock Exchanges: Organized securities exchanges for the New York Stock Exchange (NYSE) and the American Stock Exchange (AMEX) that deal mostly in securities having a local or regional flavor.

Registered Bond: A bond registered on the books of the issuer's transfer agent. The owner receives the interest by mail instead of by coupon and must endorse the bond to transfer it.

Registered Representative: Also known as "customers' broker" or "customers' man." An employee of a brokerage firm registered with an exchange or the National Association of Securities Dealers as having passed certain tests and met certain requirements authorizing the representative to serve the public.

Registration: Before a public offering of new securities may be made by a company, or of outstanding securities by controlling stockholders—through the mails or in interstate commerce—the securities must be registered under the Securities Act of 1933. The application must be filed with the SEC by the issuer. It must disclose information on the company's operations, securities, management, and objective of the public offering.

Regulation T: Federal requirement on the amount of credit which may be advanced by brokers and dealers to customers for buying of securities.

Regulation U: Federal rule on the amount of credit which may be advanced by a bank to its customers for the purchase of securities.

Reverse Stock Split: A division of shares into a lesser number.

Rights: The right given by the company on the additional issuance of its stock to buy the new shares before others in proportion to the number of shares owned. In general, the stockholders pay less than the public. The rights enable existing stockholders to retain pro rata ownership interest.

Rollover: Reinvestment of proceeds from an IRA account. The rollover period is 60 days to avoid taxes and possible early distribution penalties.

Round Lot: A unit of trading or a multiple thereof. On the New York Stock Exchange the unit of trading is generally 100 shares in stocks and $1,000 par value in the case of bonds.

Royalty Trust: An investment in oil and gas production, structured like a REIT.

R-squared: A measure of how much of the fund's performance variation can be traced to movement of the overall market. For example, a fund with an R-squared of .9 is 90 percent as diversified as the market. This means 90 percent of the fund's risk is market-related and 10 percent is due to the fund's unique characteristics.

Secondary Distribution: Also referred to as a secondary offering. This is the resale of a block of stock from a major owner or owners, instead of the company itself. It is usually sold through an underwriter or syndicate at a stated price near the stock market's valuation of the shares, but without sales commission or odd-lot differential.

Sector (Mutual) Fund: Or *specialized fund* or *specialty fund*. A mutual fund that invests in one or two fields or industries (sectors). These funds are speculative because price fluctuates depending on how the individual fields or industries perform.

Securities and Exchange Commission (SEC): The overseer of the financial market, established by Congress to protect investors. The SEC administers the Securities Exchange Act of 1933, the Securities Exchange Act of 1934, the Trust Indenture Act, the Investment Company Act, the Investment Advisers Act, the Public Utility Holding Company Act, and the amendments to some of these contained in the Securities Acts Amendments of 1964. SEC rules attempt to protect the public from malpractice and negligence in the securities market and force companies to disclose information pertinent to investors.

Securities Market Indexes: Indexes measuring the value of a sample number of securities to reflect the behavior of the overall market.

Selling Against the Box: A short sale to protect a profit in a security and to defer taxes to a later year. For example, an investor owns 100 shares of XYZ Company which has gone up and which he believes may decline. As a result, he sells the 100 shares "short" and keeps them. If the stock declines, the profit on his short sale is exactly offset by the loss in the market value of the stock owned. If the stock advances, the loss on his short sale is offset by the gain in the market value of the stock he retained.

Shadow Stocks: Small stocks with low institutional interest that have had positive annual earnings for the two previous years. They are out of the spotlight and in the shadows of Wall Street.

Short: This is when an investor sells borrowed stock, expecting to buy it back at a lower price. In options, an investor who has written options has a short position in them.

Short Covering: Buying stock to cover a short sale when delivery is required.

Short Position: Stock sold short and not covered as of a specific date. On the New York Stock Exchange, a tabulation is issued a few days after the middle of the month listing all issues on the Exchange in which there was a short position of 5,000 or more shares and in which the short position had changed by 2,000 or more shares in the prior month. Initial margin requirements for a short position are the same as for a long position.

Short Sale (Selling): An investor sells a stock he or she does not own, hoping to buy it later at a lower price before having to return it to the lender.

Small Investor Index: An index published by *Money* magazine that measures gains and losses of the typical investor. It is based on a portfolio including types of investments held by average small investors.

Specialist: A stock exchange member who maintains an orderly market in a particular stock by buying or selling on his own account when bids and offers by the public are not suitably matched to maintain an orderly market. The specialist is the broker's broker and receives commissions for executing other brokers' orders.

Speculation: The employment of funds by a speculator. The safety of principal is a secondary concern.

Speculator: An investor willing to take greater risk to make substantial gain. The investor's major concern is capital appreciation instead of dividend income. The speculator may buy and sell the same day or speculate in a company he does not anticipate to be profitable for years—for example, by investing in a penny stock.

Split: Increasing the number of outstanding shares proportionately. A two-for-one split by a company with 1,000,000 shares outstanding would result in 2,000,000 shares outstanding. Each holder of 1,000 shares before the two-for-one split would have 2,000 shares, although the proportionate equity interest remains the same. A company sometimes declares a stock split to make the market price per share lower to attract smaller investors. A stock split may arise if the market price of stock has significantly increased and the company wants to lower it.

Spread Order: A type of order for the simultaneous purchase and sale of two options of the same type (calls or puts) on the same underlying security. If placed with a "limit," the two options must be traded for a specified price difference or better.

Spreading: Engaging in two or more futures contracts to earn profit while capping loss exposure. You buy one contract and sell the other.

Standard Deviation: A measure of a security's total risk. It is the sum of security-specific risk and market risk (beta). The more volatile the returns, the higher the standard deviation.

Standard & Poor's Corporation (S&P): The publisher of financial and investment reports and services, including *Corporation Records*, *Stock Guide*, and *Bond Guide*.

Standard & Poor's 500 Stock Composite (S&P 500): The 500 Stock Composite Index computed by Standard & Poor's. It is different from the Dow Jones Industrial Average (DJIA) in several respects. First, it is value-weighted, not price-weighted. The index thus considers not only the price of a stock but also the number of outstanding shares. It is based on the aggregate market value of the stock; i.e., price times number of shares. A benefit of the index over the DJIA is that *stock splits* and *stock dividends* do not impact the index value. A drawback is that large-capitalization stocks—those with a large number of shares outstanding—significantly influence the index value. The S&P 500 consists of four separate indexes: the 400 industrials, the 40 utilities, the 20 transportation, and the 40 financial.

Standardized Yield: Or *SEC yield*. A method of calculating a fund's yield, assuming all portfolio securities are held until maturity. The SEC requires all fixed-income funds to calculate this measure of return.

Stock Dividend: A dividend issuable in stock, not cash. The dividend may be additional shares of the issuing company or shares of another company (usually a subsidiary).

Stock Index Futures: Futures contracts written on broad-based measures of stock market performance like the S&P Stock Index.

Stock Index Option: A call or put option written on a particular market index, such as the S&P Stock Index.

Stock Split: see Split.

Stockholder of Record: A stockholder whose name is registered on the books of the issuing corporation.

Stop Order: An order to buy or sell stock or options at a price other than the current market price. It becomes a market order when the stock or option trades at the price specified.

Straddle: Combining a call and a put on the same security with the identical strike price and expiration date.

Street: The New York financial community located in the Wall Street area.

Street Name: Securities held in the name of a broker rather than a customer. This occurs when the securities have been bought on margin or when the customer wants the securities to be held by the broker.

Striking Price: Or *exercise price*. The fixed price per share stipulated in the option contract.

Stripped Treasuries: Zero-coupon bonds issued by the U.S. Treasury and created by stripping the coupons from a Treasury bond and selling them separately from the principal.

Switching: Selling one security and buying another, or going from one fund to another in the same mutual fund.

Syndicate: A group of investment bankers underwriting and distributing a new issue of securities or a large block of an outstanding issue.

Tangible Assets: Tangible items of real and personal property that usually have a long life, such as housing and other real estate, automobiles, jewelry, cash, and other physical assets.

Tax Equivalent Yield: The yield on a tax-free municipal bond stated on an equivalent before-tax yield basis, because the interest received is not subject to federal income taxes.

Tax-exempt Bond: A bond that pays no federal taxes because it is issued by a state or subordinate division thereof.

Technical Position: Refers to the internal factors affecting the market; as distinguished from fundamental forces, such as economic expansion or decline.

Tender Offers: Offers by an outside party to buy shares directly from current shareholders, usually with the intent of gaining a controlling interest in a corporation.

The Wall Street Journal: A daily financial newspaper published by Dow Jones.

Thin Market: A market in which buying or selling a few shares can affect the security's price disproportionately, either upward or downward.

Third Market: Trading in the over-the-counter market of securities listed on an exchange.

12B-1 Fees: Fees of a mutual fund that cover advertising and marketing costs, but do nothing to improve the performance of the fund. Their main purpose is to bring new customers to the fund, and ultimately more money for the fund's management to invest.

Tick: The term used to describe each incremental change in a stock's price.

Ticker: The device that prints prices and volume of security transactions in cities across the U.S. within minutes after each trade is executed on the exchange.

Time Value: The amount that the premium of an option exceeds its intrinsic value. It incorporates the statistical possibility that the option premium will increase in value. If an option is out-of-the-money, then its entire premium consists of time value.

Tips: Supposedly "inside" information on company affairs.

Total Return: The return earned on a security investment over a given time period. It equals dividend (or interest) income and capital gains (losses).

Trader: One who buys and sells for his own account for short-term appreciation. Also applies to brokerage employees who buy and sell in the over-the-counter market.

Trading Post: Trading locations where securities are bought and sold on the exchange floor.

Transfer Agent: The bank employed by mutual funds to prepare and maintain records relating to fundholder accounts.

Treasury Bill: A short-term (91- to 360-day) debt instrument issued by the federal government. It is safe and marketable.

Treasury Bond: A federal government obligation, typically payable to the bearer, issued at par, with maturities exceeding five years and interest paid twice a year.

Treasury Note: A debt of the federal government, usually typically payable to bearer, with a fixed maturity of not less than one year or more than seven years. It is issued at face value, with semiannual interest payment.

Treasury Stock: Stock issued by a company but later bought back. It may be held in the company's treasury indefinitely, reissued to the public, or retired. Treasury stock receives no dividends and has no vote while held by the company.

Triple Witching Days: See Program Trading.

Turnover: The volume of business in a security or the overall market. If turnover on the New York Stock Exchange is reported at 5,000,000 shares on a particular day, 5,000,000 shares changed hands. Odd-lot turnover is computed separately and typically is not included in reported volume.

Uncovered: An investment in which the written options are not matched with a long stock position or a long option position that expires no earlier than the written options. The potential loss of this strategy is unlimited.

Underlying Stock: This is the stock specified in an option contract, which is transferred upon exercise of the option contract.

Underwriter: See Investment Banker.

Underwriting: The buying of securities from the issuing company, thus guaranteeing the business the capital it wants and in turn selling the securities, at a markup, to the investing public or institutions.

Underwriting Syndicate: A group of underwriters (that is, investment banking firms) assuming the task for selling a new security issue.

Unit Investment Trust (UIT): A closed-end investment company created by investment bankers in which the proceeds from the sale of original shares are invested in a fixed (and unmanaged) portfolio of bonds and held until maturity. Similar to a mutual fund, a unit investment trust offers small investors the benefits of a large, professionally chosen, diversified portfolio. Unlike a mutual fund, however, its portfolio is fixed; once structured, it is not actively managed.

Unlisted: A security not listed on a stock exchange.

Uptick: Or *plus tick*. A price higher than the preceding transaction in the stock. A stock may be sold short only on an uptick, or on a *zero-plus tick*. A zero-plus tick is a transaction at the same price as the preceding trade but higher than the preceding different price. Conversely, a downtick, or *minus* *tick*, is a transaction made at a price lower that the preceding trade. A *zero-minus tick* is a transaction made at the same price as the preceding sale but lower that the preceding different price. A plus sign, or a minus sign, is displayed throughout the day next to the last price of each company's stock traded at each trading post on the floor of the New York Stock Exchange.

U.S. Savings Bonds: Bonds issued in various denominations and maturities by the U.S. Treasury to aid in financing federal government activities.

Value Averaging: An alternative approach to *dollar-cost averaging.* The strategy is to make the value of investment holdings go up by some constant amount (such as $100) each month. It is a little more complex than dollar cost averaging but can typically provide higher returns at lower per-share costs.

Value Line Composite Average: A stock average, published by Value Line, that reflects the percentage changes in share price of some 1,700 stocks traded on the NYSE, AMEX, and OTC markets.

Value Line Investment Survey: A weekly subscription service covering some 1,700 of the most widely held stocks and mutual funds.

Vertical Analysis: Financial statement analysis that presents all other accounts on the financial statement in percentage terms as relative to a base value. For example, in the balance sheet, total assets equals 100 percent and each asset is expressed as a percentage of total assets.

Volatility: A measure of price and interest rate variability. Stocks with greater volatility show wider price swings and their options are higher in price than less volatile ones.

Voting Right: The stockholder's right to vote his stock in the affairs of the business. One common share usually has one vote. A stockholder may assign his vote to another through a proxy.

Warrant: The right to buy a security at a fixed price, either for a stated time period or indefinitely. A warrant is usually offered with another security as an inducement to buy.

Wash Sale: Sale of a security to establish a capital loss and then repurchase the same security within 30 days after the sale.

When Distributed: A security trading in advance of the printing of the certificate.

When Issued: A short form of "when, as, and if issued." It is a conditional transaction in a security authorized for issuance but not as yet issued. All "when issued" transactions are on an "if" basis, to be settled if and when the actual security is issued and the National Association of Securities Dealers or an exchange rules the transactions are to be settled.

White Knight: A slang term for an individual or company who saves a corporation from an unfriendly takeover by acquiring it first, thus rescuing the targeted corporation is rescued from the unwanted bidder's control.

Wilshire 5000 Index: Measure of the total dollar value of 5,000 actively traded stocks, including all those traded on the NYSE, AMEX, and OTC markets.

Write: An investor who sells an option contract not currently held (selling the option short) is said to have written the option.

Writer (of Options): A person who writes the options to be bought or sold by the option buyer.

Yield: Or *return*. The dividends or interest paid by a company, stated as a percentage of the current price. The return on a stock is computed by dividing the total of dividends paid in the prior 12 months by the current market price. For a mutual fund, yield is interest or dividends plus capital gain or loss in the price per share.

Yield Curve: A graph of the term structure of interest. It shows bonds' yields relative to their maturities. The yield curve is positive (upward sloping) when long-term bonds yield more than short-term issues.

Yield to Call: A yield on a bond to be called. Not all bonds are held to maturity.

Yield to Maturity (YTM): The fully compounded rate of return on a bond, presuming it is held to maturity.

Zero-Coupon Bond: Or *original issue discount (OID) bond*. A bond purchased at a deep discount. The interest is added to the principal semiannually and both the principal and the accumulated interest are paid at maturity.

INDEX

Other books of interest to you from Irwin Professional Publishing . . .

SOROS
The Life, Times, and Trading Secrets of the World's Greatest Investor

Robert Slater

Discover why abandoning traditional economic theory and recognizing chaos in the marketplace is key to Soros' success and how Soros' understanding of history, psychology, and social behavior led to him becoming "The Man Who Broke the Bank of England."

ISBN: 0-7863-0361-1

THE MUTUAL FUND MASTERS
A Revealing Look Into the Minds and Strategies of Wall Street's Best and Brightest

Bill Griffeth

In a series of revealing interviews, Bill Griffeth, the host of CNBC's acclaimed "Mutual Fund Investor", elicits the philosophies, strategies and formative experiences of 20 of today's most successful and most popular fund managers.

ISBN: 1-55738-583-1